Languages of Care in Narrative Medicine

Maria Giulia Marini

Languages of Care in Narrative Medicine

Words, Space and Time in the Healthcare Ecosystem

Springer

Maria Giulia Marini
Department of Healthcare Innovation
Fondazione ISTUD
Milan
Italy

ISBN 978-3-030-06907-0 ISBN 978-3-319-94727-3 (eBook)
https://doi.org/10.1007/978-3-319-94727-3

Softcover re-print of the Hardcover 1st edition 2019

Cover illustration: Johannes Vermeer - Woman Holding a Balance, Date 1664. Courtesy: National Gallery of Art, Washington

This Springer imprint is published by the registered company Springer Nature Switzerland AG
The registered company address is: Gewerbestrasse 11, 6330 Cham, Switzerland

"This is a trail-blazing book, bringing health care and "human understanding" closer than ever before. A key feature of the book is the use of shared human concepts (the "Natural Semantic Metalanguage") which can help humanise the relations between sick people and the caring professions by offering a new "language of care": Basic Human. It's a language that facilitates empathy and deep human connection. This is the first book to take this perspective on illness and care. Reaching other people through shared concepts is an art which can help us at many times, but perhaps especially when we are ill, or care for the ill. I strongly recommend this book."

—Anna Wierzbicka, *Australian National University*

Foreword

In the *Language of Care*, Maria Giulia Marini sets out both a theory and a method for applying narrative to foster health and healing. While this study has relevance to a variety of relationships, Marini's particular focus is on the clinical encounter, where gaps in knowledge, authority and experience tend to exacerbate stress and suffering.

Marini draws on her prior scholarship in the realm of the health humanities to argue that stories, told formally and informally, can build bridges to overcome these divisions with improved communication, insight and empathy. Using multiple examples, she demonstrates how Natural Semantic Metalanguage can be used as an accessible framework to facilitate the development and exchange of stories between the various constituents of the clinical encounter. Patients or providers may be unsure of where to start, or how to structure a narrative in such a way that it can be expressive not only "of" one's experience, but expressive "to" an audience; NSM functions as the template or script, which gives shape to thoughts and emotions for the benefit of both storyteller and interlocutor.

What makes Marini's argument in favour of this humanistic bridge so persuasive is the way in which the entire text is suffused "with" the humanities, applied as theory, rationale and demonstration. Marini employs varied examples from literature, art, music and popular culture, to first illustrate where healing is needed, and why—from the patient who is terrified of his illness to the physician whose efforts to provide care with limited resources have left him stressed and burned out—and then to demonstrate how a structured sharing of narratives can facilitate healing: listening, exchanging, comprehending, empathising. Synthesising scholarly sources, interviews with health humanities practitioners, poetry, music, fiction and non-fiction, Marini demonstrates that the Language of Care is one that we all already "know"—and, with the guidance provided here, that we can apply to enrich our relationships in the clinic, the classroom and beyond.

Carol Ann Farkas
Massachusetts College of Pharmacy and Health Science
Boston, MA, USA

Preface

Healthcare is a complex ecosystem comprising care providers, patients and their families, buildings and facilities, medical and communication technologies, competences, management, waiting times and performance times. Among such variables, we must recall the central position of a patient, a person who unwillingly sees his/her role within this ecosystem suddenly redefined by a disease and inevitably impacted by its internal variables.

Narrative medicine (NM) and narrative care—which extends to all providers of clinical settings—concerns the exploration of disease as experienced by the person who is ill (beyond the mechanistic view of the human body) and shaped by its sociological and cultural collocation. Apparently in contrast with evidence-based medicine (EBM), NM integrates the approach to disease and our current way of understanding and managing disease. Providing a new perspective, this new discipline (minimised to 'current of thought' by some) enables us to look deeper into a disease and focus on its components, illness and sickness, and their role in the care of the disease.

EBM can be more effective and efficient by integrating narrative care, leading to less uncured patients, more satisfied patients and a better quality of life and satisfaction for all healthcare providers.

During these years, we witnessed the policies concerning healthcare narrative research by WHO. These policies rely on real, authentic narratives of all healthcare providers, from patients to carers and from administrative staff to citizens. These guidelines suggest a strong integration of EBM with the narratives originating from all stakeholders for an improvement in healthcare.

Following the WHO guidelines, this book focuses on the scientific approach to implement NM. It embodies the classic medical and health humanities, including literature, philosophy, ethics, history, spirituality, mythology, social sciences, anthropology and psychology, in addition to new insights from linguistics and the neurosciences.

I aim to provide a broad multiple approach to NM, which should be called 'narrative healthcare' considering the complexity of the healthcare ecosystem.

The first new input comes from a linguistic point of view based on the concept of natural semantic metalanguage (NSM). According to this theory, all spoken languages across the globe share a core number of universal words, which stem from the ancestral development of perception and reaction to experiences common to all humankind. It can be viewed as our innermost and authentic language that allows individuals to reach out to others and connect beyond any cultural, social and historical upbringing and barriers. It is an important component of a human being and can play a central role where there are 'natural conditions of fragility' in particular.

The second new input comes from an excursus among new discoveries in neuroscience to investigate the effectiveness of the use of such metalanguage on our emotions and rational mind, evaluating the influence of the systematic application of the 'good words', 'right time' and 'comfortable space' on a person's health.

Finally, we consider the perspective of spirituality that goes beyond the normal 'biopsychosocial model' to encompass the 'biopsychosocial spiritual model' of care.

An Experiential Journey

The chapters are structured as a journey. The first chapter is more theoretical, focusing on the methodology of NM, language and storytelling. This book is like an inner journey for the reader, exploring *Time, Space Environment, Trauma, Emotions, Shame and Hope.* The basis of these chapters is beyond scientific, social and narrative literature. It involves field research on NM and humanities, carried out by Fondazione ISTUD, and main players in this field, in a healthcare setting.

In my opinion, beyond the learning of NM and its application, this book will help us understand the meaning of language, its importance, the ways to improve it and the need for language in vulnerability time. Furthermore, it includes other languages, beyond words, as body language, art, colours, architecture, music and sound, developed during these centuries, and explores the existential questions of illness and wellbeing, the cycle of life, with death and new life again. I hope that this book represents an experiential journey. Some suggestions have been provided for reflection and practice at the end of each chapter.

Human Dimension and Universe of Care: Squaring the Circle

Appropriately fitting the individual and collective human dimensions into the universe of care is a challenge for the stakeholders interacting in the healthcare ecosystem. Understating and improving healthcare is similar to facing the challenge of 'squaring' a circle or fitting different variables and dimensions into just one geometrical shape: on the one hand, EBM is based on signs, symptoms, digits and plots; on the other hand, narrative healthcare is based on words, space, time, feelings, thoughts and beliefs. This reminds us of the dilemma faced by Leonardo Da Vinci in finding the ideal proportions of man in relation to a universe governed by perfect mathematical models. In drawing his Vitruvian Man, he envisioned a man reaching out to (and yet enclosed by) the universe and abstracted such a challenging concept of a 'squaring circle'.

The narrative turn is a human need in this contemporary age when technology becomes technocracy and digits and protocols want to command, with a reductionist approach, without assigning adequate meanings to human facts. Thus, the divide between medical sciences and medical humanities is getting smaller day by day, and an increasing number of scholars and healthcare providers are now actively engaged in integrating NM and EBM.

Target Audience

This book targets those interested in caring for and curing others: in particular, it is dedicated to all providers of care, physicians, either general practitioners or specialists, nurses, psychotherapist, counsellors, social workers, providers of aid, healthcare managers, scientific societies and scientist and social academics or expert. Moreover, it is a handbook for students of medicine and nursing, especially for farsighted universities that have fostered the interest in and understanding of NM as well as medical humanities and ethics.

It is dedicated to patients, families and citizen associations and companies that work in the life sciences domain and develop technology by making patients a part of their corporate mission.

Structure of the Book

Each chapter is divided into two main sections: the first chapter reports on recent outcomes from research in this field based on my perspective as an expert in NM. The second chapter is a proposal of practical tasks for the reader, directing us from theory to practice. The book entails interviews with experts in different fields, such as one of the authors of the WHO guidelines on qualitative research, the expert in EBM as well as a specialist in music therapy and experts in NSM.

Chapter 1 begins with a brief state of the art of narrative methodologies in healthcare, reporting the guidelines of WHO, publications on narrative research in scientific journals and reflections of methodology. In Chap. 2, I explain NSM, with 65 universal prime words. In Chap. 3, I use the terms of NSM to create subtitles that summarise the most meaningful concepts of each chapter as a practice of the use of universal language.

Finally, I wish that this book seeks a balance between 'order' in classifying method (which finds its best expression summarised in the Glossary) and 'fresh air', innovation, a little bit of chaos. As statisticians teach us, chaos allows all degrees of freedom. The trick is to balance order and chaos. I chose Johannes Vermeer's painting, 'Woman Holding a Balance' as the cover of this book because this indicates a sense of stability and rhythm. A woman dressed in a blue jacket with fur trim stands serenely at a table in the corner of a room. The scales in her right hand are at equilibrium, indicating her inner state of mind. The woman is focused on seeking the balance; thus, I consider her as my model in writing this book.

Milan, Italy Maria Giulia Marini

Acknowledgements

Before extending my gratitude to the people who helped me to reach Ithaca, the homeland and the dreamland, the peaceful and quiet place that I wish for all patients and all carers, I would like to get inspired by this poem, Ithaka, composed by Costantino Kavafis.

As you set out for Ithaka,
hope the voyage is a long one,
full of adventure, full of discovery.
Laistrygonians and Cyclops,
angry Poseidon—don't be afraid of them:
you'll never find things like that on your way
as long as you keep your thoughts raised high,
as long as a rare excitement
stirs your spirit and your body.
Laistrygonians and Cyclops,
wild Poseidon—you won't encounter them
unless you bring them along inside your soul,
unless your soul sets them up in front of you.
Hope the voyage is a long one.
May there be many a summer morning when,
with what pleasure, what joy,
you come into harbors seen for the first time;
may you stop at Phoenician trading stations
to buy fine things
mother of pearl and coral, amber and ebony,
sensual perfume of every kind—
as many sensual perfumes as you can;
and may you visit many Egyptian cities
to gather stores of knowledge from their scholars.
Keep Ithaka always in your mind.
Arriving there is what you are destined for.
But do not hurry the journey at all.
Better if it lasts for years,
so you are old by the time you reach the island,

wealthy with all you have gained on the way,
not expecting Ithaka to make you rich.
Ithaka gave you the marvellous journey.
Without her you would not have set out.
She has nothing left to give you now.
And if you find her poor, Ithaka won't have fooled you.
Wise as you will have become, so full of experience,
you will have understood by then what these Ithakas mean.

Keep Ithaca always in your mind, and if you find her poor, Ithaca wont' have fooled you. These are words that have inspired my writing. I wish that by reading *The languages of care,* everybody of us would have found a little piece of Ithaca as homeland, as a place to discover, as the ultimate aim and as the place of good boundaries.

I extend my gratitude to the team in Fondazione ISTUD: Luigi Reale, Paola Chesi, Antonietta Cappuccio, Valeria Gatti, Silvia Napolitano, Matteo Nunner, Nicola Castelli, Tania Ponta, Delia Duccoli, Morag Mc Gill, Andrea Guarini, Roberta Geusa, Marella Caramazza and Francesco Alleva—all people engaged in adventure to seek new insights for creating a better eco-friendly healthcare system. I'm sincerely grateful to Selena Pampalone, who took care of the glossary of this book and editing, wishing her all the best for her oncoming child, Orlando.

I'm grateful to the people I met in most continents who endorsed the writing of this book: Carol Ann Farkas from America, USA; John Launer from Europe; Susana Magalhaes and Isabel Fernandez in Portugal; Vera Kalitzkus from Germany; and Silvia Rossi in Paris. In Australia, I was honoured to have met a wonderful woman, Anna Wierzbicka, who empirically developed the concept of NSM together with Cliff Goddard. My particular gratitude goes to Bert Peeters with whom we have collaborated across the continents to establish the illness plot written according to a universal or semi-universal language. I'm grateful to the WHO, Europe, which gave me the honour to review the narrative research document, together with the other reviewer Brian Hurwitz, with guidelines written by Trisha Greenhalgh, a doctor who always believed in the complementarity between EBM and NM for a better healthcare system. I'm grateful to Silvio Garattini who was an eye opener in trying to integrate EBM with NM; he believes that good words are drugs. As far as the other languages of care are concerned, I'm grateful to June Boyde-Tillman for her knowledge on curing with music, to Rita Mangano for her artistic work in the place of care, to John Ballatt for having explained the concept of a coping factor, which allows us to reach Ithaca, the intelligent kindness, that one used by Odysseus in his last part of the journey to prey the Pheacis to bring him back to his motherland, and to Colin Jay who was open to understand that NM is a wonderful tool to expand and vehicle spirituality beyond the stiffness of historical religions. I'm grateful also to Cristina Mameli who supported me through the counselling, Letizia Ragusa who is a wonderful life coach and to Bruno Brugnoli who designed the ideogram of the listening.

I'm grateful to all the students of the Master in Applied Narrative Medicine, to the students of the Master 'Scientists in Enterprises', to the students at Hunimed, future physicians and nurses I met in Italy during these years and to the people I met at the congress and at the patients' associations meetings. I'm grateful to Antonio Virzì and Stefania Polvani of the Società Italiana di Medicina Narrativa who are really allowing to build a network of complicity in disseminating medical humanities.

I'm grateful to the people I met in the companies, pharmaceutical and biomedical ones, and to the institutions which have funded our independent research and educations. I am sincerely grateful to all the people who confuted my approach since they have been the best stimulus to go on and to deepen, become more curious and have changed my view from a simple opinion to a more reflective discourse, based, whenever possible, on evidence. It is true that one learns both from the friends, as in the poem of Kavafis from *Laistrygonians and Cyclops and Poseidon*, because it is also through the debate that culture might evolve.

I can't say the commotion in words about the people who have followed me during these pages: my cherished man, who stimulated the writing of this book and my discovery of linguistic and sound; my son, Gabriele, who now studies philosophy because he thinks that there is too much technology in this world and world needs 'better thinkers'. Gratitude to the women of my family and to my niece, Evelyn, a baby girl, who owns the same name of my grandmother, revealing the importance of roots, even if our family is spread all over Europe. And to my loved father.

A special thanks to Manuela Walker who reviewed the editing of this book: but more than this, she asked me, *What is the target of this book? What do you want to get out?* I stayed still, in silence and then I muttered an answer: *I want to expand, to bring in healthcare new disciplines, to prove that they work, metaphorically to go for a long journey, with many stops before reaching Ithaca, which might be the healing, the coping and caring and curing; having good relationship in the eco-friendly system, with people, beauty and nature.* My gratitude was also to Louella Pay, a wonderful nurse who helped me in reviewing part of the English as well from Perth. And thanks also to Enago, for the English proofreading. My gratitude to Rajesh Gopalakrishnan and Donatella Rizza of Springer who believes in the dissemination of the Medical Humanities in the Clinical Practice.

I dedicate this book to all people who had a trauma, wishing them their recovery from the so-called post-traumatic stress disorder: maybe, some Cyclops are just inside our souls, but we can try to make them blind so not allowing to interfere with our current life. Seize the day. *Carpe diem.* Gratify ourselves with *sensual perfume of every kind.* Live the moment. Gratitude to Pamela Wible, who is trying to make better and more enjoyable the life of the carers.

Above all, I dedicate this book to all the nurses, doctors, volunteers and other providers of care who are working to make this ecosystem more friendly, open and more natural and beautiful. We have learnt that beauty is a healing factor. Let's search for beauty, *pearl and coral, ebony and ivory*. Even if fake, they are beautiful as well. We need rest sometimes and beautiful places to converse with people in this

Ithaca, which Homer described as full of stones, goats and olive trees with a wonderful sea. A simple island where to rest: *If you find her poor, Ithaca wont' have fooled you.*

A particular acknowledgement is referred to Selena Pampalone, neurobiologist, who has been co-author of the glossary.

Contents

1 Narrative Medicine and Narrative Care: Developments in the Field—The State of Art of Narrative Methodologies in Healthcare, Success and Pitfalls as Well as New Perspective on Methodologies 1
Practice Time 11
References 12

2 Narrative Medicine Encounters on Language and Linguistics: Natural Semantic Metalanguage and the Role of Universal Words in Health and Illness 13
A Short History of the Origin of Oral and Written Communication 14
So Much in a Name 14
Views on Narration 16
Human Experience Through Universal Grammar and Protolanguage . . . 16
Practice Time 24
References 24

3 Narrative Medicine Across Countries: Bridging the Gap of Cultural Differences Through Linguistic Methodology, from Universal to Local Cultural Scripts of Illness. The Narrative of an Intercontinental Collaboration on Linguistics 25
Value of Structured Narratives 25
Story of an Emerging Collaboration: Natural Semantic Metalanguage, Minimal English and Narrative Medicine 28
The Pilot Study: An Early Report 31
Final Remarks 39
Practice Time 41
Appendix: The New Narrative Medicine Storyline, Written in Minimal Italian/English 42
References 43

4 Between Narrative Medicine and Storytelling in the Healthcare Ecosystem: Narrative Medicine and Medical Humanities and Their Impact on Education and Training of Healthcare Providers 45
When Fiction Is Necessary to Make the Unpleasant Truths of Narrative Medicine More Soothing 48

The Core Concept ... 50
Practice Time ... 55
References ... 56

5 **Among Health, Illness and Time: Chronic Disease, Waiting Time, Recovery, Perception of Time and Resting Time** ... 59
The Long Time: Feeling Bad for a Long Time ... 61
Orlando, Virginia Woolf ... 61
A Long Time to Feel Good ... 63
Modern Life ... 65
When Time Is Back and Forward: Cyclic Time and the Hours ... 66
The Natural and Eco-friendly Nobel for Medicine ... 69
The Narrative of Time: I Feel My Time, You Feel Your Time, I Say My Time Is... and You Say Your Time Is ... 72
Time, Young and Elder People ... 72
What About Patients' Perception of Time? ... 74
Practice Time ... 76
References ... 76

6 **Curing the Language of Care: The Heaviness of the Prescriptive Jargon, Moving Towards a Lighter Language for Better Caring and Better Outcomes—Language, Music, Sound and Colour** ... 79
The Example of Smoking ... 81
From Torture to Empathy ... 82
The Lightness of a Wish ... 83
The Lightness of Smile ... 83
Other Languages of Care: Music and Sound ... 84
Practice Time ... 96
Point of View of Healthcare Providers ... 96
Point of View of Patients and Family Members ... 96
References ... 97

7 **The Environment for Wellbeing: The Need for Therapeutic Places of Care and the Languages of Proportions and Colours** ... 99
Practice Time ... 112
References ... 113

8 **Trauma and Coping Activation of Patients and Curers: Learning from Humanities Mythology (Odysseus and the Minotaur) and Fairy Tales (the Beauty and the Beast), Suicides and Recovery Practice** ... 115
The Minotaur in the Labyrinth ... 115
The PTSD Migrants and the Odysseus Syndrome ... 119
The Point of View of Neurosciences on Trauma ... 121
The Beauty and the Beast ... 122

Far Inside the Trauma: 'To Want to Live' and 'to Want to Die' (Where Are We in the Society?) . . . 124
To Want to Live . . . 124
Do Not Want to Die . . . 126
Do Not Want to Live . . . 127
To Want to Die . . . 129
The Case of *to Not Want to Live* in Doctors . . . 129
Practice Time . . . 138
References . . . 139

9 Language of Emotions, with a Focus on Shame to Be Defeated: The Flower of Emotions and Their Role in a Post-contemporary Society . . . 141
Classification of Emotions According to Robert Plutchik . . . 142
Shame: An Undesired Emotion Not Enough Rewarded and Respected . . . 145
Patients' Narratives on Shame and Coping . . . 146
Shame and Cancer . . . 148
Shame and the Healthcare Providers . . . 150
Medicine in Contemporary Society . . . 151
Practice Time . . . 152
References . . . 152

10 The Language of Spirituality in the Pathway of Care. Hope, Good Relationships, Setting Priority, Inner Space and Divine Space, If Any. Patients' Beliefs as a Starting Point to Engage in the Pathway of Care, Kindness and Compassion . . . 155
The Coping Factors . . . 156
Religion and Spirituality as Coping Factors for Recovery in Illness Time . . . 157
Religion . . . 158
Spirituality . . . 159
First Petal: Loving Relationship . . . 160
Second Petal: Being in the Present Moment . . . 161
Third Petal: Meaning and Purpose of the Things We Value . . . 161
Fourth Petal: Inner Freedom and Wellbeing and Peace . . . 163
Fifth Petal: Flourishing and Finding Hope . . . 163
Practice Time . . . 172
References . . . 173

Glossary . . . 175

Appendix . . . 205

References . . . 217

About the Author

Maria Giulia Marini I am an epidemiologist and a counsellor in transactional analysis, with 30 years of professional life in healthcare.

My classic humanistic background, including the knowledge of ancient Greek and Latin, helped me to study languages and arts. Subsequently, I followed scientific academic studies, chemistry and clinical pharmacology. During the first years of my career, I worked in a private international environment and medical research and gradually moved to a healthcare organisation, acquiring specialisation in epidemiology. Later, I engaged in consultancy and healthcare education.

With its humanistic management, Fondazione ISTUD could integrate humanities with healthcare.

Currently, I am a member in the board of the Italian Society of Narrative Medicine, tenured professor of narrative medicine at Hunimed, Milan, and teacher of narrative medicine at other universities in the world.

In 2016, I have been referee for the World Health Organization Europe on the guidelines Narrative Research for a better quality in health care.

I have written the book titled *Narrative medicine: Bridging the gap between evidence-based care and medical humanities*, an international publication on narrative medicine edited by Springer. As a lecturer, I have focused on different international contexts, including academic and public and private foundations. I have written books in Italian titled *The open organisations in healthcare* and *The evolved organisations in health care*, edited by Sole 24 Ore.

1 Narrative Medicine and Narrative Care: Developments in the Field—The State of Art of Narrative Methodologies in Healthcare, Success and Pitfalls as Well as New Perspective on Methodologies

In 2014, the Lancet published a landmark report entitled *Culture and health* (Napier et al. 2014). In the report, the authors defined culture as 'a set of practices and behaviours defined by customs, habits, language and geography that groups of individuals share'. Accordingly, they acknowledged that although much progress in medicine was made through epidemiological and basic science research, a significant shortcoming was the lack of systematic attention to culture. They made several recommendations: they suggested that medicine should accommodate the cultural construction of wellbeing, culture should be incorporated in health and healthcare provision and there should be a better understanding of agency (i.e. human intention and action) in light of cultural imprint. This led to the inception of the 'cultural context for health' taskforce. This taskforce was entitled to write a document on the research concerning healthcare improvement by adopting the methodology of narrative medicine (NM) in 2016.

This achievement represented a milestone: after more than 15 years from its foundation (Greenhalgh 1999), NM, or narrative research, was finally acknowledged by WHO—the global ruling institution establishing policies for healthcare. By introducing it to the health evidence network, it established the equal dignity of evidence-based medicine (EBM) and its validity outside humanistic disciplines. *Cultural context of health: the use of narrative research in the health sector, WHO Europe* (Greenhalgh 2016) represents an exhilarating victory for all people who believed and still believe that NM is as important as EBM. Personally, I have always considered EBM to be the best way to organise and evaluate the outcomes of the pathways of care. However, I strongly believe that efficacy figures are inadequate to uncover the true needs of individual patients and explain their inner complexity. Narratives from patients as well as from their care providers are important to capture a glimpse into the lives of the people involved in care and focus on their illness within a specific context. Without these parameters of real life against which we can 'adjust' results from evidence-based studies, it would be difficult to advance care to the next level. Humankind is so complex that we cannot restrain it to fit clinical studies, where the pursuit is to confirm to which extent 'one size fits all'. Figures of

M. G. Marini, *Languages of Care in Narrative Medicine*,
https://doi.org/10.1007/978-3-319-94727-3_1

EBM provide measures of generalisability, indicating an individual's proximity (or lack of) to the average characteristics of a heterogeneous population. Accordingly, EBM cannot be an exact science unless it considers those parameters making each of us so unique. NM can provide these 'new' parameters and the tools for their measurement. If well conducted and applied in its methodology, NM can integrate traditional medicine with a more proper application of EBM. Symbiosis between EBM and NM should be the best achievement, a cohousing made by sharing technologies, arts and competences. I emphasise this point because some physicians, nurses and healthcare providers at national (Italy) and international levels think that by embracing NM, EBM can undermine the medical quality of making diagnoses, providing treatments and ensuring rehabilitation. However, I believe that NM helps a better application of EBM if it is well conducted and applied in its methodology.

Along with Trisha Greenhalgh, University of Oxford, and, an external reviewer, Brian Hurwitz, King's College, I had the unique opportunity to review the policies in the report *Cultural context of health: the use of narrative research in the health sector* before its issue in 2016. This report aimed to provide a consistent and thick methodology for conducting proper research and integrating the outcomes of NM with those of EBM. In reviewing the document, we felt the need to explain the clear distinction between narratives and storytelling (or fiction) and their differences in terms of applicability: narratives involve a setting in everyday care, while stories (also those inspired to real facts) involve a setting in healthcare campaigns.

The following are the sources of narratives as per the policies in the report:

- Traditional clinical case study, a clinician's reflections on a real clinical case (told from the perspective of the clinician)
- Individual accounts of illness, captured through qualitative interviews
- Case study narratives of a healthcare organisation or system that forms the institutional context for individual illness experience and treatment
- Cultural-historical narratives within which particular illness stories are embedded (e.g. the metanarratives of disadvantaged and/or displaced communities)
- Policy discourses (particular framings that drive action or justify inaction)
- The social drama of participatory research
- The shared, multivoiced narratives of online communities and social movements

How to conduct a good quality research in narrative medicine?

Narrative research must meet the general criteria of high-quality research (Greenhalgh and Wengraf 2008), *including the following*:

- Originality, clarity and importance of the research question
- Appropriateness of the study design to answer the research question

- Sample size and representativeness (note that a maximum variety sample selected to incorporate a range of viewpoints may be more appropriate than a statistically representative one)
- Robustness of the data collection process, including choice of instruments or tools, experience and training and supervision of research staff
- Quality and transparency of the analysis (including coherence of theoretical framework and an identifiable unit of analysis)
- Extent to which conclusions are justified by findings
- Awareness of the possibility of error and steps taken to minimise or explain this throughout the research process

Rigour in narrative research is more about producing a convincing interpretation than technical procedures (e.g. ensuring that two observers independently check the data). In addition to the generic criteria of good research listed above, rigour is demonstrated through evidence of the following (Loh 2013; Golden-Biddle and Locke 1993):

- Trustworthiness, where researchers go beyond a superficial approach to collecting data (through measures such as prolonged engagement, triangulation and disconfirmation of cases) to provide rich detail (what anthropologists call thick description) and include a cycle of member checking by research participants.
- Plausibility (verisimilitude), where researchers, in their account, are able to 'recruit the reader … smooth contestable assertions, build dramatic anticipation, and differentiate the findings' (Golden-Biddle and Locke 1993); hence, the account rings true and allows the audience to enter the world of the research subject(s).
- Criticality, where the researchers show a high degree of reflexivity, questioning their own findings and considering alternative interpretations for them.

Storytelling (and story interpretation) belongs to the humanistic disciplines and is not a pure science. However, scientific linguistic methods can be applied to the collection and interpretation of the text. The storyteller might use rhetoric and other literary devices to give a version of events from his or her own perspective.

In narrative research, the story should, therefore, be anchored in some way (Greenhalgh and Wengraf 2008), *for example, through the following:*

- Collecting multiple stories about the same event or comparable experiences
- Linking the story to other sources of empirical data (e.g. biomedical data about the severity and time course of a person's illness)
- Including a thorough and critical review of the relevant literature

Ethical duties arise for those who collect and use the stories of others (Charon 2006). *Requirements of the researcher role include the following:*

- Honesty in being explicit and transparent about the purpose of the research
- Non-malfeasance, i.e. intending to do no harm (unless balanced by a greater benefit)
- Obtaining consent and undertaking only those activities to which the storyteller has consented
- Confidentiality and protecting the identity of the storyteller (if that is his or her desire) and those implicated in the story

While anecdote is rightly placed at the bottom of the evidence hierarchy in evidence informed medicine, narrative research should not be equated with anecdote (Greenhalgh 1999) more than quantitative data should be equated with truth. Epidemiological studies and trials help make predictive statements about the frequency of events in populations and the likelihood of particular outcomes; narrative research helps make sense of experience. Both can be done effectively or badly and produce findings that are more or less trustworthy.

The box indicates the core of the policies concerning methods of narrative research. The same quality and intellectual honesty that apply to a well-performed research in EBM is requested in NM. After the official recognition of NM, EBM can mutually benefit, and they can complement each other to help the interpretation of facts, emotions, thoughts and life events.

As a general comment, many times I was asked the questions: 'Why it is called narrative medicine? To whom is it addressed?'. Since I envision an integrated eco-friendly healthcare system, I wish we could embrace the concept of narrative healthcare in the future, including all the healthcare providers, not always subsegmented in narrative medicine, narrative nursing, narrative psychotherapy and so on. The entire multidisciplinary equipe benefits from narrative practice. However, if we insist on the term 'narrative medicine', we exclude the nurses (as I was told by them) and other fundamental actors in care. I think that the same issue was valid also for EBM. The neologism evidence-based healthcare was defined in 1997 [Gray] to underline the extent to which the practice of caring and curing is centred on medicine; however, this has been poorly used. Therefore, NM, or, in my opinion, narrative healthcare, is addressed to every professional dedicated to the service of giving care. I would mainly focus on this stream.

In the following lines, I include two interviews: first, with Trisha Greenhalgh, a general practitioner, Oxford University, and second, with Silvio Garattini, director of Istituto Mario Negri, one of the most acknowledged centres in the world for EBM. Both the interviews focus on the importance of methods and the discussion concerning NM and EBM.

MGM. What is the importance of the WHO document 'Cultural context of health: the use of narrative research in the health sector' in your opinion?

TG: The document represents an important shift in WHO's thinking about evidence. Many issues that WHO seeks to address are what might be called 'grand challenges'. While the results of randomised trials, meta-analyses and large routinely collected quantitative datasets are crucial in addressing some aspects of these grand challenges, there is growing recognition that there are also different kinds of questions for which we need a broader range of research methodologies. This was expressed very well recently in the introduction to a book on qualitative research methods in public health:

Over the last several decades, there has been an increasing recognition of complex forces that contribute to the public's health—factors that interact at individual, family, community, population, and policy levels. Social, economic, political, ethnic, environmental, and genetic factors all are associated with today's public health concerns. Public health problems are complex not only because of their multi-causality but also as a result of new and emerging domestic and international health problems. Consequently, public health practitioners and researchers recognize the need for multiple approaches to understanding problems and developing effective interventions that address contemporary public health issues (Tolley et al. 2016),

MGM. How do you explain this attention to the research on narrative methods?

TG. As I explain in the monograph, 'narrative truth' is a different kind of truth from the logico-deductive truth of scientific evidence. A narrative (story) is a subjective version of events; it also has an intersubjective dimension—the storyteller's dialogic (teller-listener or writer-reader) relationship with a real or imagined audience. Narrative is about making sense of what happens in our lives as well as conveying meaning and highlighting (or questioning the lack of) moral order. Let me give you an example. Hundreds of randomised trials have been undertaken concerning patient education in the management of type 2 diabetes. Educators emphasise the importance of 'healthy behaviours' (taking exercise and restricting diet to certain healthy foods and small portions). We know that diabetes education works a little for some people but has limited efficacy in changing the behaviour of some people—especially those from certain cultural and social groups. Through narratives, we can identify what the suggested 'healthy behaviours' actually mean to the target population. Sometimes, we find we are asking them to undertake social practices that have a negative cultural meaning (e.g. rejecting a gift, arguing with one's mother-in-law, acting in an immodest way). Of course, people resist pressure to follow such recommendations. Systematic attention to the cultural storylines that shape and constrain people's actions will allow us to design better public health programmes with greater chance of success.

MGM. Which are the main points of attention in this document?

TG. There are three key points. First is the aforementioned point about narrative being an important form of evidence that can complement and extend traditional forms of health evidence. The second point is that narrative research is a broad church. A wide range of approaches can be used to capture cultural contexts through stories. They include the traditional clinical case study (especially when closely analysed from a scholarly perspective), sociological studies of the 'illness narrative' (usually captured through narrative interviews), more contemporary sociological studies of the multivocal narratives of online communities (typically captured by narrative analysis of website text), anthropologically informed studies of cultural practices (using techniques such as ethnography and photo-elicitation), the construction of organisational or community case studies and the study of storylines or metanarratives that frame policy (using discourse analysis). Key quality criteria for such research include measures to assure trustworthiness, plausibility and criticality. Third, like all research, narrative research can be done well or badly. People need to be trained in the methodology and quality standards of narrative research; otherwise, the research findings will not be valid. If WHO uses narrative research to successfully enrich its written reports and inform its future strategies, systematic attention must be given to capacity-building and researcher development.

We need to be wary of the misuse of narrative research. Last week, a group of homoeopathic practitioners cited my work on narrative to claim that homoeopathy 'works'. Their line of reasoning was that if narrative research is a legitimate approach, then we do not need randomised trials to evaluate the efficacy of a drug and can just take individual patient stories. Of course, this is nonsense. To evaluate the efficacy of a drug, you need a randomised controlled trial. This example illustrates why we need to focus on quality standards and match the research question to the appropriate methodology. If the research question is of the format 'what is the meaning of…?', then narrative is likely to inform the answer. But if the question is a quantitative one ('what is the effect size…?'), then narrative is not the way to go.

As a brief comment to the interview with Prof. Greenhalgh, I would emphasise that there is a method for conducting qualitative research and this method is evolving from previous ethnographic studies: with the advancement of technology, we can analyse more narratives. I am not an admirer of digital NM, i.e. the stories collected by web, even though it works perfectly with certain population of patients such as teenagers, adults who work or disabled people who can benefit from augmented communication system to leave their experience. However, it does not work with old people, digital analphabetic persons and those who prefer to leave his/her experience by talking or reflective writing. However, technology helps in research, when one is seeking for clusters, or vice versa, the impossibility to gather words in groups, of hundred stories. Thus, I claim that the ethnographic approach is still valid in terms of observations, but 'big data', as a metaphor, can be collected and analysed through multiple stories. Hence, we will transform words in quantitative trends: the danger is to lose the poetry of each story, which should be honoured, anyhow, in its original version.

Development in NM is now rapid, the document *Cultural Context: Narrative Research for a Better Quality in Health Care* written for WHO received the 2017 BMA medical book awards under 'highly commended' recognition in the public health category. This was announced at a ceremony on 11 September 2017 in London, United Kingdom. The prestigious BMA Medical Book Awards recognise significant work and contributions to medical literature. Over 630 books competed this year for awards in 20 categories. This document demonstrates the importance of narratives in public health research. By focusing on storytelling and conveying the individual experience of illness and wellbeing, narrative research becomes an important tool for reporting on the cultural contexts of health. This award, given 1 year after the issue of the document in September 2016, indicates the importance of narratives in an evidence-based world and positions the scientific society in favour of expanding their methods and perspective.

Moreover, the scientific journals have started to publish enlarged studies of NM: by enlarged, I mean not simple case reports but stories that generate digits after clustering narratives by gender, age, severity of the illness, coping skills, emotions, used language, style and pathways of care. Proofs are the recent publication of our study on narratives of parents of premature newborn: *Digits and narratives of the experience of Italian families facing premature births* (Marini et al. 2017). The objective of the research was to understand the experience of families living a premature birth and outline the current care plan in Italy. The survey was addressed to 150 parents of children born in the 34th week of pregnancy. Topics of the investigation were the implications on their family as well as social and working contexts determined through a questionnaire enriched by a collection of narratives. Written testimonies were clustered through an NM method and matched with quantitative information. The main respondents were mothers of severe and moderate preterm children. Results indicated that except for the kangaroo care, services were not uniformed among the centres and few home care supports available for families. Sixty-seven per cent of the mothers could not obtain a prolonged maternity leave and described the impact on their working activities. Narratives revealed a low level of prevention, information and awareness of the risks of prematurity among families; few local networks among neonatal intensive care unit teams, gynaecologists and paediatricians; and the shortage of support for parents at work. These actions were collected in a position paper. Findings showed the integration between families' coping strategies and the offered care services for preterm births.

Another published experience is a study on the international journal of COPD: *Narrative medicine to improve the management and quality of life of patients with COPD: the first experience applying the use of the parallel chart in Italy* (Banfi et al. 2018). In short, poor adherence to therapy and the failure of current smoking cessation programmes evidence issues in current management of COPD and potential for improvement through new approaches to patient care. The parallel chart is a narrative medicine tool that improves the doctor-patient relationship by asking physicians to write about their patients' lives, thereby encouraging reflective thoughts on care.

Between October 2015 and March 2016, 50 Italian pulmonologists were involved in the collection of parallel charts of anonymous patients with COPD. The narratives were analysed according to the grounded theory methodology. In the 243 parallel charts collected, the patients (mean age: 69 years, 68% men) were described as still active and as a resource for their families (71%). The doctor-patient relationship was considered to be difficult in 50% of cases, and younger age and smoking were the main risk factors. The conversations turned positive in 78% of narratives, displaying deeper mutual knowledge, trust in the clinicians' ability to establish effective therapy (92%), support efforts to quit smoking (63%) or restore patients' activities (78%). All the physicians concurred that the adoption of innovative parallel charts was useful for improving clinical care and worthy of official inclusion in protocols for the management of COPD.

A third example of publication in a peer-reviewed journal, *Clinical Practice*, was the research titled *Narrative Medicine, a Model of Clinical Governance: The Experience of the Local Health Authority of Florence in Italy* (Polvani et al. 2014). In summary, this work evidenced the fact that modern medicine is faced with the ever-increasing need to consider the existential qualities of patients during the process leading to diagnosis and choice of therapy, in addition to relying on technological progress.

NM has gradually entered the routine of clinical work, aiming at improving patient-physician relationships and adherence to therapy as well as reducing direct and indirect health cost. Accordingly, the Local Health Authority of Firenze (Italy) has launched an innovative process for the integration of narrative practices into health services. This initiative aimed to spread the culture of narrative-based medicine among health professionals and increase the quality and appropriateness of care (NaMe project).

The following interview presents the dialogue I had with Prof. Silvio Garattini, an expert in EBM and the one leading a 'temple' of science in Italy, in the last summer of 2017. However, he wants to do it in a very innovative way.

This is a very short list; however, beyond single books and case reports, an increasing number of scientific papers are exploring narrative medicine, worthy of being published only in humanistic journals. Narrative is evolving in healthcare, but it has to meet the criteria to be acknowledgeable from a scientific point of view. I will discuss this topic in the next interview.

Prof. Garattini is a chemical expert, a medical doctor and an academic of chemotherapy and pharmacology. He is the founder and director of the 'Mario Negri' Institute for Pharmacological Research, established in 1963. He has authored hundreds of scientific works published in national and international journals. He is part of the Group 2003 and founder of the European Organisation for Research on Treatment of Cancer.

MGM. Professor Garattini, what is your position on narrative medicine?

SG. Narrative medicine does not have a good reputation.

MGM. You're right professor. Unfortunately, narrative medicines have been often corrupted by fiction. However, WHO itself wrote narrative research 'policies' (Cultural Contexts of Health: The Use of Narrative Research in the Health Sector) in September 2017 to establish some guidance on conducting good quality narrative research that can be used towards healthcare improvement. These policies officially established what can be considered 'narratives', the calculation of the sample size and the method for interpreting the patient stories. For example, it claims that sources of narrative must be patients and caregivers rather than from a literary genre. So, it narrows the scope, excluding narrative in medicine or narratives in medicine but narratives collected in the clinical practice. Other two aspects are the requirement for sample size calculation contemplating epidemiological factors and blinding in the interpretation of narratives to limit as much as possible the interference of the reader in the interpretation of narratives.

SG. I totally agree with the first point: we have to distinguish between what is literature and what is the real patient's narratives. Regarding the second point, the sample size calculation, I would like you to think about the idea of giving voice to all the possible kind of patients, considering age, earnings and social, professional and cultural factors. Patients most willing to adhere to these initiatives are the 'active' patients. These include those belonging to associations, the most privileged, cultured and maybe wealthy. Therefore, we have to carefully section 'sick' people if we want to select a representative sample divided by age, earnings, gender and ethnicity. Only in this manner can we obtain a collection of patient's narrations useful for planning an egalitarian and universal healthcare system.

MGM. Yes, indeed. Sometimes, we are able to access adequate information, which is truly representative of people experiencing a disease first hand, and sometimes not. Unfortunately, mostly working with observational and transversal studies and not enough perspective and longitudinal ones, this is a risk.

SG. If there was a bigger effort in the hypothetical formulation a priori of how many patients are needed to be listened according to the different socio-demographic factors and to the seriousness of the disease, we would already be on a better road. The problem of the interpretation of narratives remains. If, for example, we collect narratives with directs interviews, we could have an interviewer with a scientific culture, another with legal skills and a third with literary culture: it would be nice to see how the same narrated story is interpreted in different ways depending on the person and his/her background. This could be an interesting study.

MGM. Professor, we usually collect narratives through a written illness script to avoid the biases of non-verbal and para-verbal language (gesture, tone of the voice), and if it's also oral, we are careful to the words in order to limit any possible bias. One example is the recent introduction of the natural semantic metalanguage in formulating our texts or questions for surveys and interviews. This consists of a core of 65 universal atoms of meaning, belonging to all the languages of the world (Goddard 2009)*; using these core words and universal concepts will keep language direct and very rarely give rise to any misunderstandings. Here's an example. We collected narratives from patients with colon tumour who had a surgical intervention for the creation of a stoma in Italy and Australia: to start the narration, we proposed some short prompts using the words of universal semantics, which are evocative but not influencing words (although they might sound a bit 'unconventional' by current spoken standards). 'Which people you want at your side', allowing the person an open answer. The question was part of a project simultaneously conducted in Australia and Italy with English and Italian patients using their respective native languages. Interestingly, the replies we received differed largely among the two cultural groups of Australians compared with those of Italians: eighty per cent of Italian people replied they would have liked to have relatives by their side, while 80% of Australians would have liked healthcare professionals or no one at all. It is clear that in the planning of interventions in Italy, we can deduce that we should take care not only of the patient but of the global family in the managing of the patient with the stoma. In Australia, instead, we have to sustain healthcare professionals, the enterostomy professional and mainly the patient. We have highlighted this through a written instrument with those universal words, those semantic atoms.*

SG. Yes, I agree that in this case, evidence-based medicine and narrative medicine could reciprocally complement each other if used with rigorous methodology.

MGM. In some fields of medicine, qualitative methods such as narrative medicine may even contribute to obtaining more accurate results. The field of pain management, which currently relies on patient reporting outcomes by numeric pain scales, still presents much need for improvement. It is now open to new instruments such as narrative medicine to help physicians adjust the dosage efficaciously and is included in quality improvement protocols at certain healthcare institutions, at least in the measurement of pain. Only apparently, Professor, it seems a neutral didactic pedagogic style, but if we will observe narrative medicine, we see that there are words such as Group A vs. Group B, survivors, failures and enrolled (recruited, the professor adds) typical of scientific literature which also recalls an epic military style. The clinical trial and the clinical study had a language that hints to competition and not to cooperation—the enemy to fight is the disease; this is why there is the need to build the therapeutic alliance.

SG. We have to be careful about the way we talk, very careful: words could be medicines.

MGM. I agree with that. Words could be medicines but unfortunately also poisons. I think about the ancient meaning of the Greek word pharmacon (Derrida 1968) *that means both medicine and remedy but also poison.*

SG. The biggest poison is to take away hope from a patient. Never take away hope.

I ended that conversation, with great knowledge and hope given to me by Prof. Garattini: a serious NM can be performed, which produces evidence certainly subjected to scientific confutations, like any research. The lightness in taking a little bit of distance from this scientific approach to beautiful poetries and novels and films that talk about the disease, for us is not NM, not in our meaning where we desire that NM is a real tool to improve the healthcare services of the entire world. However, they are wonderful medical humanities, which can mingle, mix and be used together.

Again, the word that strikes in my mind is balance, like the girl in the cover, observing the reaching of the point of equilibrium with calm, serenity and peace, balance between science and interpretation of the narratives, between digits and tales, between the robustness of the many narratives and between the oddity of each specific illness story. Hence, I recall another art based on balance, i.e. ikebana, literally kado, the way of flower (Davey 2015). It looks so far away from the above written line, but I think it is such a tremendous metaphor to explain the need for something, the ground on which we walk, sleep and live; the sky above us, to look at, to be inspired and to dream; and the human being in the middle as the connection agent among the stone, rock, soil of EBM and air, the light and dark of the NM and the human being as a flower in the middle. Three levels are the basis of this art: the concrete of the ground, poetry of the sky and the human figure in the middle (McArthur 2016; Stamm 2010). The point of balance is human carers and patients at the human being level. This is where the word 'humanitas' originates from.

Practice Time

Did you know about the existence of a position paper by WHO on narrative research?
Do you think that you may use it?
Do you think that you want to read it?

Do you want to write down how to use this document within your professional work?
Do you have a strategy to integrate NM with EBM?
Do you have a strategy to integrate medical humanities with numbers and digits?
Do you want to organise some educational sessions in your work on these topics?
Have you ever remarked the style in which EBM is written?
Would you like to try to conduct a narrative research project, considering multiple viewpoints, the socio-demographic aspect, giving emphasis to the context?
Are you interested in the art of balance?
Would you like to try to prepare an ikebana masterpiece?

References

Banfi P, Cappuccio A, Latella ME, Reale L, Muscianisi E, Marini MG (2018) Narrative medicine to improve the management and quality of life of patients with COPD: the first experience applying parallel chart in Italy. Int J Chron Obstruct Pulmon Dis 13:287–297
Charon R (2006) Narrative medicine: honoring the stories of illness. Oxford University Press, Oxford
Davey HE (2015) The Japanese way of the artist: living the Japanese Arts & Ways, Brush Meditation, The Japanese Way of the Flower. www.michipublishing.com
Derrida J (1968) Plato's pharmacy. First version published in Tel Quel, nos 32 and 33
Goddard C (2009) The natural semantic metalanguage approach. In: The Oxford handbook of linguistic analysis. Oxford University Press, Oxford
Golden-Biddle K, Locke K (1993) Appealing work: an investigation of how ethnographic texts convince. Organ Sci 4(4):595–616
Gray J (1997) Evidence-based healthcare. Churchill Livingstone, London
Greenhalgh T (1999) Narrative based medicine in an evidence based world. BMJ 318(7179):323–325
Greenhalgh T (2016) Cultural contexts of health: the use of narrative research in the health sector. WHO Regional Office for Europe; Health Evidence Network synthesis report 49, Copenhagen, viii + 54 pages. http://www.euro.who.int/en/publications/abstracts/cultural-contexts-of-health-the-use-of-narrative-research-in-the-health-sector-2016
Greenhalgh T, Wengraf T (2008) Collecting stories: is it research? Is it good research? Preliminary guidance based on a Delphi study. Med Educ 42(3):242–247
Loh J (2013) Inquiry into issues of trustworthiness and quality in narrative studies: a perspective. Qual Rep 18(33):1
Marini MG, Chesi P, Bruscagnin M, Ceccatelli M, Ruzzon E (2017) Digits and narratives of the experience of Italian families facing premature births, vol 22, pp 1–7
McArthur M (2016) The Buddhist roots of Japanese flower arrangement. https://www.buddhistdoor.net/features/the-buddhist-roots-of-japanese-flower-arrangement
Napier AD, Ancarno C, Butler B, Calabrese J, Chater A, Chatterjee H et al (2014) Culture and health. Lancet 384(9954):1607–1639
Polvani S et al (2014) Narrative medicine, a model of clinical governance: the experience of the Local Health Authority of Florence in Italy. Clin Pract 11(5):493–499
Stamm JD (2010) Heaven and Earth are flowers: reflections on Ikebana and Buddhism. Wisdom Publications
Tolley EE, Ulin PR, Mack N, Robinson ET, Stacey M (2016) Qualitative methods in public health: a field guide for applied research. Jossey-Bass, San Francisco

2 Narrative Medicine Encounters on Language and Linguistics: Natural Semantic Metalanguage and the Role of Universal Words in Health and Illness

One of the aims of NM is to remove the background 'noise' from healthcare communication to capture the authentic signal feelings, hopes and thoughts of the patient. The noise we refer to here is related to the excessive use of technology. Certainly, the application of technology in medicine has been beneficial; however, it is being used when not required, diverting the physicians' attention from other more appropriate tools available for understanding the human nature and illness. Whenever healthcare providers are unable to listen to their patients and speak to them in a constructive manner, technology creeps up time and again as if it were a Pavlovian automatism. In fact, when we analyse the language spoken by physicians during medical consultations, we most often encounter technical jargon made up of complex terms, which the patient can rarely comprehend or relate to.

Today, health and cure are primarily taught in the academic world through Kleinman's concept of 'disease', which is reflected both in the 'biomedical model' and technical jargon (Kleinman 1988). The patient is transliterated to represent a biomedical object ruled by laws of physics and biology as something *broken* in which *something has gone wrong* and which must be fixed or adjusted back towards *normalcy*. The disease becomes an object of the healer. Yet, 'repairing the broken part' is often not enough, particularly if seen from the patients' perspective. Thus, language is so important in healthcare, and students need to be trained to communicate in simple words of everyday language which the patient can understand. During their training, medical, nursing or psychology students learn to identify pathologies with their technical definition and jargon but are not trained to transfer those concepts into true-life experience and the language of emotions.

As Aristotle wrote, a man is something 'biologically alive', as well as a 'politicon zoon', a *political animal* intrinsically characterised by social interaction (Aristotle n.d.). Accordingly, the language of care must foster this aspect of human nature through a more meaningful instinctive form. Patients are human beings whose actions and existence are driven by feelings and emotional adaptation, which are expressed to each other through words.

M. G. Marini, *Languages of Care in Narrative Medicine*,
https://doi.org/10.1007/978-3-319-94727-3_2

A Short History of the Origin of Oral and Written Communication

A short history of the origin of oral and written communication According to the research findings of evolutionary biologist Mark Pagel from the Centre for Linguistics of the University of Reading (UK), the roots of a common protolanguage developed at least 40.000 to 50.000 years ago, during the period of the migrations of the *Homo sapiens* (Pagel et al. 2013). Communication most likely spanned from primordial needs such as survival, in addition to sharing knowledge on events, dangers, rules, food, animate objects in nature, cooperation and trade. The development of the skill of speaking was a distinctive evolutionary feature. Human language allowed to express thoughts 'compositionally' through sentences with defined functional grammatical elements and verb tenses and to recount a story. As described by Steven Pinker, a psychologist and cognitive scientist at Harvard University, the spoken language is extremely instinctive due to its direct wiring to the voice mechanism (Pinker 1994). Although thought may be convulsive at times, the construction of words and sentences is sequential as the larynx and pharynx system can only send forth one sound, a phoneme, at a time. Accordingly, it appears that evolution itself favoured the development of words and language as a process of setting order to chaotic thought into something more meaningful to others.

Different from spoken communication, written language developed after many millennia probably induced from the transition from the hunter-collector society to the shepherd-agriculture society. Archaeological findings date back to 5000 BC and likely functioned both as a management control tool, i.e. for counting the goods, as well as to transmit a lasting testimony of stories. In fact, *narratives* date back to over 30,000 BC across the paintings of the scenes of hunting as facts of the daily life in deep caves, which might have been sanctuaries for live and death ceremonies. The sign, which is sober and abstract, of the letters of different alphabet, at least in our Western tradition, was perhaps born in coincidence with the calculation.

From an etymologic point of view, it is interesting to notice the derivation of the verb 'to narrate' from 'gna to na', whose suffix is linked to *gnosis*—'knowledge'—and its ending *-ate* which likely derives from 'to act/to do', suggesting the meaning of 'letting one know something'.

Hence, to narrate means to express someone's own thoughts and actual states of mind, memoirs (past time), aspirations (future time) and emotions: the communication through narratives is part of everyday life, and it belongs to our relationships and is an evolutionary tool to improve the quality of our way of living.

So Much in a Name

On the same note, the expressions 'to name' and 'to give a name' are derived from the Greek term 'kaleo', which share the same root of the adjective 'kalos' that means *beautiful*, suggesting the aesthetic experience behind the process of inventing a name. The concept was also extensively discussed by Plato (the scholar of Socrates) in the fifth century BC in his dialogues *Cratylus*, one of the first written texts on language (surely the first in our Western culture) arguing the criteria that determine the correct choice of name for any given object through the dialectic tool of 'dialogue'. The same dialogue, taught by Socrates, with its question-answer dyad allows to achieve a wider truth and increases one's awareness regarding life (May et al. 2010).

Daniel Pennac, a renowned writer and elementary school teacher, reminds us of the aesthetic experience in a word in his modern-day chronicle *School Blues* (Pennac 2007). He described the meticulous effort and concentration the child puts in writing his first words in the specific case 'maman', mother. After all the concentration set into tracing waves and bars and writing the word, the child eventually sees the fruit of his labour and admires his accomplishment with a sweaty smile. *Mother* has come out of the pen, opening the child's way to narration through the new skill he learned. A new technique that involves one's brain, muscles, fingers, hand, arm and shoulder, engaging the neck and the eyes that follow the text: it is not any more a fast and instinctive shooting of an oral narration that serves for communicating above all the contingency. It is something more mechanical, more filtered and selective. Indeed, the act of handwriting activates the cortical circuitry involved in refection and logic within the brain.

In the setting of NM, the choice of words and their relevance can be connected to many linguistic and emotional aspects. The foremost, perhaps surprisingly, is that of giving a name to a condition or illness. On the one hand, patients are often frustrated by the difficulty in grasping the technical terms and jargon used by healthcare providers. On the other hand, they are relieved once their illness, disease or condition has been identified and given a name. This does not imply that the name of the disease is an aesthetic experience, but rather it underlines the value of calling things by their name, which establish order and provide a reference point. For many patients, especially the asymptomatic ones, to come to terms with an uncertain or less than positive prognosis is a shock, but most of them express relief to know the 'beast', 'the enemy', 'the invader' or 'the roommate' of their body and mind. They stress it is *better to know, to face the truth: denial does not help in many cases in coping*' (Marini 2016). As we will learn, trauma of whatever reasons blocks the capability to speak, the instinct of 'letting the other know'. Finally, we cannot avoid mentioning the connection between words and human existence. Indeed, ancient literature offers several examples, one for all the written testimonies contained inside the sacred books such as the Bible and the New Testament, where the 'word' is used in reference to divinity. John, an evangelist, wrote 'In the beginning was the Word', (*logos*, in Greek) 'and the Word was with God, and the Word was God' (The Holy Bible: King James Version 2004), emphasising that without the 'word' there would have not been a beginning, and indeed, history of mankind has developed by word.

Hence, narration, which is the conscious choice of words and an elaboration into a logical structure of sentences and paragraphs, along with the intellectual and physical effort involved (just as in the case of Pennac's schoolboy), can represent a cathartic enlightening experience that connects us to our inner being as well as to mankind. The aesthetic experience of narrating 'letting one know something' leaves people healthier, and reflective writing can offer the key to balancing chaos and order in life, with its turmoil of health and illness.

Views on Narration

Not everybody, however, views narration in this way. Galen Strawson, an analytic philosopher and literary critic, refuses to accept the concept of narrative being and claims the possibility of existence in an *antinarrative* way. According to Strawson, narration is countless because someone can serenely meet particular existential truths, perhaps in a less neurotic way, through 'contemplation' rather than the spasmodic use of words or the search for accurate language (Strawson 2004). Terms may complicate comprehension among people as language is often inaccurate and redundant, with messages that depart from a source but barely arrive to a recipient unless through interpretation. In short, the language is extraordinarily ambiguous and correlated to the point of view of who speaks and listens.

Such relativity in points of view and subjectivity is highlighted by Umberto Eco, the Italian semiologist known worldwide for his novel *The Name of the Rose*, with this paradoxical story. According to the known experiment of Pavlov, a dog produces saliva when stimulated by the sound of a bell by virtue of a mere conditioned reflex. The scientist feeds the dog. There is a tale that narrates the meeting of two dogs in Moscow: one is fat, and the other is thin and hungry. The hungry dog asks the other, 'How you do to find food?' The other dog answers, 'Easy'. Every morning at noon, I go to the Pavlov institute and start salivating; here, a conditioned scientist rings a bell and someone brings me a bowl of soup.

However, going beyond the ambiguity of truth and the words, according to Strawson, individuals can be separated into two categories: 'synchronic', those who live in synchrony with the facts and do not feel the compelling need to find a meaning in what's happening in their life, and 'diachronic', those who perceive their personal story as part of a continuity across time, (past, present and future) as living a biography. The diachronic people reflect on what has happened and happens and might even condition what will happen.

Human Experience Through Universal Grammar and Protolanguage

Noam Chomsky, an American linguist, cognitive scientist, historian, social critic and political activist, has done extensive research on the existence of universal grammar (Cook 1988). He proposed that as long as an individual is brought up under normal biological conditions, not those of extreme sensory deprivation, it will always develop language featuring specific basic properties (e.g. distinguishing nouns from verbs or distinguishing function words). His theory proposes that there is an innate, genetically determined language skill that knows these rules, making it easier and faster for children to learn to speak than it otherwise would be. This skill is not associated to the lexicon of any specific language; rather, language-specific words and their meanings must be learned along with other non-language-specific parameters that vary among languages (such as whether adjectives come before or after nouns).

Occasionally, aspects of universal grammar seem describable in terms of general details regarding cognition. For example, if a predisposition to categorise events and objects as different classes of things is part of human cognition and directly results in nouns and verbs being created across languages, then (according to Chomsky) it could be assumed that universal grammar is embedded in human cognition.

Anna Wierzbicka, professor of linguistics and founder of the natural semantic metalanguage (NSM) approach (together with Cliff Goddard), provides a somewhat revolutionary perspective on language (Goddard and Wierzbicka 2002). NSM is based on empirical evidence that all languages of the world share 65 simple core words (the 'primes' or atoms of meaning). Using English words (since this essay is written in English), let us briefly spell out some of these semantic bricks that are found worldwide: *before, now, moment, after, feel, think, say, do, know, happen, hear, see, touch, want, don't want, big, small, good, bad, something, someone, body, you, I, people, mine, kind, can, maybe, if, inside, live and die.*

Just as these words are common to all languages, so are the human experiences collected in the narration of stories of illness, daily life and care. As human beings, we are subject to the biological laws of life and death; we start out small, grow up, live and communicate (i.e. say things to other people), get old and ill and die. Nobody or few escape illnesses. Nobody escapes death. All people can feel good things and bad things. People do not want bad things to happen to them.

In NM, one of the challenges when collecting illness narratives is choosing the proper tool for the oral or written interview. We can either opt for soliciting free-flowing stories without guiding the storyteller in any kind of way, or we can provide a guided series of prompts, which diachronically unfold from 'the falling ill' to 'being ill' and to 'future expectations'. At ISTUD, we use both methods: unrestricted narratives that allow patients' total freedom in telling their story and the guided plot. We use the latter because we are committed to collecting the entire process that unfolds from beginning to the end, without leaving out important elements such as how a person copes with changes affecting the body or the mind (or both), how that person experiences the treatment or cure from the very early stages and how his/her life changes at all levels, considering the people close to him/her, at home, at work or when engaging in social activities. The purpose is to provide prompts that are meaningful to the person who is narrating to encourage the person to write openly, with the least possible restrictions. Hence, our prompts must be easy to understand (across languages and individuals speaking the same language) and void of sources of potential biases or misinterpretation, which arise more easily with the use of 'closed prompts'.

Thus, we undertook a collaborative research involving the Australian National University and Fondazione ISTUD. It aims to establish a dialogue between NM and the NSM approach, setting the basis for a new way of listening to patients' thoughts, feelings and actions when coping with the 'illness' or to express it in the words of NSM primes, the 'bad things we do not want to happen in/inside the body'. Accordingly, we put together an illness plot mostly written using NSM—the universal words—plus a few so-called minimal English words, semi-universal words such as *doctor, home and work* and scientific words such as *specialist* and *nurse*, which, as a result of globalisation, are now presumably understood in a similar way in all countries of the world (Goddard 2017).

Looking beyond our current use of NSM in collecting patients' narratives, we can see other fascinating and useful applications of the metalanguage. One of them relates to the definition of illnesses from a patient's rather than a doctor's point of view. In recent times, the 'bible' psychiatrists rely on documents such as DSM-5 (American Psychiatric Association 2013) for the definition of mental diseases such as depression and anxiety. At an NSM workshop in Canberra, Australia, on 17 and 18 March 2017, Professor Wierzbicka shared some of her insights on the DSM-5 criteria used to diagnose depression. One of them referred to the 'feelings of worthlessness or excessive or inappropriate guilt (which may be delusional) nearly every day'. Wierzbicka claims that no patient, even in the most technological and technocratic country, would ever use such a statement. I fully agree with her. The best way to talk to a depressed person is not by asking questions such as 'Do you feel worthless?' Questions such as these miss the point, as they relate to an external or outside perception of sickness and the societal perspective. These are unable to address what is inside the patient. The question is quite apparently a 'closing' element for any further conversation. A much more appropriate question would be, 'How do you feel?' This opens more broadly onto depression and leads to a variety of possible answers from which a true dialogue can take off.

Associating depression with feelings of worthlessness is assuming it is something that is not related to personal and profound sorrow. The emphasis is shifted away from the inner realm of the patient, making depression become 'a social status', a sickness and a perception from the outer world. In other words, DSM-5 provides a definition that does not focus on the nature of the illness but unduly favours a societal perspective, namely, that of a demanding society where all that matters is being productive, being a winner. This is a Kleinman 'sickness' approach: someone who is a loser, not able to do anything good and not worthy of belonging to the society of good performers is 'labelled' as depressed (Van Poppel 2004). It is astonishing to realise that DSM-5 provides a 'sickness' definition for depression, one of the most common mental illnesses. It relates depression to social failure, to guilt, to a moral judgement passed by others and imposed on the patient, whereas it should describe what is inside the patient. This is where NSM can provide good leads. Using NSM, Wierzbicka tells us the kind of words a depressed patient is likely to use: 'I can't do anything, I can't do anything well'. When the depression becomes really severe, the patient may use: 'I don't want to live anymore'. Like in a loop, as we will see the danger of this label of depression, 'somebody does not want to live anymore' not because of his/her 'depression' but because he/she does not want the world around to label as depressed; this person continues until it might become too late, with possible risks of suicide.

Let us examine the word 'trauma': it has more than one meaning, but the one we are referring to is defined by the Merriam-Webster dictionary as 'a disordered psychic or behavioural state resulting from severe mental or emotional stress or

Table 2.1 Semantic primes of natural semantic metalanguage (English exponents) (Goddard and Wierzbicka 2014)

I, you, someone, something–thing, people, body	Substantives
Kind, part	Relational substantives
This, the same, other–else	Determiners
One, two, much–many, little–few, some, all	Quantifiers
Good, bad	Evaluators
Big, small	Descriptors
Think, know, want, don't want, feel, see, hear	Mental predicates
Say, words, true	Speech
Do, happen, move	Actions, events, movement
Be (somewhere), there is, be (someone/something)	Location, existence, specification
(Be) mine	Possession
Live, die	Life and death
When–time, now, before, after, a long time, a short time, for some time, moment	Time
Where–place, here, above, below, far, near, side, inside, touch	Space
Not, maybe, can, because, if	Logical concepts
Very, more	Augmentor, intensifier
Like	Similarity

physical injury'. This is not how NSM goes about it. The NSM definition (or explication, as we call it, since it is meant to make things *explicit*), as defined by the Wierzbicka's school, has de-structured the word trauma in its atomic meaning by a precise, logical use of the selection among the 65 prime words (Goddard and Wierzbicka 2014), reported in Table 2.1.

Hereafter, from a to i, the whole linguistic de-structuring is a procedure, including from a to d—the 'person who is in charge to speak about trauma'. If we focus on sentences from 'e to i', we can really understand the 'core' of what a trauma is and what inevitable and long-lasting consequence it has in the life of every person.

Trauma

(a) Something.
(b) People can say what this something is with the word trauma.
(c) Someone can say something about something with this word when this someone thinks like this.
(d) It can be like this.
(e) Something very bad happens to someone for some time.
(f) At this time, this someone thinks like this.
(g) I want these bad things not to be happening.
 I want to do something because of this.
 I know that I can't do anything.
(h) Because of this, after this, this someone feels something very bad for a long time.

(i) This someone can't say anything of this to other people for a long time.
(j) This someone does not want to think about it for a long time.
(k) Because of all of these things, this someone is not like this someone was before, and because of all these things, this someone can't feel many good things like this someone could before.

'Can't say anything': this person is not as he/she was before and keeps on wearing the mask in front of the society. Indeed, the coping factors that we are looking for in people who underwent a trauma are the first signals of talking of what happened in an objective or subjective way. Chapter 8 is dedicated to trauma and coping.

These are examples of how NSM can be used towards improving the psychiatric formulations in DSM-5, replacing them with more accurate and realistic formulations that are certain to create better channels of communication between carers and patients. Let us consider another example: the definition of *intrusive thought*, which is at the basis of obsessive compulsive disorder. Intrusive thought is based on 'unwanted memories' (often related to a trauma), 'violent thoughts' (where someone imagines doing violent/aggressive things) and 'sexual thoughts' (Cassidy 2016; Baer 2001). Through the narratives from many patients, we have been able to identify intrusive thoughts that can be different from the above. Personally, I think the DSM-5 list of intrusive thoughts is quite short. Unwanted thoughts can arise from fears of an undefined future—anxiety—moral judgement of oneself and others, fear of poverty, fear of disease without any underlying trauma, lack of trust in the society, fear of being object of violent actions and many other possibilities, all of which can be summarised in NSM via the statement 'I do not want to think about some kinds of things; when I think about these kinds of things, I feel something bad'. As for the widely used word *anxiety* itself, from a patient's perspective, using a first-person perspective, it could be paraphrased as follows:

(a) I don't know what will happen to me after this.
(b) Very bad things can happen to me.
(c) I don't want this.

Taking the simplicity and universality of NSM seriously, a doctor could avoid falling into the trap of asking the patient: 'Do you have unwanted memories? Any violent thoughts? Any sexual thoughts?' There are myriads of unwanted thoughts in the different cultures of the world, whereas the intrusive thoughts that are the focus of DSM-5 mainly refer to possible undesired social behaviours, again focused on sickness—violence and sex—without exploring the thousands of other unwanted thoughts in people's brains that are at the basis of an illness.

To sum up, NSM is an enabling tool allowing us to understand ourselves and others using everyday words that really matter. This is as true in the health sector as anywhere else. By the way, *true* is also one of the semantic atoms for which there is a word in every language. Steven Pinker is right in talking about the instinct of language and to say the words are universal (Pinker 1994). Maybe something universal has an instinctive basis in the neurobiology that brought us with the need to communicate.

We conducted an interesting interview about NSM with one of its main promoters, Professor Bert Peeters, associate professor at the Australian National University.

He is also an adjunct associate professor at Griffith University, Brisbane. His main research interests are in French linguistics, intercultural communication and language and cultural values.

MGM. As a linguist, you have examined 'natural semantic metalanguage' in several publications. But what, exactly, is 'natural semantic metalanguage'?

BP. Natural semantic metalanguage or *NSM*—as it is called by those who use it or have at least heard of it—is a tool or an instrument made *out of* language and used to talk *about* language, which is why it is called a metalanguage. Whenever we need to talk about language or the properties of language, or as soon as we want to say something about one or more languages on the other, we have no choice but to do so by means of a language. The latter is then referred to as a *metalanguage* (I'll come back to that in a moment), and the former could be called the *object language*, i.e. the object of the metalanguage.

NSM is used for 'doing semantics', as understood by linguists, i.e. for describing meaning: meaning of words, meaning of word segments, meaning of phrases and meaning of the entire sentences. It is also used for describing ways of thinking that are culturally specific, i.e. so-called cultural scripts. I won't go into that here, but you have seen the application of NSM to the word trauma. The complex words are not necessarily any clearer than the word that is being defined. The NSM explication is very different: it is long, and provided you read through it carefully, it is easy to grasp. Reading it, you get a real feel for what a trauma is and what it feels like, something you can't say about the definition provided by Merriam-Webster. This brings me to the adjective *natural* in 'natural semantic metalanguage': NSM explications, when done properly, are rather good at what they are meant to do because they are couched in natural, or naturally occurring, language, as opposed to artificial, technical or esoteric language.

Unlike many other metalanguages, NSM is also natural in a different way. It is as natural as its object language. It shuns all kinds of formalism and relies entirely on *existing* vocabulary (other metalanguages often use symbols, abbreviations or newly developed concepts or use existing vocabulary in idiosyncratic ways) as well as on *existing* grammar (other metalanguages often have no grammar whatsoever or use logic instead; in Italian, they would presumably be referred to as *metalinguaggio* rather than *metalingua*, as from a linguistic point of view, they are very much a matter of vocabulary only—no naturally occurring grammar). Its *vocabulary* and *grammar* are rigorously defined on the basis of empirical research on dozens of typologically and genetically unrelated languages that stretch back decades. The only vocabulary and grammar used is vocabulary and grammar that, until proof to the contrary, is truly universal, i.e. expressible in all the languages of the world—except in very particular circumstances on which I will say a little more later on. This means that NSM has as many guises as there are languages in the world, and all these guises are fully translatable into each other, without semantic distortion. What can be said in one version can also be said in any of the others, and end users understand exactly the same thing, irrespective of the actual language that is being used. To put it in more technical terms, all external guises of the NSM are meant to be fully isomorphic.

MGM. What about languages other than English?

BP. For practical reasons, the language most often used for formulations phrased in NSM is English, but several strictly isomorphic versions have been developed relying on the resources of other languages, including those that are being used by practitioners of narrative medicine. The words and phrases used in NSM are known as *primes*. On current count, on the basis of the empirical research I referred to, the number of primes stands at 65: 65 words or phrases that are translatable in all the languages of the world and that are semantically simple, which is why they are called *primes*. These 65 words or phrases cannot be defined any further, unless we allow the definition to be more technical than the word or phrase we are trying to define, which goes against the very spirit of a definition. The primes are the bedrock that underpins everything else: all semantically complex words and phrases can be defined—and ought to be defined—in terms of semantic primes and their universal combinations (i.e. their grammar). The only concession that is made is the occasional reliance, not on primes but on so-called semantic molecules, which are fully definable in terms of other molecules and/or primes. This concession is made to prevent explications from becoming unwieldy and uninterpretable. But I am concerned I am becoming uninterpretable myself. Am I?

MGM. Not at all. What would be an example of an explication containing molecules?

BP. Let's stay in the medical world and look at the word *temperature* as used in *body temperature*. The explication that follows is based on that of the word *temperature* as used in sentences such as *What's the temperature?* and *The temperature was dropping fast.*

(Body) temperature

(a) Something.
(b) People can say what this something is with the word temperature.
(c) Someone can say something about someone's body with this word when someone wants to know something of one kind about this someone's body.
(d) At many times when people want to know something like this, people say things like this. 'This someone's body is (hot) *m* at this time. This someone's body is very hot at this time.'
(e) At some times when people want to know something like this, the people say things with (number) *m* words.

There are two molecules in this explication identified through a lowercase *m* added between square brackets. One is the word *hot*, and the other one is the word *number*. These words are not semantically simple, they can be explicated further. I will not attempt to do here. *Hot* and *number* are used in the explication for *(body) temperature* as it would probably be impossible to work the explications for them into the explication for *(body) temperature* without rendering the latter unintelligible. Molecules are not created or posited haphazardly…

MGM. This is exactly what I was going to ask next. What is the process for discovering the primes and the molecules?

BP. You wanted to know more about the process for discovering the primes and molecules. For the primes, that process has been ongoing for several decades. It is not a *scientific process*, if by 'scientific process' you mean a process that is outlined from the start and then rigorously followed until the end. Instead, NSM scholars have relied—there really is no other way—on trial and error. We have always tried to find the simplest concepts, which we have then tested against other languages to see if these concepts exist there as well, i.e. are lexicalised in those languages as they are in the languages we have already looked at. Over the years, we have abandoned some presumed primes because we found they could after all be defined in simpler terms; but above all, we have added many more (we started off with about a dozen or so…), which we discovered were needed to define or explicate more complex concepts. We have always cross-checked against other languages to see whether the newly added primes were lexicalised there as well. To our great relief, we have mostly found that they were, and we have not been obliged too often to give up on a prime we thought we needed but that turned out not to be lexicalised in language X or language Y.

For *semantic molecules*, the process is different. Here, we do have some criteria we can use, such as usefulness (we do not want to posit a molecule unless we will really need to use it on a number of occasions), frequency (we do not want to posit a molecule that hardly occurs in the language) and cultural salience (we do not want to posit a molecule language that users cannot relate to). The latter criterion points to a crucial difference between primes and molecules: the latter are not necessarily universal, but as I mentioned before, they must lend themselves to explication in terms that are ultimately universal…

The interview develops further introducing the topic of the next chapter, the structured illness plot.

I want to add my personal experience discovering this metalanguage and applying the 'logical' decomposition of molecules up to the building elements: it is a therapeutic process, unveiling all possible over-construction and going deeply at the core of the human being's way of expression. It might look like an evolution of humankind through the simplicity and impossibility to be misunderstood. It is a wonderful tool to communicate with patients and carers the primes as keywords. Being so meaningful and powerful, I have chosen them as a *fil rouge* for the other chapters of this book.

Practice Time

Read to yourself the 65 semantic primes, the universal words of all languages.
What did you feel while reading them?
What ran through your mind while reading them?
Are they too many or too few?
Which words would you like to add related to your personal and professional life?
Think about a word that is not included in this list and try to it *de-structure* it at an atomic level (perhaps you might like to try 'happiness, stroke, sky, boundary'), the same way shown above.

References

Aristotle. Politics. 384–322 BC
Baer L (2001) The Imp of the Mind: Exploring the Silent Epidemic of Obsessive Bad Thoughts. Plume. http://www.ocdaction.org.uk/forum/obsessive-compulsive-disorder-ocd/intrusive-sexual-thoughts-and-false-memories
Cassidy A (2016) The Psychology behind Intrusive thoughts. http://www.drarthurcassidy.com/the-psychology-behind-intrusive-thoughts/
Cook VJ (1988) Chomsky's universal grammar: an introduction. Basil Blackwell, Oxford
American Psychiatric Association (2013) Diagnostic and statistical manual of mental disorders, 5th ed. https://psychiatry.org/dsm5
Goddard C, Wierzbicka A (2002) Meaning and universal grammar: theory and empirical findings (2 volumes). John Benjamins, Amsterdam/Philadelphia. https://www2.griffith.edu.au/arts-education-law/school-humanities-languages-social-science
Goddard C, Wierzbicka A (2014) Words and meanings: lexical semantics across domains, languages, and cultures. Oxford University Press, Oxford
Goddard C (ed) (2017) Minimal English for a global world: improved communication using fewer words. Palgrave Macmillan, New York
Kleinman A (1988) The illness narratives: suffering, healing, and the human condition. Basic Books, New York
Marini MG (2016) Narrative medicine: bridging the gap between evidence-based care and medical humanities. Springer, Cham
May J, Baum M, Bewley S (2010) Plato's Socratic dialogues and the epistemology of modern medicine. J R Soc Med 103(12):484–489
Pagel M et al (2013) Ultraconserved words point to deep language ancestry across Eurasia. Proc Natl Acad Sci U S A 110(21):8471–8476
Pennac D (2007) School blues. MacLehose Press, London
Pinker S (1994) The language instinct. William Morrow and Company, New York
Strawson G (2004) Against narrativity. Ratio 17:429–452
The Holy Bible: King James Version (2004) Hendrickson Publishers
Van Poppel M (2004) Effects of resistance and all-round, functional training on quality of life, vitality and depression of older adults living in long-term care facilities: a 'randomized' controlled trial. BMC Geriatr 4(1):5

3 Narrative Medicine Across Countries: Bridging the Gap of Cultural Differences Through Linguistic Methodology, from Universal to Local Cultural Scripts of Illness. The Narrative of an Intercontinental Collaboration on Linguistics

Value of Structured Narratives

Narratives can be collected in various ways: orally, through an open interview (with no fixed questions letting the speakers follow their stream of consciousness) or through written text using either under the form of free narrative without prompts. These can also be collected using semi-structured illness plots (related to the broader meaning of illness, i.e. of disruption from a previous state of wellbeing), with prompts that follow the diachronic unfolding (past, present, future) of illness. Nonetheless, our experience shows that those who narrate eventually develop their narrations by spontaneously following what is identified as the mental illness plot, which unfolds from past to present to future. Using free narratives and a semi-structured illness plot, we found no major differences. This is probably because most of us live with the 'continuity of the self', i.e. a consciousness of continuity in time, with memories of the past, here and now of the present time, and the uncertainties of the future (Ramachandran 2012).

From an operative point of view, compared to their free-flowing narratives, structured narratives based on pre-established prompts are easier to analyse and classify feelings, thoughts and development of the patient's story. It clarifies throughout the story of the stages of disease and illness and the healing process.

At ISTUD, the NM research team generally solicits narratives from patients in a way to allow stories unfold chronologically. Stories move diachronically from ancestral past to recent past to present and beyond, providing patients with a structured opportunity to talk or rather write. Patients start from their initial symptoms, the treatment, and how they are feeling at the time of writing, as reported in Table 3.1 (i.e. whether their condition has got better or worse), leaving at an open-ended field for developing their narration further, without any prompts (Goddard 2017). In addition, there is an untitled section in the original version, prompting patients to explain whether and how writing about their condition has helped them cope with the situation they are in at the moment of writing.

M. G. Marini, *Languages of Care in Narrative Medicine*,
https://doi.org/10.1007/978-3-319-94727-3_3

Table 3.1 List of headings in the original version of the storyline followed at ISTUD

	Original headings
1	Something has changed
2	The journey in care
3	Today

Table 3.2 Prompts following the first heading in the original version of the storyline

Prompts gathered under the main heading 'Something has changed'
I was ……
when I started to feel not well ……and it happened that ………………………… So to understand what was going on, I decided to go to ………………………..… At the end the experts told me that …………………………… The moment they told me about the disease, I felt.…………………………, and I thought that ………………………… and decided to ………………………… At home, it happened that ……………………………………… At work, it happened that ………………………………………With my loved ones, I used to ……………………………………… My body ……………………………....

Each heading is followed by a series of prompts. No questions are asked; each prompt comprises few words, followed by a dotted line enabling patients to freely express themselves. Table 3.2 provides the original prompts used under the first heading 'Something has changed'.

When we use this plot, patients are given no explicit instructions nor bound to any requirement of completeness: there is no obligation to fill all the dotted lines, and there are no expectations that patients tell their story using the exact prompts provided. In fact, not all participants fill in all the fields, and some even replace some prompts with other ones that they believe more relevant to their story, even providing extra paragraphs on the back of the form or on separate sheets. Over the years, during which we have collected over 6000 narratives, the responses received and the way they were returned provided a wealth of information to help us refine the prompts and adapt them to disease- or condition-specific situations (Marini et al. 2016; Cappuccio et al. 2017; Gatti et al. 2017; Marini et al. 2017; Banfi et al. 2018). Such adaptation was also extended to the route of story collections, making the storylines available through Internet (http://www.medicinanarrativa.eu) and providing patients even more freedom to express themselves with the type of information they wish to share.

What follows is the English version of the bulk of a story provided to ISTUD's NM team by a female patient, aged 25, diagnosed with multiple sclerosis in 2008. The story was recorded in Italian in 2014 via the web interface. The English translation was checked against the original by the first author of the research.

I noticed that I was not seeing well through my left eye; everything seemed blurry, as if were foggy; and everyone told me that I probably had vision fatigue because of too many hours spent on books. I waited for a few days before going to the emergency room… From there, I was admitted for 15 days to the neurology department for further assessment and to treat inflammation of the optic nerve with cortisone. Since 2005, every year at the same time, around February/March, I would experience optic neuritis, which would always be treated with cortisone, just as on the day hospital of the center for sclerosis. I kept asking if I had that disease, but nobody would confirm it for me… Then, in 2008, I changed hospitals, doctors, and therapies and finally got the diagnosis.

The moment they told me I had MS, I felt I was dying… I didn't know well what this disease was, so I started searching on the Internet… at 17 years of age, every road seemed the right one to get information… I wanted to know at all costs what I was about to go through.

I decided to look for news anywhere I could, reading blogs, encyclopedias, and anything else. I was angry with the whole world… no one understood how I felt… I hated my family because, until that point, they hadn't told me a thing. I felt alone overwhelmed by something much bigger than me.

In the days immediately following, I was always full of anger in my heart, I pretended I was feeling well, and that the whole thing did not affect me in the slightest way, and instead, every night, I was alone crying in my bed.

I was angry with the people, with my close family in particular, and as for my friends, I never told them anything… I felt different… a loser… who would no longer be able to have as much fun as they would.

Others around me were silent… nobody said anything, never any word of comfort, any help, any explanation. I felt ignored by the doctors because they wanted to talk to my mother and not to me… she always had to be present, even after I turned 18… and that was something I just could not stand… it was like retaliation: since she hadn't informed me about anything, now I was the one who did not want to inform her about anything going on with me. […]

I did not know what would become of my life, my relationships, my future… I was afraid of no longer managing to study and of not being able to find a job.

MS for me was a sentence, a punishment I did not understand.

I gave up a thousand evenings with friends; I passed up high school trips and holidays because of the therapy. At age 18/19, my life was organised around therapy and assessments.

My achievements have been numerous… I enrolled in a law degree, I continued to study, I had a few minor jobs, I met many people, I found new friends that I could talk to about my illness, and who were always ready to encourage me and help me when I felt tired, and I continued to go swimming at least twice a week.

I talk about sclerosis only with those who can give advice or suggestions and understand my mood and my difficulties.

My family talks very little about it, and, when they do, they talk about 'that disease of yours'… in short, it is the great nameless thing. […]

MS, for me, is a fixed thought… every day I wonder if the therapy is working, if I can continue it for life, if and when I will have other relapses… it is a never-ending source of questions I'm not always able to answer.

My everyday life is fairly quiet… when I study, my concentration is not always at its best, when I do some work at home or in the garden, I have to stop because I'm tired… but, after all, everybody is entitled to a break sometimes…

I think the support I received during my journey has been full of obstacles…

self-injection therapy made me feel sick; the intravenous one seemed to work well, but because of the risks involved, it has been suspended until the arrival of oral therapy, about which I was not told much… and as always I had to search on the web… […]

I'm not thinking about tomorrow… I live one day at a time.

Story of an Emerging Collaboration: Natural Semantic Metalanguage, Minimal English and Narrative Medicine

The cross-disciplinary dialogue between NM and the NSM approach in linguistics got underway in May 2016, when I established contact with Anna Wierzbicka. Several decades earlier, the latter had sown the seeds of what would eventually, under the impetus of Cliff Goddard, be referred to as the NSM approach. Some of that work had come to my attention as I was working to improve the English version of ISTUD's NM storyline, shortly after publishing my own book on NM (Marini 2016). The need for a correctly phrased English version was becoming particularly pressing in view of the dissemination of results from NM research and practice at international conferences, where English is the default language for proceedings. ISTUD-style NM was mainly locally acknowledged, and the research team was keen to share its findings with the international scholarly community. In addition, an ever-increasing number of non-Italian-speaking refugees arrived at Italian shores, and elsewhere in Europe, via the Mediterranean. These refugees are not always in the best state of health; they are medically screened upon arrival and often have a story to tell. However, they cannot tell their story in Italian, as they do not speak the language.

In the process of making improvements to the English translation, we came across Wierzbicka's work and realised how much our team had actually, but unwittingly, relied on NSM semantic primes (such as I, BODY, MOMENT, FEEL, HAPPEN, THINK, WANT and NOT in the prompts in Table 3.2), when drafting the original version. Further reflection soon convinced the whole team of the importance of using simple language (Banfi et al. 2018) and of the type used within the NSM approach. We realised that the use of unnecessarily complex language would cause unnecessary problems for patients from a variety of cultural backgrounds. Therefore, we wanted to make the storyline easier to understand for people whose English is rudimentary at best. In addition, as mentioned previously, I suspect that during physical and/or mental discomfort, people will spontaneously use simple language, including a greater number of semantic primes and molecules. Relying on prompts written in simple English in the hope of collecting data that are also expressed in relatively simple language seemed appropriate and is entirely in line with the assumptions of communication theorists working within the framework of communication accommodation theory.

Given the scarcity of relevant publications, I was not aware of the recent work on minimal English, an expanded mini-language, which goes beyond the 65 primes and includes semi-universal words such as doctor, house and family. However, it did not take long for Wierzbicka to realise that it was the latter, rather than the NSM in its purest form, that would be more likely to play a potentially ground-breaking role within NM. A preliminary presentation of the basic tenets of NM and the potential of minimal English for its ongoing development took place at an NSM workshop at the Australian National University in July 2016 held by Professor Bert Peeters, roughly 2 months after the initial contacts between Wierzbicka and myself (Goddard 2017). It sparked a lot of interest among workshop attendees and provided further encouragement for a collaboration, by now, which is well underway between Prof. Peeters and myself. It is by no means an exaggeration to say that innumerable e-mails and half a dozen or so Skype sessions, each extending well over 1 h, have successfully overcome the tyranny of distance to draft the illness plot in minimal English/NSM.

As it turns out, Bert Peeters and myself had little trouble finding common ground. We soon enough agreed that the way to go was to critically assess both the Italian and English versions of the storyline to bring them in line with the principles underlying minimal English (and minimal Italian). The original prompts were redistributed over and expanded from the initial three to six, as seen in Table 3.3.

Table 3.3 The new headings (Italian and English) compared with the original English ones

1	Something has changed	Before the illness
2		Then something happened to me
3	The journey in care	Things/some things were not like before
4	Today	Now
5		Tomorrow
6		Writing my story

The new headings comprise a mix of primes and molecules. *Illness*, in heading 1, is a word that could not possibly be avoided in a version of minimal English compiled for NM. The same is true for words such as *doctor*, *nurse* and *specialist* (used in the revised prompts, under the third heading). Heading 2 avoids the verb *change* and uses the simple past. The correspondence between heading 3 and the metaphorical 'The journey in care' may seem to be far-fetched; however, the full version of the storyline in the appendix shows that the prompts in this section are as much about reactions and fears as following the diagnosis as they are about the diagnosis itself. The heading 'Today' was replaced with 'Now', as this section is not just about the day when the patient tells his or her story. Nevertheless, 'Tomorrow' was chosen as the heading for the fifth part of the storyline as we could not think of a convincing option. We need to keep in mind that the text should not appear to be written in stilted, clumsy or unidiomatic English. A compromise between the rigours of NSM and the freedom of ordinary English had to be found.

Each section in the storyline was painstakingly rewritten in both languages, with all possible precautions to ensure that the distance between the original storyline and the improved versions would remain as minimal as possible. There was a simple rationale for this. Before the ISTUD team and I 'discovered' NSM, and subsequently minimal English, she and her team in Milan had already collected several thousands of narratives in Italian from patients suffering various medical conditions. For these narratives, of which many have already been subjected to analysis, the original storyline was used. To cast aside this wealth of data and start again from scratch was simply unimaginable. From the outset, the idea was to go on collecting and analysing data, without having to give up on the work that had already been done. Despite the differences between the original and the revised storylines, the 'old' and the 'new' data have been comparable and could be analysed together. In due course, the amount of new data will of course significantly increase, and it will be possible to focus more and more on data that are fully consistent.

As of today, one major achievement from using translated illness plot is that of having a harmonised tool that does not require any localisation process of the translation and back-translation. It is suitable for authorisation applications to the ethics committee of the hospitals and other setting of care and is ready for being used in narrative research, due to the use of NSM and words of minimal English (semi-universal language). Using this illness plot, with these universals of language (NSM) or semi-universal (minimal English, minimal Italian, minimal French, etc.), the action of linguistic back-translation is not needed anymore, and neither cultural validation, as it was necessary, for instance, in quality of life standardised questionnaire. NSM and minimal language are particularly effective in setting of care visited by foreigners, migrants, students, tourists, international business people and family members reconnecting to the person who live in a different country, and other possibilities here are not contemplated.

Table 3.4 shows, side by side, the original English version of the material under the fourth heading ('Now').

Although the differences are significant, the general thrust is the same. The main difference is that the text has been simplified and made relevant for larger numbers

Table 3.4 A partial comparison of the prompts before and after the rewrite in minimal English

My body and my feelings..	Now, I feel... ....
I feel I can do.. ....I think that the care has been..................... .... and in particular therapies were.. .... When I'm at home, I can/cannot .... With my loved ones.. ....At work I can/ cannot.. Away from home I can/ cannot... With friends................................	The illness.. My body.. I can do.. Many/some people have done things for me... When I think of them.................................... .... They have.. Now, the illness is... ..../is not... anymore At home, I can/ cannot... When I am not at home, I can/ cannot... Now, with the people in my life,.................... ....

of patients. References to 'at work' have been avoided since not all patients have a job away from home: some may be permanently disabled, retired or unemployed. We also wanted to include an opportunity for patients to talk/write about what they can and cannot do when, instead of being at home, they are in a shopping centre or on a holiday, rather than at home.

Space limits prevent us from presenting a detailed comparison between the original and the revised storylines. The full version of the new storyline (in minimal Italian as well as in minimal English) can be found at the end of this chapter in the appendix. It became the cornerstone for the pilot study described in the next section.

The Pilot Study: An Early Report

After the revision of the storyline, we launched a pilot study. It aimed to assess the translatability of the new version, make further changes and collect some newly written narratives originating in a number of countries. An invitation was sent to medical researchers in ISTUD's NM network based elsewhere in Italy, as well as in the UK, the USA, Australia, France, Germany, Portugal and Chile.

At the time of writing this book, expressions of interest had been received from Italy, France, Portugal, the UK and the USA. Silvia Rossi, community and content manager of the association *Cancer Contribution* (Paris), and Susana Magalhaes, professor of medical humanities at the Catholic University of Porto, had produced local versions of the storyline (in French and Portuguese, respectively) to be checked for accuracy before being used for data collection. Agreement was reached to focus on oncological patients from Italy, France and Portugal, writing in Italian, French and Portuguese, respectively. Marina Mariani, counsellor, has been reviewing the illness plot and collecting Italian narratives of women with breast cancer, together with the oncologist, Prof. Francesco Scanzi. Pamela Jofre from Valparaiso in Chile agreed with the oncological team to collect narratives in minimal Spanish. NM researchers in Australia accepted to participate in the study using a slightly modified tool targeting patients with colon cancer who had undergone an ostomy: the 'Australian storyline' presented several commonalities with the one prepared in minimal English, in addition to some peculiarities related to living with the ostomy. David Tomasi, from the University of Vermont, wanted to test the illness script with his patients from the mental illness department.

Thus, all patients whose narratives were collected in the course of the pilot study in the various countries were mainly cancer sufferers whose condition represents a source of frailty that, we think, is best approached through simple and easy-to-understand language. NM researchers in the UK and the USA positively reacted to the call for expressions of interest but made no undertaking to put the new tool to the test and use it for narrative collection.

Currently, France completed the collection of 10 narratives, Portugal is on the way, and Italy has collected 20 narratives. They consider this tool so useful that they wanted to expand the survey to a process to be used, in this case, by oncologists.

Now let us consider three countries, Portugal, Italy and France and the narratives of three individual women living with breast cancer. The illness plot was the same, written originally in minimal Portuguese, minimal Italian and minimal French, of courses with the fundamentals of the atoms of the NSM.

Below is an example of narrative collected using the guided illness plot. The excerpts are from the written narration of a 54-year-old *Portuguese woman* diagnosed with cancer in 2014:

My story

Before the illness

I was a person with some problems of health but they were solved. I was 19 years when I detected a cyst in the left breast, with palpation, hurt me a lot. It was analysed, and it was always benign. Three years ago they diagnosed me breast cancer, already with three children, breastfed up to the 12 months the cyst increased and I had to remove liquid two times but I didn't make any biopsy again. Starting from the age of about 40, I began to do yearly mammograms and echograms. When, in December 2012, I turned 49, these exams showed the presence of tumors in the breast and in the armpit. I went to have the biopsy to .... and it shown that I had cancer. I didn't want to believe it, I had always done checkups, and now a discovery of a tumor? I underwent mastectomy of the left breast, 6 chemotherapy treatments and 28 radiotherapies. The last three chemotherapy treatments were very violent. I had a lot of pain in the body, a panic attack, but always continued eating. In this period, the people that had family relatives with cancer, people who went through the same situation visited me and suggested some reading about healthy nutrition because they believed that some products that could have helped working as antioxidants, but the family, husband, children, siblings and parents are those who gave energy and force to react and to face the physical pain, the interior pain! I'd like to say that the doctor that gave me the news of the disease as well as what to decide for eliminating it was extremely sincere and distant, he showed me two treatment options: surgery first or chemo, and later after studying the result of the size of the tumor and surgery, together with radiotherapy. Then they give me 2 days to think about it, I decided for the radical mastectomy with emptying of the lymphatic vases. I was operated in …, it went well, I was admitted to hospital on Monday, and I left on Wednesday, with draining but everything under control. I've been always followed because I have a sister who is a nurse, and the treatment plan ran how I explained before. Then I had no hair, having a lot of difficulty in using the wig because I couldn't feel it, I used many scarves but I always tried to put on makeup and be beautiful. I always liked to do the chemotherapy treatment, and there was a volunteer who gave me reflexology massages and made me smile. I learnt a lot with him, it was wonderful. In the radiation treatments, just 2 min in the machine but 2–3 h waiting. On the days of consultation, sometimes the waiting was 8 h, sitting in very hard chairs trying to read, while I would have liked to lie down or to lean, and I didn't have that luck! I don't remember when I began physiotherapy, I know that when I went to the gym of center, after doing a treatment of radiation, I said to myself that I should already have begun to move the left arm much more. During the physiotherapy, I felt a lot of pain, I felt 'strings' in my armpit, little mobility but the physiotherapists were excellent. At the same time, I attended a gym MamaHelp, where I was able to exercise twice a week guided by a physical training coach, always careful to my limitations but very expert on the importance in the physical exercise during the cancer treatments. I continued to undergo examines, to do the follow up tests and was followed by the doctor at the Clinic of the Breast of… For 2 years I took tamoxifen, I had polyps in the uterus removed at the center, and I am taking …, which provokes terrible pains in the bones of the hands, feet and knees. On February 13, 2014, I underwent breasts reconstruction, protocoled at the center, also removing the right breast, inserting prostheses but keeping my own skin. It was the operation which caused so much pain as well as the post-surgery: after removing a cyst in a thigh, having done three Caesareans, having lost two foetuses, having had a small cerebral hemorrhage and having been operated to my head. I was admitted in hospital for 6 days, had eight drainages, but I did very well in spite of a small wound in the right breast that took a long time to heal, 1 month. This whole disease brought me to think and to live to thank everything that the Universe gives us! At this time, after 5 years, I don't feel like a sick woman, I am working, I just rested 2 years and, in spite of the fatigue, I feel physically well but more fragile psychologically!

Now

Now, I feel the enormous absence of my breast, my belly and my breasts are numb, sexual intercourse started to be much more painful, I tend to do immense treatments, I have pain, daily stabbings of the scars.

The disease allowed me to get the most out of every second of the day.

My body changed but I like it.

I can do everything that I want, I have much more physical fatigue.

A lot of people have been doing things for me; they have been helping me to be more cheerful, to laugh more, they hugged me and have been more and more careful to my needs.

They haven't treated me as a different person but what costs me the most is the changed in my features, those who don't see me every day don't recognise me.

Now the disease is normal.

At home, I can cook, make the beds, hang clothes that I adore, relieve my arm. I cannot carry weights.

When I am not home, I can't help but swimming.

Now, with the people of my life, I need affection, attention, love.

Tomorrow:

When I think about tomorrow, I think that I have to prepare myself to die since pain is a burden and death comforts.

I want to have people friends, affectionate, playful and to feel that only the facts of already breathing me is enough!

Writing my story:

When I wrote my history, I felt a big comfortable.

To me, this narrative is breathtaking: a woman who from the youth is hit by the disease; she submits herself to all therapies and controls, as in a 'restitution' mode, according to the Frank classification (according to which if one submits like a 'disciplined soldier' to invasive treatment as chemotherapy and radio, he/she will be rewarded back by health).

But life for this woman decides to take a different turn, and the cancer keeps on growing. The surgeon described in her story seems very competent but detached, whereas the physiotherapist is trying to instil some joy. She uses different styles of language: on one hand, she describes her disease very carefully, in a didascalic way. On the other end, she writes in a very romantic style about her family. Finally, she is very sharp in concluding that 'pain is a burden, death comforts'. It may look like a 'no coping attitude', but it may look like I gave everything; now deliberately I say stop. In this narrative, a human being is telling her own story, with the richness of the ambivalence of the emotions, even accepting the potential conflicts; on one day, she feels the joy of tasting every minute of life, and on the other, she wishes to die. This has to do with narrative, which is very often complex and full of inconsistencies as human life could be especially after so many traumatic years.

Below, we have another narration following the same illness plot, written using the words of the NSM and minimal Italian. It is a narrative on a 69-year-old *Italian woman*, divorced with two children, living in a different cultural context and different marital status. Let us see how the open illness scripts are able to pitch the differences.

Then it happened to me that

One day, I got a tumour, making the hypothesis that I had perhaps put into account become true more for luck that for conviction. All the imaginary that I had built inside me on this disease suddenly became a reality that I had to face.

What happened to me is more or less what happened to many women of my age, a more deepened breast palpation after a shower, during a summer evening set off an alarm, a suspicious swelling and the idea that it could be a tumour immediately filled my night.

For days, I forced myself to think that it wasn't going be anything serious, but the doubt keep haunting me.

I am aware of the dynamics in facing the problem, a bit from picking up prevention information, a bit from stories I heard from friends who lived the same experience before me.

At this point, I decided to have my first visit at a centre I had heard about from women I am in contact with.

The oncologist of the centre, a woman, after seeing the mammogram and the echogram that evidenced a suspected nodule, recommends its removal to better identify its nature, she also said that the test could be done using a needle aspiration but that test was not always reliable.

No one spoke about tumour, and there was no immediate urgency to refer me to surgery.

The summer is near, as a project I have a trip to Nepal, but on the wave of the events, I prefer being in the countryside, staying with some friends who make curative medicines with herbs, and search together for a possible remedy to reduce the nodule. It took me 1 month before I decided if and where I wanted to undergo to surgery.

I really enjoy the countryside because there are always a lot of things to do during the day, the harvest in the orchard, making jam, the long lunches and suppers, time for gossiping, and then the silence of the night broken by nothing else but animal sounds.

I love to live a part of the night without sleeping: it is the time that I devote to reading, to thinking. I realise, when I reflect on what is happening to me, I don't feel panic of it anxiety but rather a strong determination to win the evil, and I begin to consider the worse scenario, so I wouldn't be unprepared.

This is how the month of August went by.

The first days of September I undergo a second visit with the oncologist, I establish with her a very essential relationship of trust, I feel her very confident, prepared, and besides, I perceive a certain complicity, I feel her by my side and this reassures me, on her side she realises that I don't feel fear she feels and my determination, we decide together to choose which surgeon among the one she recommends me will operate me.

It's the time of Cinema Festival in my city, so one day between a movie and another, I find myself in the study of the surgeon with all the performed tests. I tell him that I don't have anyone as caregiver and that I want and to know the truth, and, above all, what I should be expecting. After the palpation and looking at my mammograms, he tells me there are 90% of chances it's a tumour and, let me any choice, and decides for immediate hospitalisation.

Up to that point, I showed all of my strength, so I wouldn't be taken over by discouragement, above all, I try not to emotionally involve who is around me, and when I talk, I minimise the fact, I say that the world diffusion of cancer now has fostered the medical research to keep this disease under control; I am aware that the fear still hasn't touched me and I try to live reality, with a great desire to overcome this dirty trick of the destiny.

In mid-September, I am operated and he removed a ductal carcinoma that invaded 2 of 36 lymph nodes removed from me.

Now

Four months have passed since the operation, I have made a cycle of preventive chemotherapy, everything is proceeding for the best, during this time I have tried not to forget important things, to be very careful to arrange what has to be done to my body whenever I have been able to, but I also had to make some compromises, seeking for the balance of the best adequate treatment which fulfilled my wish and the scheduled oncological protocol.

I have tried not to give too much importance to stereotypes and the attitudes that have inevitably touched me.

When I think about the behaviour of the oncologist, a woman, of the public hospital where I was been admitted, who with a snobbish attitude accused me of not doing mammograms every year, offended me with the statement 'you women neglect yourselves', associating me with an undetermined number of incapable women, despising the category to which she herself is thought to belong, or when I think about the surgeon who perhaps (?), just for the sake of encouraging me, tells me before the operation. 'you will see, I'll make your breast look like that of a 15-year-old'. Too bad that now I have one breast lower than the other, but I don't want to launch myself in this useless list of common sayings, pronounced out of convenience or out of habit.

I would want to say instead how much anger I have built up listening to those people, that, with words or only looks, blamed me with punishment, or they were felt authorised to compassionate attitudes, forecasting me diseases that I didn't even perceive, attitudes that annoyed me, especially because they denied my difference, reducing me to a prebuilt sick person in their imaginary, to commiserate and to comfort, a thing that I didn't absolutely appreciate.

This behaviour annoyed me to the point to provoke in me a consequent position of resentment and defeat to make me pronounce words of arrogance that didn't mirror my true state of mind.

I did a huge work effort for not making me oppressed from the cancer and for maintaining a careful and fighting attitude: this real attitude that I had decided to adopt was put to silence by these people, who perceived me as an arrogant and almighty person.

Then, reflecting, I told myself: what is it that makes me exceed towards uncontrolled attitudes and above the lines, by the way, a journalist was speaking of some women who in phase of divorce become extremely aggressive—well this "losing control" is due to a sense of retaliation on someone or something that offends and hurts.

I don't' know if this strategy is correct or not, I think it is an attitude that I use in an uncontrolled way in certain moments, perhaps because it is more effective to create distance, certainly it takes away the joy and the dignity to show myself for what I am and I feel really.

The chronological order of the event is displayed here: longer the past with the suspicion of cancer, a term which is written only at the end, and called as tumour for the entire story. While the narrative starts with kindness and strength and even in a sort 'of Garden of Eden' that beautiful countryside, the woman is able to show between the lines that there are pleasant oncologist to trust and people with the white coat who blamed her like she was the culprit, together with all women, who are not able of taking care of themselves and who are not following the right screening programme. The doctor might be right in his/her thinking, but, personally, reading this narrative, we understand that this woman was already doing the preventive breast palpation, under the shower. And in any case, the moral judgement by the oncologists could have been staying out from the therapy, *You women neglect yourself.* Her narrative evidences how important it is for her to be acknowledged as a responsible and strong woman, in her uniqueness, and how she hates the easy generalisations and the easy jokes on the plastic surgery to rebuild her breast.

This is the power of the diachronic narrative illness plot, which starts from the past up to the present. Yes, through this narrative, we learn what we should not do, the way we should not talk with this woman affected by cancer.

This third example is the narrative of a 55-year-old *French woman* diagnosed with breast cancer in 2007, when she was 45.

Before the illness,

I felt dreadfully tired. One day while I was having a shower, I happened to feel a hard area on my right breast.

I felt terrified.

To know what was happening, I spoke to my gynaecologist who prescribed me a mammography and an echography, which though did not detect anything abnormal. Doctors told me I had a mastitis and that my extreme fatigue was due to my negative state of mind.

After 6 months, the mammo/echo tests were still negative, a surgeon decided to do an IRM (Internal Reflection Microscopy): the diagnosis fell from above: infiltrative lobular cancer in the breast. Affected ganglions. Capsule disrupts.

I felt wiped out because the symptoms had been present for more than 6 months before, and nobody had listened to me.

I lost 10 kilos in 6 months. I was on my knees, exhausted. I knew that there was something wrong but what was I to do if doctors were saying that this was psychological? The news brought on great fear, yet at the same time relief as well as I came to know the reason I was so exhausted.

I thought I was going to die in the next months, and I wanted to organise everything for my children and my husband, with least worries for the time when I would not have been with them.

I became stronger by staying at home and avoiding people. I wanted to stay as long as possible with my family. When I was not at home, I was searching and looking for nature, and the sky, I head a terrible fear of leaving all this.

All the doctors and nurses of the hospital with whom I socialised were extraordinary people. The illness was a move towards a new life, a second life.

A friend of mine who had a cancer before me guided me through all the treatment.

Now

It's not completely over. I have a lymphatic oedema which reminds me of the cancer, but I go on. I exploit every moment since I know that life is so fragile. I benefited from a surgical breast reconstruction. …

Some people have really helped me, and a whole lifetime is not enough to thank them. Others turned away when they knew about my illness. This really annoyed me at the beginning, but now I'm happy. I cut some relationships.

For the future: I'm happy to make projects and I hope to live so long to see my children growing up.

This is the last story collected with the illness plot I wish to share within the healthcare ecosystem: again, this is an evidence of how important the patient's voice is across the pathways of care. She wrote *nobody listened to me*, so the global healthcare service lost 6 months of time before intervening actively. The next chapter, in fact, is on the topic of 'listening'. It is through this kind of narratives, which are not merely an autobiography, but a biography of the illness, that we can work to improve the service of care.

Quantitative data, together with qualitative date, are necessary to assign a meaning to a story: this woman was 44, with small children when she got ill: if we don't know when the illness occurred in her life, we have a blurred vision, and we cannot understand the length of her path in care, that is, a continuum of pain for recurrence and joy for recovery, up to now, that when she writes is 55 years old. Due to these narratives, Cancer Contribution, in Paris, was able to redefine the orientation for the oncological services.

Final Remarks

The ultimate aim of NM, as we know it today, is not to replace evidence-based medical practice but to *supplement* it, bringing benefits to both sides. For the time being, the relationship remains rather rocky, but specialists of NM believe that EBM and NM will eventually be able to live together as a harmonious couple, with NM's narratives lending increased credibility to EBM's statistics and providing their own quantifiable evidence. It is indeed misguided to believe that only EBM works with 'real data'. NM works with a different type of real data, considering patients' lives in a broader setting, rather than with the kind of evidence (clinical research, lab tests, results of treatments…) that EBM has traditionally focused on. Within NM, the focus is on narrative, i.e. how patients talk about their illness and their health, how they react to a poor diagnosis, how they learn to cope with their illness and what they feel and how they consider the therapeutic approach, including procedures, drugs, visits and surgery. The belief is that analysing the way patients talk about their illness can provide a different kind of evidence that can be used to improve healthcare.

The dialogue between NM and NSM has just started 2 years ago, and the current indications are that a fruitful collaboration, far from being merely possible, is already well underway. While linguists have shown for decades a keen interest in the oral and written discourse that takes place between medical specialists (doctors, surgeons, nurses) and patients, the interest shown by medical practitioners for the work done by linguists has been less pronounced. The medical humanities, a broadly defined and relatively new area of research of which NM is an integral part, are set to play a pivotal role in building more and stronger bridges between medicine and linguistics for the common good of both (Hurwitz and Dakin 2009).

In the last year of experience, what we have remarked is that NSM is not only important in collecting structured narratives but also in clinical practice.

During our education and training with healthcare providers, we found that the list of 65 primes fascinates doctors, nurses, social workers and all care providers.

The words are so simple and so far from being misunderstood that the carers are increasingly choosing this new approach to keep things simple to explain patients an illness and to share with them the decision to be taken and to understand by actively listening not only to their medical history but also to their short biography. If the doctor starts to use a simple and unstructured language, patients will open himself/herself more freely.

The illness script that we have written together with the Australian National University is a simple tool to collect narratives respectful of the different cultural backgrounds, of the individuals and the biography of every person living with an illness. As we have seen from narratives, some people will focus more on the past facts, some on the here and now and some on the future. Of course, here, the narratives shown are of strong women facing cancer, and this is the common denominator. All we have to do, as Rita Charon teaches us, is to honour these narratives by observing the told and untold, or better, in this case, the written and unwritten, with all the emotions and thoughts generated by these intersubjectivity between the writer (or the teller) and reader (or the listener) (Charon 1993, 2001a, b, 2006; Charon and DasGupta 2016).

In the case section, there will be the consideration of a group of patients affected by COPD, a name that is harshly pronounceable and poorly understood in its fatal threat by the patients and is the fourth cause of death nowadays, according to WHO (WHO Website n.d.): patients were very poorly aware of the risks given by this condition, and 30% of them continued to smoke when the COPD was still in a mild phase. Using our illness plot, we came to know that at the prompt 'With the person/the people who had spoken to me, I felt … (doctor/physician/nurse)' at the moment of the communication of the diagnosis, there were few emotions of fears, and anxiety, and 30% of patients did not feel anything particular. That 'name', 'chronic obstructive pulmonary disease', which in Italian is 'broncopneumopatia cronico ostruttiva', introduces a further distance between physicians and patients, citing anatomical term 'bronchi' and the Latin-origin technical term of 'pneumopatia' used in pathology handbook to refer to lung disease. A term, whose stiffness hardly evokes an imminent personal danger able to release the right amount of adrenaline, which triggers in the patient the following idea, using the universal and core language: 'Something very bad can happen to my body'.

'I can die because of it'

'Now, I know it'.

'I want to do something about it'.

'I want to feel good for a long time'.

They can stop dependence on smoking and start to cure themselves properly. These occur only in few cases and with few pulmonologists who will translate that 'odd' name of a disease in something understandable. Otherwise, COPD will become more and more severe, and more patients will live with a worsening lung condition. As expressed by patients in their metaphoric language, 'suffocating in the fog', 'being hit by a tsunami', 'strangled by a pillow' 'or living in an iron cage', these are the definitions given through narrative method by the very same patients who were unaware of the risk of this disease at the beginning. They underestimated the first signs and symptoms likely because of the name of the disease, which was given to this illness blocking or changing the lung's capability of breathing. Could we change the name of this disease? This is a question I wish to address to the scientific community.

With this short case, which we will expand further in Case 2, I simply wanted to stress how words are not just a matter of 'being politically correct' to foster empathy with patients: words represent meanings, information and knowledge that should be delivered to the patients.

In the following pages, the reader will find the 'universal' plot, which follows the phases of an illness, from 'before the illness', 'something' has happened, 'things were not like before' to 'now' and 'tomorrow'.

We can decide whether to listen to the people following their *stream of consciousness*, made by flashbacks, here and now, and flash-forward all mixed together or to try to unravel the knots using a semi-structured proposal for an illness narrative. There are pros and cons in both tools: in the totally blank paper, the degrees of freedom are infinite; however, things lost in memories can come to the surface, and the smallest details can assume an important role. In the latter, the illness plot is somehow conducting the development of the narrative, like the banks of the river that is the patient's story: it is thought to follow the whole world of the person, crossed by the occurrence of the disease.

Practice Time

Now you have the illness script in your hands. Do you envision any possibility of application?

If your work occurs not in one multicultural setting, do you think that you could use it?

You can choose what to leave in and what to eliminate for your own purposes. You can build your own plot using the NSM going backwards instead of forwards.

You had the chance to read the three narratives of women with cancers: they were collected proposing the same plot.

What did these narratives mean to you?

Were you moved by these narratives?

What would you have done if you were there with these women?

Appendix: The New Narrative Medicine Storyline, Written in Minimal Italian/English

La mia storia/my story

- Prima della malattia/before the illness

Ero...	I was...

- Poi mi successe qualcosa// Then something happened to me

Successe così: Ero .... quando sentii qualcosa di .... Mi sentii .... Allora, per sapere cosa stesse succedendo, parlai a .... Dopo qualche/molto/poco tempo, mi dissero che .... Mi sentii .... perché .... Il mio corpo .... Pensai che .... Volevo ....; perciò	It happened like this: I was .... when I felt something .... I felt .... Then, to know what was happening, I spoke to .... After some/a long/a short time, they said to me that .... I felt .... because .... My body .... I thought that .... I wanted ....; because of this, ...
A casa .... Quando non ero a casa .... Le persone nella mia vita	At home .... When I was not at home .... The people in my life ....

- Dopo, le cose/alcune cose non erano più come prima/after that, things/some things were not like before

Nel luogo dove mi avevano detto cosa mi era successo, ... Con la persona/le persone che mi aveva(no) parlato, mi sentivo .... Il medico/L'infermiere/ Lo specialista .... Volevo/ Non volevo parlare ad altri specialisti perché .... La malattia era	In the place where they first told me what had happened to me, ... With the person/the people who had spoken to me, I felt .... The doctor/the nurse/the specialist .... I wanted/I didn't want to speak to other specialists because .... The illness was ....
In casa, parlavo a .... perché .... Quando non ero a casa .... Le persone nella mia vita .... Perciò, mi sentivo .... Le cose erano	At home, I spoke to .... because .... When I was not at home .... The people in my life .... Because of this, I felt .... Things were ....

- Adesso/now

Adesso, mi sento .... La malattia................................. Il mio corpo .... Posso fare	Now, I feel .... The illness .... My body .... I can do ....
Molte/alcune persone hanno fatto cose per me; hanno .... Non hanno	Many/some people have done things for me; they have .... They haven't ....
Adesso, la malattia è .... / non è più	Now, the illness is .... /is not .... anymore
A casa, posso .... /non posso .... Quando non sono a casa, posso .... /non posso .... Adesso, con le persone nella mia vita, ...	At home, I can .... /I cannot .... When I am not at home, I can .... /I cannot .... Now, with the people in my life, ...

- Domani/tomorrow

Quando penso a domani, ... Voglio	When I think about tomorrow, ... I want ....

- Scrivendo la mia storia/writing my story

Quando ho scritto la mia storia, mi sono sentito	When I wrote my story, I felt ....

References

Banfi P, Cappuccio A, Latella ME, Reale L, Muscianisi E, Marini MG (2018) Narrative medicine to improve the management and quality of life of patients with COPD: the first experience applying parallel chart in Italy. Int J Chron Obstruct Pulmon Dis 13:287–297

Cappuccio A, Limonta T, Parodi A et al (2017) Living with chronic urticarial: a study through Narrative Medicine to improve the quality of care. Acta Derm Venereol 97:81–85

Charon R (1993) Medical interpretation: implications of literary theory of narrative for clinical work. J Narrat Life Hist 3(1):79–97

Charon R (2001a) Narrative medicine: form, function, and ethics. Ann Intern Med 134(1):83–87

Charon R (2001b) Narrative medicine: a model for empathy, reflection, profession, and trust. J Am Med Assoc 286(15):1897–1902

Charon R (2006) Narrative medicine: honoring the stories of illness. Oxford University Press, New York

Charon R, DasGupta S (2016) The principles and practice of narrative medicine. Oxford University Press, New York

Gatti V, Amaducci S, Banfi P et al (2017) Faro: far luce attraverso i racconti di persone con bpco sul loro vissuto e sulle esperienze di cura. Poster Congresso Nazionale Della Pneumologia Italiana XLIV AIPO 2017, Bologna

Goddard C (ed) (2017) Minimal English for a global world: improved communication using fewer words. Palgrave Macmillan, New York

Hurwitz B, Dakin P (2009) Welcome developments in UK medical humanities. J R Soc Med 102(3):84–85

Marini MG (2016) Narrative medicine: bridging the gap between evidence-based care and medical humanities. Springer, Cham

Marini MG, Chesi P, Guazzarotti L et al (2016) Creating through stories of experiences of care for GH deficiency the empowerment toward the excellence—the C.R.ES.C.E.R.E. project, Stories about life with GH deficiency. Future Sci OA 2(1):FSO82

Marini MG, Chesi P, Bruscagnin M, Ceccatelli M, Ruzzon E (2017) Digits and narratives of the experience of Italian families facing premature births. J Matern Fetal Neonatal Med 22:1–7

Ramachandran VS (2012) The tell-tale brain: unlocking the mystery of human nature. Windmill Books

WHO Website. http://www.who.int/respiratory/copd/en/

4 Between Narrative Medicine and Storytelling in the Healthcare Ecosystem: Narrative Medicine and Medical Humanities and Their Impact on Education and Training of Healthcare Providers

NM is based on real stories in the healthcare ecosystem, whereas storytelling is based on fiction, inspiring artistic re-elaboration/movies/literature and entertainment based on true facts. Storytelling and NM in the education and training of healthcare providers change their mindset and behaviour for providing care.

The best seller *The Life-Changing Magic of Tidying Up: The Japanese Art of Decluttering and Organizing* was written by the Japanese writer Marie Kondo (Kondō and Hirano 2014). The principle is to set a new order: to make space to organise things and to catalogue them according to colours, use, feeling and reason. In short, Kondo clarified and suggested to inspect each room, drawer and box to understand what is necessary; if useless, the item must be thrown away or given to some charity.

Kondo also suggested deleting from the phone book names of long-time acquaintances of people we no longer find interest in. Although I was not able to complete all the suggestions, I personally appreciated it. For 2 months, I threw away and eliminated stuff to do what? To make space for the new that was preponderantly entering but not breathing enough. This was the easiest part: it is not merely a New Year procedure; it is more complex.

What does Marie Kondo have to do with storytelling and NM? It is all about setting order. The more I participate in conventions and conferences and read press and literature, the more I feel the urge to put order, in this case, between storytelling and NM. Whenever I explain that I deal with NM—the collection of narratives of patients, their families, doctors and GPs—it generates a great confusion. Many people find no difference between storytelling and NM: 'both are stories'.

And it is true, both are stories. So, let us apply what Kondo tells us, and let us try to put some order: the point here is the difference in how these stories are built, where they are collected and who writes or tells them.

In storytelling:

- Stories may be inspired by true experiences, but are most often factitious, and belong to the world of medical humanities (O'Hara 2014).

M. G. Marini, *Languages of Care in Narrative Medicine*,
https://doi.org/10.1007/978-3-319-94727-3_4

- Stories are narrated by an individual and are generally oriented to a large audience (Neeley 2016).
- Stories are not collected in clinical practice, but they belong more to free time and performance.
- Stories are perpetuated through many artistic forms such as movies, drama, comedy, books and artworks (Turow 2010).
- Essentially, the narrator is a 'storyteller' entertaining a large public (Silverman 2017).

In NM:

- Narratives recount authentic experiences as perceived by the narrating subject, and they are not told to impress but to share a personal experience relating to disease and the pathway of care (Launer 2007).
- The narrations are often the result of the interaction between patients and healthcare professionals and can be written either by the patient or by the healthcare professional (Greenhalgh 2016).
- Narratives are collected not as material with literary value but rather as a means for gathering insight into experience (Marini 2016).
- Carers' narratives about their clinical cases likewise are real (Denzin 1989), without literary devices, and are reflections to understand more deeply what writing about a case allows to take care of the patient as good as possible.
- It is a spoken or written dialogue between who writes and a few listeners/readers.

The difference is borderline and subtle: medical storytelling would not exist without NM. But I would like to put order in this sequence: first is NM, a daily practice, which is based on the intersubjectivity of carer and patient, interdependence or encounter. This is followed by storytelling, which is extraordinarily emotional, and it is the artistic interpretation expressed in a film by a writer or a director after having read and listened to what happened to a patient.

Another perspective on such difference can be found passing from medicine to philosophy: back in Ancient Greece, Socrates used to practise narrative on the streets of Athens where he would often engage in conversations with the lay people he met and speak about life, existence and humankind in search of the absolute truth. Not only would he listen, but he would also encourage the speakers to ask questions, reflect deeper into the topic and find answers through a maieutic process. This process would result in bringing more awareness, more lightness and happiness to those involved in the conversation, which helped him create an alliance between the speaker and listener (Hanke 1990). Another great philosopher of the ancient Greek culture, Plato, left us extraordinary texts of story telling (Macdonanld 2016).

The Greek word for 'truth' is *Aletheia* whose etymology, paradoxically, means 'the words that cannot be said' (Florensky 2004).

We are quite familiar with the sad ending of the trial to Socrates: condemned to death, he drank the herbal poison hemlock. Is there a risk of drinking a bitter and dangerous liquid by being too narrative, too introspective and too intrusive for going so close to the truth, even in the healthcare system? Plato, we said he was a storyteller, reported through the art of dialogue some reflections inspired by his teacher's thoughts, Socrates. However, the wonderful dialogues of Plato, which are quite calm, with a steady pace and reassurance, comforting our spirit about the pre- and post-existence of the soul after death put the life of the philosopher in danger. Plato was not there, in jail, when Socrates drunk the hemlock; on the contrary, he escaped away to travel, taking distance from the biography of his teacher. After some years, he returned to Athens where he was able to create the academia. He was rewarded and praised in his entire life. Storyteller, Plato, runs less risks than true seekers, as Socrates. Most likely, balance is the best choice. Through this analogy, I wished to have explained that healthcare providers, as patients, as carers and all of us, have different level of awareness and different wishes to know the most plausible reality of things. To get into their brain, their heart and their souls, we cannot use standardised slide kit or a unique message. A part who wishes to become user of NM to improve quality of care seriously will work with every type of verbal and written narratives, including praises and complains, and another part who does not wish to get in real relationship with the patients will still focus on the disease, and if they want to listen stories, they have to be from another world.

Socrates was a 'narrator', and Plato was a 'storyteller'. You can choose which philosopher you like the most or understand if you are employing both: maybe, you can make more order on the street you are travelling. Through 'maieutic', Socrates was building a new reality, an alliance, with people he was talking to, and both were coming home with an increased awareness, more lightness and happiness. Plato was writing for posterity, for the academy, searching for a large public.

It is good to make order not only in one's phone books, wardrobes, books, photos and maybe on social networks but also in definitions and names, an aspect neglected by Marie Kondo. Everyone is free to write as he/she wants, for him/herself, for the 'performance' or in a hybrid way.

Perhaps I am too *linnaean*, with the need for categorising things, as Linnaeus, the botanist and zoologist who lived three centuries earlier than Kondo. But after I made order, I felt I was breathing fresher air and felt dynamic and powerful. Likewise, I feel this need to be done here as well to set some order. Let us accept storytelling as a great tool for inspiring prevention and educational campaigns which need to work on high emotional impact stories, while we assign NM to integrating the daily practice with real patients, helping physicians, nurses and all healthcare professionals. As an example, storytelling would be most fitting for creating prevention campaigns against HIV transmission, nonsmoking and car accidents, while NM would be most appropriate for interacting with patients who experienced the real trauma of HIV infection, severe lung disease or car accidents.

When Fiction Is Necessary to Make the Unpleasant Truths of Narrative Medicine More Soothing

As the readers might have understood, I am in favour somehow of the real patient's narratives because they are so colourful, intense and vivid that they do not need particular changes of reality to be more fascinating. For years, I have been struggling with some healthcare providers, asking them to collect patients' narratives and write their true own narratives; sometimes, I encountered resistances in healthcare carers to write the full chronicle of the patients because they can talk of something not pleasant, which nobody will discover in the routine clinical chart.

Some truths are harsh to know, and courage is a gift to face them. I later understood by my own harsh experience that there are some cases in which 'knowing' that some cases are fictions, just remotely inspired to true facts, is much better than working on true cases. Even if this 'truth' is totally anonymous, and names of healthcare providers, places and patients as well, some facts—real facts or at least perceived real by patients—are so strong that some carers refuse to face them and prefer to refugee in imagined narratives, belonging to the world of medical humanities. *The Death of Ivan Il'ič* (Tolstoj 1886), a classic of medical humanities**,** talks about a patient left to die alone instead of a true narration. Both texts lead to the same issue: the dignity of dying. However, the Tolstoy's pen protects us: it looks like an act of pure invention, while seeing a real letter written by a desperate and angry son to the hospital where the death of his father occurred leads us to a difficult reality to swallow. This holds particularly true when narratives tend to be full of 'moral judgement' and 'criticism' to both patients and carers.

In a study using parallel chart, that is to say, free narratives of doctors of patients and their family, by paediatricians who are curing children suffering from asthma, we read not only of wonderful doctors who are fully dedicated to children and their caregivers, but we have to come to terms also to this 'ironic/cynic style' of a minority of doctors: *dear whale, the patient told me she was completely invalidated in doing her daily activities. She could not walk without shortness of breath, she never went out alone. The mother, very glamour, high society, was super anxious… in my opinion that girl should go and live with her father.*

Short black humour verbatim in physicians' narratives is hopefully very rare. If these few people write in this way, they probably think in this way: no one is free from judgement; everybody is contaminated by prejudice; but, here, strong stigma is given to our patient and caregiver 'whale' and 'a glamour mother', rhetoric to say that with these premises, these families will abandon their doctors. Beyond these, when we had used these parts or even the whole parallel charts in training classes, some (always a minority) doctors were mutinying, defending their unknown colleagues and remarking that they study how to ask the anamnesis and how to develop empathy at the university.

I proceed further: in a letter written by an angry son who had to face his father's death in the hospital, which took place without any relatives near the old man, the son had asked many times if he could stay that decisive night of the death; the doctor told him 'everything will be okay, just go home'. Things went unfortunately different, and in the middle of the night, the son received the phone call by the hospital 'come, your father is getting worse', 'Is he dead?', 'I only can tell you that he worsened'. The son ran to the hospital, but the father was not anymore in his bed. A nurse, not looking at him but continuing to put in order some blood samples, said to him: 'Do you know that your father has deceased?' The son asked to have a formal dialogue with a doctor; however, nobody came. Eventually, the personal belongings of the father were delivered to the son in an unpleasant bag.

This is a narrative that we used in an anonymous way during the class training in a course entitled 'taking care of the relationship of care', causing a virtual earthquake. This case induced an earthquake. The class split in two: a part which was happy that finally these things related to poor communication and wrong setting were coming out, at the light of the sun, but another part was too scared to consider this case as happening in a real place. The latter part was saying that the son invented the whole series of facts: he was still in grief for the sudden and unexpected death of his father, and he had to find an escape goat, which was the hospital. This is a very complex situation, with no right or wrong position to be taken. However, anyhow, it has to do with the dignity of dying, and all guidelines of end-of-life care mention the possibility to have family members at bedside, possibly in a better and more humane place. This has to do with the fact that perhaps there might be more suitable containers than bags (even if resources are scarce) to collect the last personal belongings of a human being. It should be coloured, with nice messages inside.

However, all of this, the dignity of death, was hidden during the discussion by a wave of rage of how these patients and caregivers can lie and bring damage to the hospital.

My first reflection: doctors and nurses overreacted because they are somehow unpleased with what they do, too scared of making possible errors and too scared of being legally persecuted. We know that 80% of doctors and nurses in Italy apply defensive medicine and are living in burn out. Not all of them, but some of them. In short, an ill healthcare system comes out with discomfort and conflict because people are overwhelmed by excessive workloads and continuous staff cuts and are struggling to have a minute more to talk about and talk to the patient.

My second reflection is that if healthcare providers cannot stand the possible true words used by colleagues, patients and caregivers, we have to use whatever works to foster empathy and relational skills (so, welcome Ivan Il'ič, the *Seven Floors* by Buzzati (1937) and 'Patch Adams' by Robin Williams (1999): use medical humanities, movies, literature, art, theatre, music or whatever is able to 'say something true' within the lines of untold and of the emotional manipulation of the performance. Use artefact tools. In my experience, I became aware that sometimes, an aversion reaction is not something only acted by patients when getting bad news, but it is acted as well by their carers. Here, the world of fiction is preferred, and, in some case, it is impossible to put things in order, as Marie Kondo (Kondō and Hirano 2014) is trying to teach us in an oversimplifying message. We all very likely return somehow to childhood when we feel that something threatening is happening, and we want to listen to nice fairy tales, where the bad wolf is far in the woods.

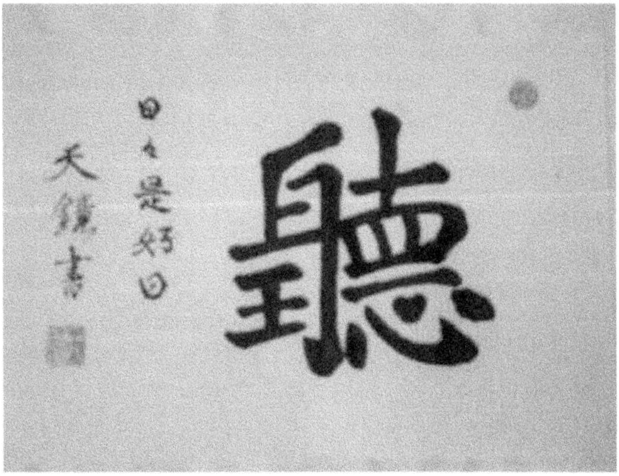

Fig. 4.1 Chinese character for listening

The Core Concept

The concept of listening is profound and is cleverly represented in its Chinese ideogram (as seen in Fig. 4.1).

If we observe this Chinese character carefully, we notice that it is divided into quadrants, with a stylised ear on the top left quadrant, an eye in the lower right quadrant and a line in between that means unit or unitary attention. There is a heart at the end of this line. To end the cycle, there is the representation of a king in the lower left part, which I also found translated in other passages as the mind. I prefer to think about the king. In summary, understanding is worth of a king (or for the sake of equal opportunities, a queen); it requires observation, listening, total attention to what happens and the heart that is the seat of the spirit Shen. If Shen is strong, the heart will be strong, the listening will be better, and the consequent actions will be straight (Lo and Li 2017).

If we then strengthen our heart and know how to use eyes, ears and concentration, we will be able to listen to everything we will be told, even the most difficult news without seeking shelter in fairy tales.

Interview of Carol Ann Farkas

To investigate the role of medical humanities and NM more in depth, we here present an interview with Professor Carol Ann Farkas, a doctorate in Victorian literature, focused on a study on late nineteenth-century novels featuring women doctors as the main characters, and teacher at the Massachusetts College of Pharmacy and Health Care Organisation (*MCPHS*) in Boston.

MGM. Professor Farkas, which courses are offered at MCPHS?

CAF. MCPHS now offers degree programmes in just about every healthcare profession you can think of beyond pharmacy, the original scope. At MCPHS, I direct the first-year writing programme and teach academic writing, nineteenth-century fiction and a course on narrative and medicine (which I need to rename narrative and health, to be more inclusive). My research has focused on health, wellness and popular culture (particularly how fitness magazines teach both health and health anxiety). More recently, I've become more involved with the scholarship of the health humanities—in particular, I've become very interested in how lay people and experts differ in their understanding of and discourse about illnesses of body and mind which elude easy diagnosis.

MGM. Considering your humanistic background, why did you decide to keep a course on medical humanities for future physicians, pharmacists, nurses and other healthcare providers?

CAF. Before I had learned much about the health humanities, I was eager to teach narrative and medicine because, frankly, I just thought it would be fun for me and a fun way to reach out to our undergraduates for whom we do not yet have a humanities degree and who consequently have relatively little preparation in studying literature. But then I started to read more of the scholarship on the health humanities and could see the rationale for the course unfolding in front of me: my students were already, somewhat simplistically, absorbing some of the more harmful lessons of the 'hidden curriculum' of healthcare practice in this country, where providers have a paternalistic knowledge of what's best and patients who don't 'adhere' well to treatment are regarded as frustrations, rather than equals. I've come to see our course and other courses in the humanities as an absolutely essential part of the undergraduate health sciences curriculum; these courses challenge the students in terms of critical thinking, imagination and empathy and demand that they pay compassionate attention to what it means for their students to be humane.

MGM. What do you mean by 'medical humanities'? Do they differ from 'narrative medicine' or do they cross each other?

CAF. Let me start by endorsing the shift in nomenclature that we're seeing, from 'medical humanities' to 'health humanities'. I like how the latter term de-emphasises the primacy of medicine, especially with its focus on just bodily disease and those who have it or treat it and instead offers a more biopsychosocial emphasis on health as it is *lived* by both lay people and experts.

Our discipline's great strength is its *inter*disciplinarity; this is also one of its great challenges, encompassing so many interests and approaches means that one definition is tricky!

What unites scholars working from a variety of disciplinary methods and theories is an interest in how health and illness function as sites of meaning in culture and as profound experiences which we humans share. Much health humanities scholarship is performed at a fairly analytical, theoretical level by doing the abstract work of understanding how discourses of 'health' or 'illness' are culturally constructed, for example. Such work is fascinating and important but pretty specialised. In contrast, I see narrative medicine as very much included within the larger category of the health humanities, but it is a much more *applied* approach, taking the theories and principles of the larger discipline and putting them into practice at the individual level as part of the healing work of the clinical encounter.

MGM. You propose close reading of medical humanities literature or 'close watching' on illness-centred movie at your course. What are the reactions of your students? What are the benefits of these activities? Do you envision any downside?

CAF. In our narrative and medicine course, we start the course with a few short stories and novels focused on the experience of the healthcare providers (mainly doctors and nurses), studying how the narratives construct different versions of 'professional identity'; in the second part of the course, we continue with short stories, novels and films, representing the patient experience. I have the students write a few short research papers, wherein they must explain how fictional narrative can influence providers' and patients' experience of illness; this work is the basis for our class discussion as well. I think the discussions go really well. Most students respond very empathetically to the various narratives, and when they don't, that generates challenging conversation: why don't you care about this character's experience? Film works particularly well; the students, as products of their time, are much more comfortable responding to film than to literature (alas!). They can readily *see* suffering when it's represented on film and definitely *feel* a response to the characters' experiences with unjust, unfeeling treatment versus caring and compassion. So there's no downside to getting future healthcare providers to be more mindful about what it means to care for their patients, at the level of the individual as well as at the level of the institution or the culture of healthcare itself. Rather than a downside, one obstacle I encounter: sometimes students just *can't* read or watch a narrative in anything other than a literal, concrete way. That is, they can encounter a story as a case study which might have a simple, direct lesson about patient care, but for some, it's very, very hard to make the leap to figurative, metaphorical readings or to use the experience of a few individuals to draw inferences about larger, abstract problems, like structural inequality, for example.

MGM. If you had the magic wand... how would you include medical humanities teaching at the university? Before university, like within the household or in school? Or after medical training?

CAF. We have the magic wand! My colleagues and I are in the process of developing an interdisciplinary, inter-institutional degree programme in health humanities! This programme will allow students to study the humanities as they might in any undergraduate degree programme, only with a thematic focus on health; we expect, however, that most students will use the health humanities degree as a preparation for further study in healthcare practice, policy and public health. I'm hoping that many (if not most) of the courses in the degree programme will not be directly focused on health. Students will take the health science courses necessary for specific career choices (e.g. pre-med) but will have a broader, more generous and liberal exposure to the humanities, arts and social sciences as the mainstay of their undergraduate degree programme.

MGM. In my opinion, there is a clear distinction between storytelling (stories inspired to facts but not written directly by patients and providers of care) and narratives of patients. What do you think about this? Do you consider it an issue at all?

CAF. I think the difference definitely matters. In particular, I'm very interested in understanding what we use different kinds of illness *for*—the social and clinical work they can or should do. To help my students think critically about the different kinds of narratives about the illness experience (being ill, caring the someone who is ill), I take a rhetorical approach: who is telling the story? To whom? What might the storyteller hope for as a result? What meaning does the audience get from the story, in addition to, or instead of, the storyteller's purpose? These questions are accessible ones to start with but can lead us to consider complicated problems of social relationships, cultural values, knowledge and authority and power.

MGM. Using medical humanities heritage, which are the writers and screenmakers of biggest impact in the hearts and souls and minds of your students up to now?

CAF. My students love a couple of texts I don't actually teach: *Tuesdays with Morrie* (Albom 1997) and *Wit* (Edson 1999). My female students enjoy *Helen Brent MD* (Meyer 1892) and *The Yellow Wallpaper* (Perkins 1980). I get a lot of good discussion going with William Carlos Williams' story *The Use of Force* (1938), which I combine with Richard Selzer's *Brute* and *Toenails* (1982). As far as film or TV are concerned, the film we watched more recently, *50/50* (2011), seemed to be a favourite. Students used to reference *House MD* (alarmingly, many would start the semester naming House as a role model), now it's *Grey's Anatomy*.

MGM. Let's move from young students to senior doctors and other providers of care. Did you have to try the experience of teaching them medical humanities? Could you tell something about their reactions? Do you think that it could be too late to teach your subject to people who already entered in their role...and they have been practising for many years and still are practising?

CAF. I've only taught undergraduates so far, and as I mentioned earlier, by just their second or third year of university, they have already acquired a lot of beliefs about what it means to practise medicine from both popular culture and their professional courses. In particular, they've learned that despite the values of patient-centred care that we espouse throughout their curricula, doctors are really the ones in charge of both patients and the healthcare team. My colleagues and I have to work really hard to challenge, or at least moderate, these beliefs! I'm not sure what it would be like to work with people more established in the health professions. Though I suspect that the kinds of health professionals who would seek out courses in the humanities would certainly be open-minded and curious thinkers.

MGM. You just published a book on psychosomatic disease. What does psychosomatic diseases have to do with medical humanities? Do you use it for teaching your students?

CAF. The anthology, *Reading the Psychosomatic in Medical and Popular Culture: Something, Nothing, Everything* (Farkas 2017), includes contributions from scholars in all kinds of fields—sociology, cultural studies, medicine and anthropology. But what situates the collection in the health humanities is that shared concern with illness as a fundamentally human experience and one which inevitably involves trying to make meaning at the individual and social level. All the contributors are interested in analysing the so-called psychosomatic as a site of unstable, disputed meaning and disrupted, if not failed, relationships. All the contributors are working towards a better understanding of the problems posed by the psychosomatic, as it is constructed in different settings through discourse in general and narrative in particular. We hope that such analysis might help both laypeople and clinicians approach psychosomatic conditions with more open-mindedness, critical insight and empathy—the qualities we value most in the health humanities.

For the reader's reference, we list the texts mentioned in the interview by Professor Carol Ann Farkas:

- *Tuesdays with Morrie*, a memoir written by Mitch Albom, later recreated by Thomas Rickman into a TV movie of the same name directed by Mick Jackson, which examines the interactions and phenomena between the human experience of living and dying, learning 'that not all stories end happily with a person going into remission and thus avoiding death. Rather, dying and death are natural processes and need to be acknowledged for what they are natural events' (Masters 2003).
- *Wit* is a one-act play written by the American playwright Margaret Edson, which won the 1999 Pulitzer Prize for Drama examining the internal life of an English professor suffering a terminal illness. Edson used her work experience in a hospital as part of the inspiration for her play. The drama highlights that while death is real and unavoidable, our lives belong to us to cherish or waste—a lesson that can be both uplifting and redemptive.
- *Helen Brent, M.D: A Social Study* is Annie Nathan Meyer's fascinating novel and still an interesting read today, which is the story of a woman who refused to give up her career for a convenience marriage.

- *The Yellow Wallpaper*, a story by American writer Charlotte Perkins Gilman, is a collection of journal entries written by a woman whose physician husband has rented an old mansion for the summer and details the descent of the young woman into madness.
- *The Use of Force* is a short story by the American author William Carlos Williams, first published in the collection *Life Along the Passaic River* in 1938. The story is narrated in first person by a physician, and the overall theme revolves around power and submission and the doctor's unnerved feeling during the forceful encounter. The main idea in the story is that the use of force itself corrupts the user, no matter the moral elevation underlying the purpose.
- *Brute* and *Toenails* belong to *Letters to a Young Doctor*, a Richard Selzer's collection of 23 stories, 5 of which take the form of 'letters' in which an older physician (not surprisingly, a surgeon) gives advice to an imaginary young surgeon. This collection of essays and tales talks about the human calling of doctoring and the lifelong learning that goes on among patients, hospitals and staff, dealing with important and difficult topics in medicine. He tells, for instance, of his own unsuccessful attempt to perform euthanasia at the request of the family of a terminally ill patient. According to Rita Charon, 'It was Richard Selzer', founder of the narrative medicine programme at Columbia University's College of Physicians and Surgeons, 'who was among the first physicians to understand the power of writing and reading fiction within medicine. He helped open up this whole territory to those of us who came after' (Stripling 2016).
- *50/50* is a 2011 American comedy-drama film directed by Jonathan Levine and written by Will Reiser. It was inspired by Reiser's own experiences with cancer in his mid-20s, and a message in the movie is that laughter is the best medicine. Finding the humour in any situation is an often-overlooked key to survival, and while the film never shies away from the pain, suffering and depression associated with an experience like this, it stays true to its core belief.
- *House, M.D.* is an American television medical drama. The series' main character is Dr. Gregory House (Hugh Laurie), an unconventional, misanthropic medical genius who, despite his dependence on pain medication, leads a team of diagnosticians. The resemblance with detective Sherlock Holmes created by Sir Arthur Conan Doyle is evident in House's reliance on deductive reasoning and psychology, even where it might not seem obviously applicable.
- *Grey's Anatomy* is an American medical drama television series focused on the lives of surgical interns, residents and attending physicians as they develop into seasoned doctors while trying to maintain personal lives and relationships.

Practice Time

Did you perceive the need for a little bit of order between medical humanities and narrative medicine? Whatever your answer is, please try to explain the reason for your answer.

What do you think about the 'border' between medical humanities and narrative medicine?

Would you like to use medical humanities tools? If so, which tools and for what purpose?

Would you like to use narrative medicine tools? If so, which tools and for what purpose?

What did the ideogram with the art of listening evoke in you? What do you think is the king in this ideogram? Do you think that you are already applying this kind of listening?

Would you enjoy practising?

If so, listen to the first person you meet until he/she will turn to silence, without interrupting them. Maybe you will be surprised that only after 2 min or at least 3 min, most of the people will stop speaking because they are looking for a dialogue.

If you wish, practise this art of listening with your carers, patients, colleagues, loved one, friends and people you don't know.

References

Albom M (1997) Tuesdays with Morrie: an old man, a young man, and life's greatest lesson. Doubleday, New York

Buzzati D (1937) Seven Floors. Originally published in the literary magazine "La Lettura", and afterwards the story was included in different collections ("I sette messaggeri", "Sessanta racconti" and "La boutique del mistero")

Denzin NK (1989) Interpretive biography. Sage, London

Edson M (1999) Wit: a play. Faber and Faber, New York

Farkas CA (2017) Reading the psychosomatic in medical and popular culture: Something. Nothing. Everything. Routledge

Florensky P (2004) The pillar and ground of the truth an essay in orthodox theodicy in twelve letters. Paperback

Greenhalgh T (2016) Cultural contexts of health: the use of narrative research in the health sector. Copenhagen: WHO Regional Office for Europe; Health Evidence Network synthesis report 49, viii + 54p

Hanke M (1990) Socratic pragmatics: maieutic dialogues. J Pragmat 14(3):459–465

Kondō M, Hirano C (2014) The life-changing magic of tidying up: the Japanese art of decluttering and organizing (First American edition.). Ten Speed Press, Berkeley

Launer J (2007) How not to be a Doctor and other essays

Lo J, Li Z (2017) The profundity of the character 'listen' in Chinese. https://www.theepochtimes.com/the-profundity-of-the-character-listen-in-chinese_2230261.html

Macdonanld H (2016) Plato on storytelling. https://thestorytellers.com/plato-on-storytelling/

Marini MG (2016) Narrative medicine: bridging the gap between evidence-based care and medical humanities. Springer, Cham

Masters JL (2003) Thursdays with Morrie: the use of contemporary literature in a death and dying course. Omega 47(3):245–252

Meyer AM (1892) Helen Brent, M.D: a social study. Cassell, New York, pp 93–94

Neeley L (2016) The value of storytelling in public health and medicine. https://www.isr.umich.edu/cps/events/Neely_20160613.pdf

O'Hara C (2014) How to tell a great story. https://hbr.org/2014/07/how-to-tell-a-great-story

Perkins GC (1980) The Charlotte Perkins Gilman reader: the yellow wallpaper, and other fiction. Pantheon Books, New York

Selzer R (1982) Letters to a young doctor. Simon & Schuster, New York
Silverman E (2017) Sharing and healing through storytelling in medicine. JAMA Intern Med 177(10):1409–1141
Stripling MY (2016) Richard Selzer: the birth of literature and medicine. Independent Scholar, Fort Worth, TX. http://hekint.org/2017/01/31/richard-selzer-the-birth-of-literature-and-medicine/
Tolstoj L (1886) The death of Ivan Ilych. Health Sciences Pub. Corp, New York. Edition 2006
Turow J (2010) Playing doctor: television, storytelling, and medical power. University of Michigan Press, Ann Arbor
Williams CW (1938) Life along the Passaic River. New Directions, Norfolk
Williams R, Potter M, Hoffman PS et al (1999) Patch Adams. Universal Studios, Universal City, CA

5 Among Health, Illness and Time: Chronic Disease, Waiting Time, Recovery, Perception of Time and Resting Time

Nobody ever seems to have enough time: there are only 24 h in a day, and yet, we continue to struggle to squeeze countless things into our already busy schedules. Healthcare professionals are no different, and as everyone else in this ever more efficiency-driven society, they are asked to push their limits constantly further. Time, or rather shortage of time, is a constant mantra. The shorter the visits are, the larger the productivity. So how is it feasible to even consider embracing a new activity like the practice of NM? Where could they possibly find the time to practise the art of listening, the tools for reflective writing, the moving forwards from disease to illness and giving each patient a central role and so right time as proposed by NM? Time is finite.

But again, *is time finite*? As other great questions of life, we can search the answer to this dilemma through the symbolism of ancient mythology. In Ancient Greece, *time* was mainly represented by two deities *Chronos* and *Kairos*: the former was envisioned as an old man who ate his own offspring (Apollodorus, 180 BC-120 BC, n.d.), symbolising future being relentlessly overtaken by the past. Time *eats* everything; thus, we are finite, and the time of the doctor's consultation with the patient is finite. *Kairos* instead was envisioned as a young winged-ankle god of opportunity. He symbolised an interruption in the flow of time and a window of instant intuition that leads to good judgement and decisions (Liddell et al. 1843). Today, we might consider it the *quantum leap*, the instantaneous infinitesimal time to reach a higher energetic level. Further, in the setting of NM, *Kairos* could be seen as the instant intuition grasping the value of patient experience.

As put by John Launer, one of the founding fathers of NM as well as a physician and an educator, good conversations inviting patients to change take just 10 min, provided one knows the appropriate questions to ask and clear the field from their *egos* and a priori diagnosis (Launer 2007). NM *does not require more time but a* change in perspective. It may be argued that training in narrative skills requires time, but if we compare the time needed for completing a core curriculum (medical humanities and NM are offered only in few universities in New York, London, Milan, Rome, Paris and few others) with the time needed to re-educate an intern or

M. G. Marini, *Languages of Care in Narrative Medicine*,
https://doi.org/10.1007/978-3-319-94727-3_5

practitioner who has been overexposed to the biomechanical aspects of medicine, we may see the advantage. Once the skills have been mastered, practicing NM and spending 5 min for writing the parallel chart (the *written room* of thoughts of doctor-patient encounter) is worthwhile the effort, especially if one considers the patient's waiting time spent waiting for the doctor. However, not all patients require the same time; some may require 20 min, while others only 5 min; it is very subjective and obviously depends on the circumstance.

To recall the concept of the Greek gods of time, practicing NM may be more a matter of *Kairos*, i.e. of reaching a different energetic level to establish a successful relationship with patients. It involves a different perception and open to different questions and different answers. Yet, reality ties us to the *Chronos* sphere, accounting for wastes of time and time-saving: here, we are time keepers with a chronometer. *Kairos*, the little god with winged ankles, is able to fly, to be light in the sky, and takes our hands so that we can learn to fly over time: if we listen carefully to some doctor-patient encounters, the 'context' is filled by tests, investigations, remedies and drugs. *How do you feel?* is a tricky question that can allow the expression of a qualitative adjective such as 'bad', 'better' and 'good' or the spreading out of the inner realm with *fear*, *anger*, *pain* or *joy*. The first kind of answer brings back to physicians, in a sort of Pavlovian's reflex, to change therapy, prescribe new tests and comment blood parameters: *Chronos* is the winner with the productivity of investigations and therapies. *Kairos* would like that we, as free children, could express our emotions so that an authentic doctor-patient relationship can start. *Kairos* shows us another way to practise as counsellors, psychotherapists, nurses and doctors.

Of course, *Kairos* is not replacing *Chronos*, but if we do not do anything to block our behavioural stereotype with patients, as defensive medicine, the defensive wall of *Chronos* will be reinforced, and daring new changes in healthcare context will not be possible. *Kairos* is an act of bright courage. It is catching messages in the patients' words, for example, the fact they might be worried for losing their job. In following a *Kairos* approach, the physician would not continue talking about the disease but would rather ask, 'What can I do in helping you overcome the fear of losing your job?'

Defensive medicine is paralysing the development of fresh and genuine doctor-patient relationship (Sonal Sekhar and Vyas 2013). It is an old conservative approach, like the old god with the beard eating his offspring: in this case, eating thoughts and feelings of physicians, nurses and patients.

Therefore, when we are questioned about how much time does the practice of NM require, we answer in a quite provocative way 'no extra time'. It is simply a different way of caring for people, built on positive dynamic patient-carer encounters, which can reduce over testing and overtreatment (the so-called defensive medicine).

Kairos involves 'active listening'. As evidenced by Langewitz and colleagues in their study on *Spontaneous talking time at start of consultation in outpatient clinic: cohort study*, patients took an average initial time of only approximately 22 s before being interrupted by the doctor (Langewitz et al. 2002). Therefore, the study assessed a sequential cohort of patients from the outpatient clinic of the Department of Internal Medicine at the University Hospital of Basel to evaluate how much talking time a patient actually needed to express their problem. Doctors were trained for 1 h on basic elements of active listening, such as pausing, using facilitators like 'hmm-hmm', nodding or echoing. They were told to simply ask the patient 'What brought you here?' and not engage in other types of questions. Moreover, they were advised to interrupt patients talking for more than 5 min to comply with their consultation schedule. Of the 330 patients, 53% were women and 47% men; the mean spontaneous talking time was 92 s (SD ± 105 s; median 59 s), and 78% (258) of patients had finished their initial statement in 2 min. Only seven patients had talked for over 5 min; yet, they had not been interrupted because the doctors felt that the patients were providing important information. No other sociodemographic variable (education, income, civil status, type of employment and sex) significantly influenced spontaneous talking time except for age ($r_s = 0.41$; $P < 0.001$; 17–29 years, 77 (105) seconds; 30–49 years, 92 (93) seconds; 50–87 years, 108 (114) seconds). In conclusion, the findings showed that most patients (when left to speak uninterrupted by the doctor) only needed 2 min.

The Long Time: Feeling Bad for a Long Time

'I'm sick to death of this particular self. I want another'.

Time though has many other facets, and Kairos is only one aspect. The time of patients, for example, the time for bringing back balance to what has become disrupted in their life, is often much longer, or rather is a much 'slower' time.

Orlando, Virginia Woolf

In Virginia Woolf's *Orlando* (1928), the main character, Orlando, is tormented in the quest for identifying and conquering his/her real 'essence'. The process is slow and is crossed by periods alternating life experiences, lethargy and metamorphosis, after which the character finally reaches understanding. Orlando was born as a male during the reign of Elizabeth I of England but ends his story as an emancipated woman at the turn of the twentieth century. He passes through two eras, two aeons, to reach his/her metamorphosis: the modern era and the contemporary one. Across the centuries, Lord Orlando takes off his clothes of a rigid male and full of false gender absolutisms in which 'every man is…' and 'every woman is…' dictated in a life of honours of great values for others, but of no value for himself, to become the 'other self' desired by Woolf. Approximately, around 1610, the triggering factor of horror and compassion for a soldier dying next to him in war will make him fall asleep in some oriental non-lieu to be born again later as Lady Orlando. From this moment, in the following centuries, he struggles to affirm the fact of 'being a woman' through the right of inclusion in conversation with male poets, such as Swift and Pope, who celebrate her beauty but ridicule her female intelligence or through the right of private property, from which she is excluded because she has no male heirs. The novel ends with the encounter with an adventurer arriving on his horse and ready to leave again for non-specified ideals in the New Continent; here, she ends the love story with the restless cavalier to conquer her freedom, autonomy and independence and thus completing her metamorphosis.

Orlando is the manifesto of the dual nature of Virginia Woolf. The peculiarity of Orlando is that in these two eras (more than 400 years), the protagonist falls into lethargy to heal from life experiences continuously affecting his/her most intimate soul and the people she/he has encountered and who have passed away. Every time Orlando wakes up as a man or woman, he/she decides to radically change his/her life by moving to other countries or changing sex, lover and profession. Thus, the novel is extraordinary: to make deep and not ephemeral changes, there must be two elements, time and sleep.

The first element, time, dilates across centuries until becoming the age, the 'Aion'—where history, as life phases, divides in centuries: for ancient Greeks, *Aion*, another of the multifaceted ways to call *time*, is translated as the succession of historical ages throughout eternity. *Aion* symbolises cosmos and its seven stellar orders (the Greek representation of the eternal universe expanding towards eternity) (Von Franz 1992).

Sleep, the other ingredient, represents a dreamless rest, an oblivion, a long pause, retreating from worldliness, becoming a cocoon to mature and give life to a new blooming. Using terms of NSM, it would be expressed as 'not doing'. Scientific and hard-working Western world based on efficacy can barely understand the transformation mystery that happens when one withdraws and creates a void as taught in the oriental approaches to life (Zen, Yoga and mindfulness).

Yet, I write about NM and ask you what Orlando's story has to do with illness narratives. We can look at patients and their familiar stories, which live with diseases not only in a 'chronic' but also in an 'aeonic' way, almost eternal in their perception—a succession of eras, phases and cycles. When Virginia Woolf started writing *Orlando*, she was feeling 'bad' (so to use a term of NSL) or, as we would label her today, 'depressed'. De facto she was an emancipated and free woman facing a very hostile society. The book was her way to understand and solve her discomfort, travelling across a 400-year aeon and reading her life through lethargy (rom *Lethes*, oblivion, and *Argos*, inertia) (Liddell et al. 1843), i.e. the inactivity in the resetting of memory. The protagonist is seesawing between happiness and unhappiness for almost the entire book. Yet, through his/her experience of young love, war, poetry, politics, society and again adult love, he/she finds his/her final happiness, open to the new experiences. For the society at that time, Virginia was considered to be 'not normal' and 'sick', as she was in love with the woman to which the novel is dedicated: this is the occasion for passing again through this suffering of being victim of social constrictions in the ancient world of unequal opportunities to arrive then in the modern world loving her diversity. There are both the real time of writing and the long time necessary for metamorphosis.

Listening to the narratives of 'sick' people, we see that they want to be 'normal' as Lord Orlando, at least initially, and they search for a key to be accepted by the others: family, friends, workplace and external environment. This happens especially in the case of disabilities. Searching for normality, yet, can be an *idiot* chimaera, if it becomes a useless obsession stealing time to the discovery of one's own real essence. As explained by Arthur Frank in *The Wounded Storyteller* (1995): *In order to cherish ourselves in our state of discomfort and the world around us, we must find our own way of living our diversity and turn that 'frailty' into a point of strength.* We cannot obtain this in the short term. It requires honesty, long time and lethargy between attempts, as taught by the great Virginia.

While above I focused on the need for an instantaneous and quick time, *Kairos*, to realise and correct pathways of patient care, I wish to stress the importance of living according to a slow and persistent maturation time, consistently with the saying, 'haste makes waste'. As Carl Gustav Jung wrote, the soul—the undefined that defines our essential nature—is much slower than the rational mind (Jung 1969). Latins, who were a people of pragmatic spirits, conciliated both time dimensions with the paradox *festina lente* (Suetonius (2nd century BC) n.d.), *make haste slowly*. We must remember that next to the voracity of infinitesimal time, our nature—above all, the suffering one—needs long times for accepting the illness condition, finding a new way to live with the disease. Decisions that may help us will be taken calmly, as choice we will take with who takes care of us. This is a juggling exercise between velocity and slowness.

A Long Time to Feel Good

The need for rest to recover and to safeguard rest is very vivid in our current society. However, as much as it is necessary, it is risking extinction: the disappearance of the time to rest after an illness means the fading away of convalescence.

Once convalescence was considered to be just as important as cure. It was needed for the body to regenerate and get strong after an illness or a surgical intervention, a trauma or any other factor that had unbalanced the body and the mind. The term 'convalescence' comes from the Latin cum—'with' and *to be worth* 'to be well' or 'with the health', as in regained health.

Nowadays, the term 'convalescence' appears obsolete and has almost disappeared from our daily vocabulary, leaving place for sentences like 'you'll return as good as before', 'as good as new in no time', 'we will immediately put you back on your feet' and 'we'll operate on Friday so he/she can be back to work on Monday'. Prescribed rest seems to be something outdated and difficult to achieve. The attitude of quick restoration though is not only manifested by the carers but by the patients as well who view checkups and medical procedures as a bothering waste of time, taken away from the duty of productivity.

In Italy, up until the 1990s, the hospitals were refunded for their services based on the total number of days of hospitalisation rather than on the number of patients or type of surgical intervention. Accordingly, hospital convalescence was a never-ending affair, with an economic gain for the hospital. Whenever a person was to undergo a procedure, admission would be scheduled approximately 1 week before so that the hospital could have enough time to (calmly) perform all the tests they needed on the patient, occupying a hospital bed and preventing its use for some other potential patients (backing up the already 'eternal' waiting list) and eventually prolonging discharge for another indefinite quantity of time. Times were endless, and the patient could no longer wait to be back home to his/her daily routine.

With the introduction of diagnosis-related groups in reimbursement procedures from the national healthcare system (as in Europe and the USA), this has changed, speeding processes towards an earlier patient discharge (Baker 2002). Time has been so compressed that the hospital convalescence has almost disappeared whatever the reason for hospitalisation (acute illnesses, planned interventions, accidents and traumas). Today, the world keeps on spinning as if nothing happened; all too often, people expect to go from the 'off' or 'sick' mode to the 'on' or healthy mode in symphony with the smiling hyperefficiency world. Despite the time of resting at home to recover one's strength, we have come to the point to feel guilty for taking some time off from our chores. This binary status between on and off is extremely evident in advertisements that show a person suffering a severe cold and sitting at their desk in front of their computer; once they have taken the medication, they return to be their own smiling self and are ready for the next business meeting. The advertising lasts for seconds, though does not obviously reflect realist timing.

Yet, convalescence is almost a taboo, hardly pronounceable in this society in which we are living: Hartmut Rosa, a German sociologist, calls it the 'Society of the acceleration and alienation' (Rosa 2010).

People can accept you sick or well, i.e. on or off. Women after delivery are discharged from hospital within 24 h, without having the time to recover from the fatigue of pushing the baby out. Patients who underwent orthopaedic surgery sometimes are asked to walk when it is premature, and then they can experience consequences of this hurry which can require further surgery. Quality of recovery is a complex construct whereby definition is heavily influenced by the opinions and biases of the individual patient, clinician or institution. As a result, recovery assessment tools differ in their fundamental definitions of recovery, breadth and assessment timeframe. Accurate assessment of recovery is essential as suboptimal recovery has both economic and prognostic implications. Quality of care is often substituted as a surrogate at the institutional level for quality of recovery, but it is ideologically distinct from patients' perceived quality of care, recovery and satisfaction. Thus, it is important to respect the uniqueness of individual time of recovery.

Alain de Botton, a Swiss-born British author and co-founder of The School of Life in 2008 says as follows: 'What's lacking is patience for convalescence'. People should not only consider recovery from important illnesses but also from work overload or stress of the daily life.

The School of Life offers a curriculum of classes teaching emotional intelligence to deal with day-to-day events of life to the death of a loved one. These classes are taught by leading authors, artists, actors and academics, combining their own experiences with ideas from great thinkers of the past to offer participants intelligent and playful ways to interpret the world and their place within it. Since the time of the publication of the book, The School of Life has attracted 3.3 million of followers around the world.

Thus, Alain de Botton insists on taking time for oneself as a system of care: the danger with stress is based on (Lundberg 2005) 'The sympathetic adrenomedullary system secreting epinephrine and norepinephrine and the hypothalamic pituitary adrenocortical (HPA) system secreting of cortisol. Their physiologic effects are also a link between the psychosocial environment and various health outcomes. The stress responses have been important for human and animal survival, evolution and for protection of the body. However, in modern society, some of these bodily responses may cause harm rather than protection. Catecholamines have been linked to cardiovascular disorders such as hypertension, myocardial infarction and stroke, cortisol to cardiovascular disease, Type 2 diabetes, reduced immune function and cognitive impairment.

Long-term health and survival requires an adequate balance between catabolic (mobilisation of energy) and anabolic processes (growth, healing). Today, lack of rest, recovery and restitution is a greater health problem than the absolute level of stress'.

In 2016, Durham University conducted the widest survey ever on rest, involving over 18,000 people from 134 different countries in the rest test, an online survey asking people what made them feel good to investigate the public's resting habits and their attitudes towards relaxation and business (BBC Website n.d.). Over two thirds claimed that they would like more rest; nearly a third said they needed more rest than the average person, while 10% thought they needed less.

The survey found that those who felt they needed more rest scored lower in terms of wellbeing. Similarly, those who responded saying that they thought they get more rest than average or do not feel the need for more rest had wellbeing scores twofold higher than those who wanted more rest, suggesting that one's own perception of rest level actually matters. Dr. Felicity Callard, principal investigator of the project and social scientist, said, 'The survey shows that people's ability to rest, and their levels of well-being, are related. We're delighted that these findings combat a common, moralizing connection between rest and laziness'.

Among the activities that the respondents considered most restful, the top five were as follows: reading (58%), being in the natural environment (53.1%), being on their own (52.1%), listening to music (40.6%) and doing nothing specific (40%) and were mostly done alone. 'It's intriguing that the top restful activities are frequently done alone. Perhaps it's not only the total hours resting or working that we need to consider, but the rhythms of our job, and rest and time spent with and without others', Callard adds.

Modern Life

The results of this survey come at a time when the urge to be busy defines modern life and the topic of rest is at the forefront of many people's minds. Rest can seem hard to find, whether in relation to an exhausted body, a racing mind or a hectic city. Rest is a much broader category than sleep and has physical, mental and spiritual components. But much less is known about the potentially restorative benefits of rest partly because it means different things to different people.

The survey asked respondents to state how many hours of rest they had within the last 24 h. The results showed that on average, being younger and having a higher household income was associated with having fewer hours of rest. Those with caring responsibilities or in shift work which included nights also reported fewer hours of rest. Claudia Hammond said, 'We had no idea how many people would choose to complete the Rest Test. More than 18,000 gave up their precious spare time to tell us what they thought about rest, which shows us what a pressing issue it is. These results show just how crucial it is to our well-being to ensure people do have time to rest. We can begin to try to work out what the optimum amount of rest might be and how we should go about resting'.

When Time Is Back and Forward: Cyclic Time and the Hours

After we learnt the importance of rest, I wish to spend some words on the need to bring back and honour 'natural time', the 'cyclic time of our world' and its impact of the human being.

Today, if one does not want to be labelled as 'reductionist' in care and medicine, medical sociology insists to move the attention from the sick organ or from the disease to the patient, or better, to the person integrated in his/her biological, psychological and social context. This 'biopsychosocial' paradigm represents an openness that distances itself from the mechanistic model—well exemplified in the man-machine metaphor, according to which disease breaks the pieces and a good mechanic-physician must repair or scrap—to reintegrate the living being in its social context, being the human (*Anthropos*), as Aristotle anticipated, a biologically living (*bion*) and social (*politikon*) being. It was and still is impossible to split our biological being from local, relational, everyday-life events. To heal in a holistic way—another word today very inflated, where *olos* means whole—the biopsychosocial model helps us (Havelka et al. 2009).

Still, in the search for a relationship among health, disease and social context, is it enough to talk about relationships, children, weddings, cohabitations, fertility, sexuality and furthermore, school, work, employment, unemployment, productivity or salary? Is it enough for us to divide everyday life in compartments at the cost of oversimplification (cosmic time, cyclic time of nature)? When a condition of fragility, insecurity or illness appears, forcing us to deal with the appraisal of our lives, does this paradigm satisfy us?

To date, quality of life questionnaire includes all these items, including sexuality and spirituality issues. Yet, are these questions able to grasp the information they are enquiring? The closed nature of the questions and their answers (i.e. yes/no; on a scale from 1 to 10, how happy do you feel today?) is embedded in the historical period we are living in: they will mirror that vague reductionist accent that will bring us to an oppositional qualification between good and evil. In short, we do not give voice to the many facets of our life and our biology, our psyche, in more or less productive relationships—in our reflections, inquiries and researches, reducing them to a mere schedule of home-work-school-hospital or another place. On the one hand, we are embedded in our current historical time (2018), and on the other hand, we are also embedded in a cosmic one. Yet, we miss a cosmology and our contact with natural time and nature itself, or better, we miss our cosmic time—where 'cosmic' means harmonious, beautiful, cyclical and biological one.

So far, we have analysed the linear time (*Chronos*), the time-opportunity (*Kairos*) and the eternal time (*Aion*) with the rest; but, we have still not considered the cyclic time of hours (*Orai*) of nature: the seasons, pacing the cyclical rhythm of nature and the 'eternal return' (Duk 2003). The Hours are the last piece of the puzzle that make up the four dimensions of time: that one that flows without return, the *Chronos*; the eternal one and the instant one, the *Aion* and the *Kairos*; and the longest time and the one of the eternal return (hours).

Time is cyclical not only for ancient Greeks but also for oriental philosophies: Japanese poems, the *haiku*, are based on the seasonal rhythm. Rhythm itself, in its etymology, indicates the flowing: *Panta rei*, 'everything flows', as Heraclitus stated (sixth century BC). Everything flows, just like hours. Nature has its precise laws: planet Earth is in aphelion, far from the Sun in summer, and in perihelion, near the Sun in winter, and—except some little realignments of the terrestrial axis or a catastrophic meteorite that destroyed dinosaurs—we have many statistical probabilities that the Sun will rise tomorrow (Hume 1711–1776) so we can serenely sleep. The humankind has been ruled so much by these Earth rotation and revolution movements since its appearance on this planet that this biological time is encrypted in our DNA (Liu et al. 1992).

Since childhood, we realise that the Sun rises day after day and time goes by with the alternation of seasons. We wait for spring through the memory of our childhood, the metabolism of our cells, or maybe because of our collective subconscious (Jung 2002).

In this cosmic time, we beat linear time, *Chronos*, the despot whom inexorably proceeds during years: we may be 30, 50 or 70 years old, yet springtime comes back for our planet and for our bodies and for plants and animals. This is a wonderful miracle. Here, in this cyclical time, the flowing rhythm triumphs, and we become immanently living in nature: Jung was right when he wondered the reasons of birth of discomfort in civilisation. He situated it precisely in the loss of contact with seasons, agriculture, the summer harvest, the autumn seeding, the winter long wait and the spring renaissance. *Primo vere*: Latins called this season the first version, the first twisting. In ancient Greek mythology, it was the first and last of the hours: *Thallo*, the blooming spring; *Auxo*, the summer luxuriance; and *Carpo*, the autumn harvest of fruits (Hyginus n.d.). The cold of winter was symbolised by a man, *Cheimon*, that means beside winter, bitter cold, snow: he was not a goddess, but—in a certain sense—the fall from goddess. The hours were the young sisters of the three Moirai, women producing the warp of the rope of the linear time: they formed the strings, and they cut them at the end of life. They were daughters of Zeus and Themis, the universal order. If the *Moirai* determine and rule the chronological time of individuals (birth, growth and death), the hours bring the cosmic time, and the cyclical laws always involve a new renaissance. It is the same tree newly growing, teaching us that the cyclical time is sovereign in the plant realm as for animals in their different mating seasons.

More ancient civilisations had actually established eight seasons linked to the astronomical movements of our planet defined by two solstices, two equinoxes and seasonal interludes as well as the variations of time we may define climate—from *klima*, i.e. the inclination of the terrestrial axis, which were all linked to human mood. In fact, our behaviour is intrinsically linked to the cycles of nature (Saeed and Bruce 1998) and adapts to the seasons just like animals and plants do through a dormant or hibernation phase. Yet, the signs of these adaptations are often taken in their extreme manifestations and classified as symptoms of medical disorders, such as seasonal affective disorder (Oginska and Oginska-Bruchal 2014). In fact, the definition of winter *disorder* reads as 'depression, lack of energies, sleepiness, weight gain, desire of carbohydrates' (Narrative Medicine Website n.d.) and is prevalent in late autumn and winter. Despite the fact that the definition basically overlaps physiological behaviour of the majority of us in winter, the tendency in Western efficiency-driven societies is to treat these symptoms with antidepressant drugs. The biopsychosocial model does not permit hibernation. The 'sabbatical' winter period for listening to our body preparing for another spring season is not an option.

In the Persian culture, people were aware of winter gloominess. To overcome it, there was the ritual of carpet weaving and looming: by creating carpets portraying beautiful spring that had a therapeutic effect. During the cold winter weather when landscapes and mindscapes are shattered by ice and snow, women used to create carpets imagining the beauty of the spring depicting the tree of life, full of flowers, leaves, fruits, nests, birds, the top standing out the blue sky and the roots embedded in a brown soil covered by fresh grass (Citati 2006).

Speaking of spring and *Orai*, it is also worth recalling the masterpiece of the renowned painter Botticelli, portraying Venus covered by a veil of flowers brought by the spring *Orai*. The painting is an ode to life, in which the dullness of autumn and winter leave place to a coloured rainbow and where life is emphasised through the prosperity of the female figures, who are all of the childbearing age.

Another interesting symbol is represented by the story of Persephone, the beautiful girl who lives with her mother in the 6 months, the harvest goddess Demeter; together, they generate spring and summer, while she lives with her husband in the other 6 months, Hades, the god-king of the underworld. There are autumns and winters without harvests (Nilsson 1941). Again nature is feminine in blossom, and its disappearance turns the world cold. No empathy, no boundaries at the light of the Sun, but just profound boundaries in the underworld.

Could we, in this long waiting time, learn to be wise and patient also from the alternation of clear and grey sky? Learn to be patient? Could we allow ourselves to mourn as Demeter does in the 6 months she is left alone without her daughter, who is 'living with the dead people'? Is it beneficial to shed tears? Yes, in one out of two individuals: tears belong to the languages of care. In an international study on *crying* (Vingerhoets and Bylsma 2007), participants across 37 countries were asked about their most recent crying episode: most reported feeling better mentally after crying compared with how they felt before crying (51.4%), 38.3% reported feeling the same and 9.7% felt worse. In terms of physical improvement, 27% felt physically better after crying, 56.4% reported feeling the same and 15.6% felt worse.

To overcome difficulties of the disease and other traumas we encounter in life, the cyclic flowing of seasons and the hours teach us the art of patience, together with art of crying and smiling afterwards, cherishing hope.

Narrating illness means having the possibility to rejoin the cosmic time, the more ancestral, and giving again this cycle of dignity and the necessary space: not for a matter of justice but because rejoining our roots brings us to a blooming awareness. Maybe it distances us from materiality and totems, but it puts us in contact with a Zen spirituality. Japanese not only stroll under blooming cherry trees, but they contemplate petals falling in the wind. In the film of Kitano, Hana Bi (Kitano 1997)—flowers of fire—the policeman's wife living with cancer at end stage asks her husband to bring her there to see cherry trees blooming, assist to a pink renaissance and to the estrangement before the awareness of death. The cosmic order is a natural law: alienation means being not able to feel the universe and the body embedded in the world.

If we want to enlarge the horizon from the biopsychosocial model, let us begin to give it again the cosmic and natural sense poorly allowed by our Western civilisation, being more and more standardised in places and continuous and identical in seasons. Narrative belongs to our human nature, and language is an instinct: in the chapter dedicated to place and wellbeing, we will see how much natural setting of care is wished by people. When I am referring to nature, I am referring to trees, water, sea, mountains, countryside, animals, flowers, colours, light, sky and ground. Nobody of our interviewed people who were asked 'what is your ideal setting of care?' mentioned concrete, as we will see in Chap. 7. The overuse of concrete in our world and society is a killer of our relationship with nature.

The sense of beauty I am feeling while writing these considerations is surprisingly found in an odd convergence of a Nobel Prize in Medicine given in last 2017: the discovery of the circadian rhythm in relationship to the Earth's revolution and rotation movements.

The Natural and Eco-friendly Nobel for Medicine

The following excerpt is from the press release of the Nobel Academy, October 2017 (Nobel prize n.d.):

> *Life on Earth is adapted to the rotation of our planet. For many years we have known that living organisms, including humans, have an internal, biological clock that helps them anticipate and adapt to the regular rhythm of the day. But how does this clock actually work? Jeffrey C. Hall, Michael Rosbash and Michael W. Young were able to peek inside our biological clock and elucidate its inner workings. Their discoveries explain how plants, animals and humans adapt their biological rhythm so that it is synchronized with the Earth's revolutions.*

The Nobel Prize in Medicine has been assigned to Jeffrey C. Hall, Micheal Rosbash and Michael W. Young (who have been working together at Brandeis University in Waltham, Massachusetts, and at the Rockefeller University) for their research on the circadian night-day rhythm and physiological functions of living beings. The Nobel Prize has shown that a gene, which is named *period* (Liu et al. 1992), controls the regular biological daily rhythm and codifies for a protein PER that accumulates inside cells during the night and is depleted during the day. Later, they find other protein-based elements of this system, revealing the mechanism that manages the self-sufficient clock inside the cell. The complexity of our biological clock is managed by two other genes, the timeless (TIM) and the double time (DBT) genes (Price et al. 1998) that modulate the 24-h regulation of the day-night rhythm. The study of the 'circadian' rhythms proved how fundamental synchronisation is important for our wellbeing.

In my opinion, this is one of the most caring Nobel about human, animal and vegetal physiology of Earth, maybe more, of the entire cosmos. If we read the first sentences of the Nobel Academy press release (Nobel prize n.d.), we find the words 'rotation of our planet': so, we, as living being, are integrated into the rotation movement, i.e. Earth's axis of 'our' planet that rotates on itself. They could write just 'of the planet': they add that possessive adjective, 'our', making all the races living on this planet responsible and sharing this soil. At the end of the first paragraph is written *biological rhythm so that it is synchronized with the Earth's revolutions*. There is that 'sibylline'—'the Earth's revolutions'. The revolution movement of the Earth is that one carried out in a solar year, 365 days, when the Earth by continuing the rotation on itself, pacing the circadian rhythm, realises its orbit around the Sun, creating the cycle of the seasons. Therefore, the topic of light and dark assumes a different dimension that touch the rhythm of the seasonal nature, where there are long days with more light and shorter nights, and vice versa. There is the *aurora borealis* and the long Austral night, and vice versa. I do not believe that the words of a press release are chosen without a reason, but the moving from the rotation to the revolution movements (How many? Of which years? Ages? Past, Present and Future?) opens to broaden breath horizons and gives a 'stellar' dynamism. That little mosquito flying around the fruit used to isolate the *period* gene, that *Drosophila melanogaster* we all studied at the high school, here is elevated in a stellar ecosystem.

This Nobel Prize reminds us that our microcosmos is inside a macrocosmos that exists through an interdependence between light, darkness, life and stars' movement. It reminds us the sense of responsibility and of belonging to our planet. Isn't this enough? It reminds us that we are human beings in a big clock: if we change the rules of nature too much, like reducing the hours of sleep to be more 'performative and productive', this involves a reduced harmonisation with the 'celestial movement' and could damage our sense of 'human being'. Richard Wiseman is analysing the sleep since decades and has written (Wiseman 2014):

> *Two-thirds of us are sleep-deprived. And this isn't just an inconvenience, making us foggy and caffeine-dependent. Lack of sleep brings with it a host of problems—an increased risk of heart attacks, cancer, diabetes and an increased risk of weight gain. You might well wonder just why so many of us are so bad at sleeping? And since the humble snooze can protect our physical and emotional health, can make us feel energetic and confident and creative, why the majority of us consistently don't get enough sleep?*

Wiseman writes that before the invention of the electric lights, people used to sleep for 10 h, an appropriate time to feel rested and to face better the next day. Nowadays, we can take pills of melatonin to overtake the jet lag, which stimulates the production of PER proteins that we will need for the next day, but only for a specific period, to protect our organism. However, beyond the occasional trips, the LED light in our bedrooms and in our bathrooms at night and the city lights damage our melatonin's production. For PER, I could add further that the period protein PER stands for performative (English term is also nowadays a trend in the people's productive efficacy evaluation).

Different studies have suggested that exposure to light at night (LAN) induces sleep disturbances, impairs melatonin section and disrupts the circadian physiology and behaviour (Boivin 2000; McClung 2013). Depression is frequently accompanied by these conditions. A greater depression risk, observed in night-shift workers, is significantly correlated to LAN exposure and circadian misalignment between internal biological and environmental rhythms (Bara and Arber 2009). Recent studies have demonstrated that in humans, 5-lux LAN exposure in home settings is significantly associated with depression symptoms (Fonken et al. 2012).

Professor Kenji Obayashi and his team in Nara Medical University, School of Medicine, Japan, enrolled 863 participants during 2010–2014 to test the association of LAN exposure with the incidence of depressive symptoms in an elderly general population. They observed that bedroom LAN exposure in home settings, including low average light intensity, is significantly associated with depression risk (Obayashi et al. 2018). The researchers visited participants' homes predominantly on weekdays, instructed the participants to maintain a standardised sleep diary and measured bedroom light intensity objectively using a portable light meter placed facing the ceiling at the head of the participant's bed. Thereafter, they assessed the depressive symptoms. Out of the 863 participants, who did not have depressive symptoms at the baseline, the LAN group exhibited a significantly higher depression risk compared with the 'dark' group (hazard ratio = 1.89, almost double). Maintaining darkness in the bedroom at night might be a novel and viable option to prevent depression.

This is another evidence about the importance of respecting the natural circadian rhythm and indicates how dangerous it is to neglect what is happening in nature for being more productive: the risk of becoming depressed.

Even with exceptions such as artists who create by night with the moonlight or women that breastfeed helped by oxytocin, dreams, as stated by Wiseman, are useful to recapture the logic path interrupted during the day and open widely the doors of creativity and possible awareness' solutions and expansions towards situations that seem hard to solve during the daylight. I believe that everyone had solution ideas in the middle of the night, then turning on the other side of the bed, restart to sleep, softly cradled by the sweet rotation of our planet.

For those who read the Odyssey (Homer n.d.), one of the trials of Odysseus was the land of the holy cows of Helios, the Sun god. They were sacred, untouchable and inedible. The number of these cows was less known: seven herds composed by 50 cows and 350 holy animals were dedicated to the Sun. Among the expressed theories, one of the most likely is that this number was a symbol of the calendar's days (in the past, around 350). Therefore, to kill one or more days was a sacrilegious action, changing the natural rhythm of rotation and revolution of the Earth towards the Sun. This is wonderful. It reminds us that we are not alone, that also plants sleep at night and that for anyone of us a sunrise grows to announce the dawn and day that will come, along with the sunset and the evening before night. It reminds us that humanisation means taking back the time of 9–10 h of sleep to be sharper and more aware during the day and switching off cell phones, TV and LED lights to prevent chronic diseases and unhappiness. It reminds us that accommodation systems exist—like the timeless gene that works also in the dark, in a situation of light deprivation, just for limited time. However, the emergency that for months the light could disappear on our planet was faced in our biological evolution.

Furthermore, it reminds us a cosmological system, which owns an extraordinary power of care. It has its own language, which has to be decrypted. Once decrypted, the benefit of pacing with the natural rhythm of light and dark as well as cold and hot will put the biological clock of the cells of our bodies in connection with the holistic system of nature.

The Narrative of Time: I Feel My Time, You Feel Your Time, I Say My Time Is… and You Say Your Time Is…

Time perception is one of the themes which philosophers and scientists have put into questioning and, more universally, all individuals, possibly, because it belongs to universal archetypes: what is behind the sensation that time flies or never goes by? Is time course different between youth and old age? What if we are sick or healthy? Moreover, are these hypotheses or prejudices originating from a lack of objective knowledge about time phenomenon true?

Among the usual clichés, or maybe through the convergence of a number of researches, we assume that 'the perception of time for young and adult people follows almost opposite tracks, where for elder people time seems to pass faster' (Gemignani 2015). Neurosciences can help us to explain this phenomenon: different awareness of time can be linked to a different capability to memorise events, more enhanced in young people, thanks to the presence of chemical mediators implicated in the processes of cerebral plasticity.

Time, Young and Elder People

For adults, time flows faster than for teenagers. This phenomenon is defined as 'telescope effect', which is the tendency to position the events inside the memory through a chronological order so that recent events result more distant in time and more remote events result nearer. Young people fix the object that is close to the telescope far away, while elder people closely investigate most distant things, getting lost in infinite details. Memory is a parallel process to how time is perceived:

'short-term memory' is very active in young people, and 'long-term memory' is that one persisting in elder people's thought, occupying space for new time.

The temporal perception appears influenced by the body and brain's biochemical conditions. In particular, dopamine is one of the main neurotransmitters involved, which contributes to that sensation by which time goes by faster. The same effect is given by substances such as cocaine, which enhances the dopamine effect. On the contrary, this effect is inhibited by neuroleptics, which are drugs used to treat diseases such as schizophrenia making time feel longer. In addition, several cerebral zones are called to account these chemical mediators: in summary, according to this theory, time perception is intrinsic in our neuronal system and ages gradually, favouring the sense of *tempus fugit* (Virgil (29 BC) n.d.), *time flies*. Other researches in psychology have confirmed this telescopic effect of perception of time, showing that only a small percentage (10%) of elder individuals escape from the temporal acceleration trap (Wittmann and Lenhoff 2005).

However, there are other kinds of time, even able to interfere with this finding: we have to train enough to concentrate on the Kairos, the 'here and now', the 'carpe diem' and the eternal and the cosmic time. However, other external incentives can deny this time perception, which bring us back to believe other possible declinations of 'time factor'.

Let us simply think about school children who get bored at school and feel that lessons are endless and tedious and the hands on the clock seem to be still in a fixed position? Yet, the same children will see time fly with some teachers. The fact that time goes faster during holidays is almost rhetoric. Hence, we can add that the perception of time is also influenced by being with other people, places and activities: there are people for whom holidays never pass; it is an empty space to be filled with the unknown, and it is better to seek refuge in an ordinary working routine, revealing the necessity to not know the mystery of unpredictable time. Maybe, having too much time to ourselves for thinking brings shock and fear and puts us in front of the extraordinary difficulty of letting ourselves free to experience the unknown, the unruled, out from strict rules not only of life but also of mindset.

Going back to science to find evidence on several ways of ageing and that an *elderly age* chased by a faster and faster time is not so unavoidable against which perhaps we can find some possible forms of human intervention.

In a study conducted by the French university *Blaise Pascal* and the English university in Keel, results contradict the fact that the older we are, the faster time flies. Young and elder individuals were given a questionnaire on time perception, and they received eight phone calls a day for five consecutive days (Droit-Volet and Wearden 2015). Such calls forced participants to stop for each call and to talk 'here and now' about their emotions, activities and feelings on time. Although the study findings did not show any perceived difference in the speed of time between young and elder people, it is likely a bias from the 'experimental' design keeping elders under pressure, in everyday life, without fearing the forward flight—in contemporaneity—and giving a particular sense of attention in a possible fragile moment, such as ageing. This research may be the key of active ageing: avoiding elders' discrimination and giving them an important role in their microcosm. This study may be a trailblazer for older age compared to the attention we give to elders, once more respected for their experience, in their world, apparently less dynamic; it gave value to their stories and so their capability to remember old story detail, the long-term memory.

Today, in this 'fast and furious' world, it is hardly permitted to look back, and elders are seen as active or inactive, heavy and useless. To 'activate' them, it is important to make them call eight times for days to acknowledge their being. Is it possible to balance between the request of being up with current time and the respect due for their single passed experiences? This is anyhow a key between a good time perception and concrete and realistic achievable behaviours.

The issue of time perception appears complex: from one side, neurosciences tell us we have an internal biological clock that goes far beyond the day and night rhythm of the PER protein, but it is a lifelong biological clock thanks to which we feel a faster time, as we are adding years to life. On the other side, it tells us we can fool our biological clock if we have a rich and stimulating everyday life and if we are a focus point for someone, at least for researchers, while instead time is a function of emotionality and participation we feel.

What About Patients' Perception of Time?

The word 'patient' has an ancient etymology, derived from pathos ('suffering', 'passion'), an ardent feeling. The patient is who suffers: while the Latin verb *patior* indicates only suffering, ancient Greeks objectified strong passion. Latins got rid of the several hints of *pathos*, keeping just a consequence: this 'suffering' was putting the person in the condition of discrimination, as 'male-aptus', not able, so 'disable', from here, the root of the word 'disease'. The Latins gave very scarce consideration to strong emotions and passions and were very much oriented to outcomes and pragmatisms.

Anyhow, nowadays, the sick person is called 'patient' that means 'suffering'. However, we can add to this meaning the feeling of time in a particular declination, that of patience. Patience is an interior quality and attitude of whom accepts pain, difficulties, adversities, troubles, controversies and death and serenely and calmly, controlling emotions and persevering in actions. It requires calm, resolution and application. The patient who pathologically (which by the way also derives from *pathos*) 'feels' has to deal with a time, which tends to be never-ending: the time of being ill. However, from patients' narratives, we remark a faster and bearable time than that one they lived when the diagnosis was unknown, as if knowing the truth on his/her own health is already a 'an accelerator of time', which drives patients to not waste no further. Time before the diagnosis is the time of uncertainty, such as waiting for the result of a test—a waiting time that objectively can last from a few hours, perceived as infinite, to some weeks. In narratives, we read 'the waiting was unbearable, finally I knew, then…' (the waiting for the result of a biopsy) and 'I spent 2 weeks passed searching for a distraction' (the waiting for the result of an amniocentesis).

Carers must not underestimate this waiting time, which increases until it becomes a colloidal magma which drives patients to be mentally exhausted: they should not minimise the waiting time of their cured ones. Often physicians and medical operators underestimate the issue of time, saying sentences such as *What's the issue, it's only for 2 days* and do not understand the anxiety given by those 48 h of waiting. Maybe it would be more opportune to say, in an empathic way, *These 2 days will be long, I can imagine, if you need, call me*. It would be fantastic. I write this in the hope that some professional will read this little tip of not abandoning the patient alone in such a difficult situation. However, also the adult patient should activate her/himself in distraction: finding something nice, cultivating an own hobby and something pleasant to distract their mind. Here the carer might help by asking the person: *What do you love to do? Which are your hobbies?* So, it is important to be a stimulator of doing something nice instead of ruminating on the obsessive thought about the outcome of a clinical test. The coping skills make a great difference about time perception: in an unpublished research of a group of psychologists working with patients with disability, contrary to what they thought before the study *that time was never-ending, and never flowing*, patients answered that they became familiar with the bothering time. They accepted the time to be themselves bothered as a coping ability. Furthermore, in their disability, some of these patients found benefits from imagination, and in this fantastic realm, there is another rhythm, a different pace of time. In this way, they feel good. They do not get bothered.

However, if a trauma occurred, and poor coping strategies are in place, in some patients living with multiple sclerosis, for instance, there is the personal regret for not having enjoyed enough life before. Therefore, the challenge, despite the trauma of the disease, is finding joy in this new, transformed dimension. Instead of staying in a conscious, still, boring patience, maybe other and funnier forms of entertainment can help us, such as music, which seems to accelerate time, independently from its emotional value.

In the study *Time flies with music, whatever is its emotional nature* (Droit-Volet et al. 2010), researchers investigated if music influences time perception in a different way from a neutral stimulus and whether emotional values of musical stimulus (i.e. sad music versus happy music) modulate this effect. Music presented in a major note (happy) or minor key (sad) induces the listening person to say that the duration of a melody is shorter than that of a non-melodic stimulus of control, confirming that 'time flies' when we listen to music. The singular thing that adds a little more complexity to time is that it is not always so true that time flies while listening to good music we love: if music is ours and is that capable to distract us really, we can arrive also to a paradoxical effect, i.e. time seems to stop (Kellaris and Altsech 1992) towards a peaceful quiet as if time itself were empty of significance because it is the music itself stripping the perception of frivolous things and therefore of tempus fugit.

It is like we found the barycentre, the extreme stability in the middle of a vortex. In the eye of the storm, space and time converge in immobility and quietness.

"*Exhausted I sought a country inn, but found wisteria in bloom*". Matsuo Basho, seventeenth century.

Practice Time

What do you think about the many facets of time? Do you believe that our living experience is something more than a matter of getting older but is also an opportunity to do, to ask and to catch the right thing at the right time? Do you think that you can apply these concepts during a visit with patients or team working?

If you want, try to 'catch the moment', living the Kairos experience.

What do you think about the long time? What about your time to get a real metamorphosis, if something changed your life? What do you think about convalescence and about rest? Please, write down the things which help you rest. Would you like to try to ask to your patients what they love to do for resting? What about convalescence after a disease?

What do you think about waiting time? Try to think in your personal and professional life to time of unbearable length, what did you do? Could you do something else to feel less the burden of time?

About the cyclic time, what are your feelings? Do you think that we could respect more our 'animal nature' and be more in tune with the Earth, Sun and moreover cosmic movements? If you think you should be more respectful of our cosmic time, what would you suggest to your closest people, friends, colleagues and patients?

If a metaphoric spring might be joyful, a metaphoric winter might shed tears. How do you consider the convalescent time and the mourning time?

What could you tell to ease patients' difficulty in mastering waiting time? Could you change something in the waiting room at your practice, introducing some activities, new people, new roles and volunteers?

Have you ever thought about the relationship between time, music and wellbeing?

References

Gemignani A (2015) www.agsm-energyinlife.com/?p=1737

Baker JJ (2002) Medicare payment system for hospital inpatients: diagnosis-related groups. J Health Care Finance 28(3):1–13

Bara AC, Arber S (2009) Working shifts and mental health–findings from the British Household Panel Survey (1995–2005). Scand J Work Environ Health 35(5):361–367

BBC Website. http://www.bbc.co.uk/programmes/b07wbjx8

Boivin DB (2000) Influence of sleep-wake and circadian rhythm disturbances in psychiatric disorders. J Psychiatry Neurosci 25(5):446–458

Jung CG (2002) The earth has a soul: C.G. Jung on nature, technology & modern life. North Atlantic Books, Berkeley, CA

Apollodorus, 180 BC-120 BC (1955) Bibliotheca, edition Adelphi

Hume D (1711–1776) http://www.philosophypages.com/hy/4t.htm

Droit-Volet S, Wearden JH (2015) Experience Sampling Methodology reveals similarities in the experience of passage of time in young and elderly adults. Acta Psychol 156:77–82

Droit-Volet S, Bigand E, Ramos D, Bueno JL (2010) Time flies with music whatever its emotional valence. Acta Psychol 135(2):226–232

Fonken LK, Kitsmiller E, Smale L et al (2012) Dim nighttime light impairs cognition and provokes depressive-like responses in a diurnal rodent. J Biol Rhythm 27(4):319–327
Frank AW (1995) The wounded storyteller: body, illness, and ethics. University of Chicago Press, Chicago
Hyginus GJ. (1st century AD) Fabula 183
Havelka M, Lucanin JD, Lucanin D (2009) Biopsychosocial model—the integrated approach to health and disease. Coll Antropol 33(1):303–310
Homer. Odyssey, most likely end of VIII century BC
Jung CG (1969) On the nature of the psyche. Princeton University Press
Kellaris JJ, Altsech MB (1992) The experience of time as a function of musical loudness and gender of listener. In: Sherry JF Jr, Sternthal B (eds) NA—advances in consumer research, vol 19. Association for Consumer Research, Provo, UT, pp 725–729
Duk KK (2003) Producer of the movie "Spring, summer, fall, winter, and spring"
Kitano T (1997) Author of the movie Hana-Bi, released in the United States as Fireworks
Langewitz W, Denz M, Keller A, Kiss A, Rüttimann S, Wössmer B (2002) Spontaneous talking time at start of consultation in outpatient clinic: cohort study. BMJ 325(7366):682–683
Launer J (2007) How not to be a Doctor and other essays
Liddell HG, Scott R, Jones HS, McKenzie R (1843) Greek-English lexicon. Oxford University Press
Liu X, Zwiebel LJ, Hinton D, Benzer S, Hall JC, Rosbash M (1992) The period gene encodes a predominantly nuclear protein in adult Drosophila. J Neurosci 12:2735–2744
Lundberg U (2005) Stress hormones in health and illness: the roles of work and gender. Psychoneuroendocrinology 30(10):1017–1021
McClung CA (2013) How might circadian rhythms control mood? Let me count the ways…. Biol Psychiatry 74(4):242–249
Nilsson MP (1941) Greek popular religion. Columbia University Press, New York
Narrative Medicine Website. http://www.medicinanarrativa.eu/importance-cyclical-time-hours
Nobel prize. https://www.nobelprize.org/nobel_prizes/medicine/laureates/2017/press.html
Obayashi K, Saeki K, Kurumatani N (2018) Bedroom light exposure at night and the incidence of depressive symptoms. Am J Epidemiol 187(3):427–434
Oginska H, Oginska-Bruchal K (2014) Chronotype and personality factors of predisposition to seasonal affective disorder. Chronobiol Int 31(4):523–531
Citati P (2006) La primavera di Cosroe. Edizione Adelphi
Price JL, Blau J, Rothenfluh A, Abodeely M, Kloss B, Young MW (1998) Double-time is a novel Drosophila clock gene that regulates PERIOD protein accumulation. Cell 94:83–95
Rosa H (2010) Alienation and acceleration: towards a critical theory of late-modern temporality. NSU Press, Malmo
Saeed SA, Bruce TJ (1998) Seasonal affective disorders. Am Fam Physician 57(6):1340–1346, 1351–2. http://www.medicinanarrativa.eu/importance-cyclical-time-hours
Sonal Sekhar M, Vyas N (2013) Defensive medicine: a bane to healthcare. Ann Med Health Sci Res 3(2):295–296
Suetonius (2nd century BC). The Lives of the Twelve Caesars—Augustus
Vingerhoets AJJM, Bylsma LM (2007) Crying and health. Popular and scientific conceptions. Psychol Top 16:275–296
Virgil (29 BC). The georgics, book 3
Von Franz ML (1992) Psyche and matter. Shambhala, Boston
Wiseman R (2014) Night school: the life-changing science of sleep. Macmillan, London
Wittmann M, Lenhoff S (2005) Age effects in perception of time, psychological reports, vol 97. Ludwig-Maximilian University, Munich, pp 921–935
Woolf V (1928) Orlando: a biography. Hogarth Press, London

6 Curing the Language of Care: The Heaviness of the Prescriptive Jargon, Moving Towards a Lighter Language for Better Caring and Better Outcomes—Language, Music, Sound and Colour

Language has a tremendous impact on our wellbeing (Newberg and Waldme 2012). This chapter analyses the power of spoken language, music and sound together and as single elements: first, we will take out the words and leave the music, and then we will take out music and leave sound eventually until reaching silence. These elements are vital to our wellbeing and affect the functioning of our brains, inducing the release of neurotransmitters involved in building our sense of belonging and approaching problems (Newberg and Waldme 2012).

Jacques Lacan, a French physician, psychiatrist and psychoanalyst, said as follows: 'the way we speak is the way we are'. According to Lacan, the human subject is constantly split between a conscious side—an accessible mind—and an unconscious side, driven by inaccessible forces. We could not have self-perception without the perception of others. Our language is structured unconsciously as a driving force to meet the missing part of ourselves—the other. That is why Lacan states, *The way we speak is the way our conscious and unconscious selves are.*

What is most basic to each human entity is what is most *alien*. We are what we are on the basis of something that we experience to be missing from us—our understanding of the others—that is the other side of the split out of which our unconscious must emerge. Because we experience this 'something missing' as a lack, we desire to close it, to fill it in and to replace it with something. For Lacan, the unconscious is that *unknown* part which drives us beyond the rational mind and is a part of our language. Thus, deeply, the way we speak is the way we are or better the way we wish things were (Lacan 1966).

Although there is a large body of literature on health psychology, emotional intelligence and patient engagement at present, many patients still deal with physicians who lack relational skills as well as tactful manners when speaking to their patients. As the narratives of patients recurrently report, one of the main elements evidenced by patients in reference to the development of the doctor-patient relationship is kindness or in many cases the lack of it.

As an example of appreciation of kindness, one woman whose husband had a brain tumour wrote as follows: *The care given to my husband during his stay at the*

M. G. Marini, *Languages of Care in Narrative Medicine*,
https://doi.org/10.1007/978-3-319-94727-3_6

hospital was amazing. The nurses and doctors went out of their way. They showed so much kindness and helped him to maintain his dignity in such a delicate moment. Or, as another story tells us: *The best thing about my treatment was the kindness.* Yet, on the other hand, it is all too common to read stories reporting of doctors mortifying patient by interfering in the patient's personal sphere, shattering dreams and tramping over personal ambitions or desires. In one story of a woman experiencing a strong maternity instinct, we read as follows: *Don't even dare considering having children, you have cancer….* While in another of a patient very fond of bike riding: *forget going on biking holidays with pulmonary disease.*

The lack of kindness though does not always come in these extreme terms but may also present as more subtle examples such as simple statements *Follow the prescription! Take your medication! Don't drive long journeys! Do these tests! Take your clothes off* that slowly erode the patient's identity and dignity. Doctors may not even perceive these simple routine sentences as an issue. As patient narratives show us, such statements can leave lasting marks in patients' memories. In fact, while pleasant situations are recalled in patient stories through generic descriptions, the harsh words pronounced by carers are reported in great details even after several years. The use of the imperative mode belongs to the culture of power, hierarchy and subjection; leaving out space to expressions of sharing, empathy and listening is absent. Yet, in some cases, the imperative power mood might also be an alibi for the carer's feeling of impotence and fear: one of not being able to get the patient out of his/her dimension of suffering. This is just as a General incites soldiers to battle giving commands aware of what his troops are risking in combat.

This, however, is not an attempt at blaming health professionals who are constantly burdened by frenetic work rhythms (fatigue, exposure to pain and sorrow, small or no privacy areas, bureaucracy and more demanding patients) but rather an attempt to come to the root of the matter: what is it that creates these situations of bad communication and of lack of kindness? Is it poor training on communication skills at the university? Is it the imprinting they have received by their predecessors? Is it the burden of seeing suffering people every day? Is it a hidden sense of impotence and guilty feelings? It may be a blend of all these factors and many more.

The analysis of typical communication patterns in doctor-patient relationship evidences a large use of imperatives (e.g. 'take your medication'), which places the carer in a position of power and establishes a hierarchical subjection of the patient. According to Berne's transactional analysis (Berne 1972), it is a typical reflection of the 'parent' and 'child' states of the ego. The parent positions itself in a top position of power; the child lets itself be subjected to a position of obedience. This latter role, however, can be distinguished into three different categories: the 'adapted child' who perceives the exhortations are for his/her own good and consistently obeys, the 'submissive child' who obeys despite considering the parent's indication as impositions that are unjust and the 'rebel child' who disobeys their parent's will. These three classifications are also found across patient narratives and reflect the unique personality of each patient and of their attitude in the doctor-patient relationship and their coping with illness. It is well known that the physician's attitude can largely influence the patient's attitude to disease as well as their engagement in treatment.

For example, the 'obedient patient' will actually expect to receive paternal suggestions (in a comforting tone of voice) from his physician, whereas the 'rebel child' patient who receives 'commands' on what he/she must do will most likely leave the doctor's surgery, thinking *This is the last time this doctor will see me again*, rather than adhering to a treatment. In fact, as evidenced in a report by the WHO, such prescriptive language does not work and is even dysfunctional; when prescription language is used without having established a trustful relationship with the patient, it is difficult to engage the patient in 'therapeutic adherence' or better (since adherence implies the patient's passive subjection) in 'therapeutic agreement' and shared decision-making. In fact, this aspect is largely confirmed by analyses of patient narrations, which evidence that the determiner making the difference between a constructive and valuable relationship and an unpleasant one is in fact the kindness factor.

The Example of Smoking

If it is true that with some patients the command works, as an example, pronouncing a sentence as "Stop smoking, that's all" with some other patients is not effective. The "stop smoking" (imperative mode) told to a heavy smoker will most likely trigger the opposite behaviour. The imperative mode enters in the unconscious of the person's inner rebel and non-responsible ego state. It will hardly move the patient's will towards the mature and conscious voluntary choice: it represents an overwhelming weight that is difficult to carry on the shoulders. Rather, a more effective approach would be the choice of different words and another tone: "I can tell you that smoking is harmful. If you continue smoking, your lungs will be filled with substances that will destroy their elasticity, and it will be harder for you to breathe, and you might risk suffocation.... Do you understand me? I imagine it is very difficult to quit this habit, but if you do choose to quit smoking, I will be here to support you. You are still on time to recover your body and your wellbeing." This is a lighter, less invasive and effective way to inform the patient about the harm of smoking, which activates awareness and responsibility, so that the patient can directly understand the benefits of ending this addiction (Banfi et al. 2018). From pulmonologist narratives' we understand that the best carers are those who ask themselves this question "What does the cigarette mean for this person?".

A recent study of ours on COPD investigated the issue of doctor–patient relationship from an unusual perspective (Banfi et al. 2018). The specialists participated in a seminar on the use of parallel charts in which they collected their thoughts about their patients in an informal and private way. However, differently from other studies on the use of parallel charts, in this study, they were then invited to enquire on what cigarette smoking meant to their patient.

The analyses of the narrations evidenced that in many cases, the specialist's approach to patients had been often biased by prejudices or moral judgements in relation to bad habits and gaining perspective onto the patient's inner dynamics helped the doctor pass from a commander enforcing their law to a coach motivating their patient towards change. In one case, the physician reported his patient's story. The patient told him that his wife had died and that cigarettes had become a friend against loneliness. Then the doctor went further and asked his patient,what do you enjoy doing? The patient answers: "chatting and playing with my grandchildren", followed by a pause and a reflective silence. Very slowly, in the next visit, the patient reports that he went down from smoking 20 to 10 cigarettes a day; he learnt to take medication regularly and started taking his grandchildren to the park, There was no need for any impositions by the physicians. What made the difference was the doctor's openness to sharing and understanding his patient's situation and re-establishing priorities in life beyond the COPD. Here, this doctor practised not only listening but 'intelligent listening', that one is able to create an alignment between the patient and the carer. The doctor has the role of the *affective parent* reassuring the scared *natural child* and of the *adult* explaining smoking consequences.

From Torture to Empathy

For some aspects, treatment can be compared with a sort of torture, starting from the doctor's enquiring and threatening statements (interrogations) to the clinical instruments (torture tools: laces, needles, retractors and pincers are present in museums, even if in a small and reduced form) and the clinical tests (frisking in search of a clue to a crime). When we are in the waiting room, as well as when a nurse commands us to stretch out our arm for a blood sample, it is hard to remain calm and quiet: we are scared by the words we will hear, by the way in which they will talk to us and by the pain we may feel for investigations that remind torture tools.

In addition to the 'torture' to the body, there are medical examinations—painful, but sometimes necessary—and carers' scaring words. These words, when used in the imperative, hurt the person's self-esteem, putting him/her in a 'not equal' position, not only physically—as there's already a hierarchy between healthy and 'sick' people (in Latin, *disease* is *male aptus* (Skeat 1888), incompetent, unsuitable)—but also verbally, with the orders *Take your clothes off, get dressed.* These are little violations of the identity and privacy, and the person finds himself/herself alone, defrauded of clothes, sometimes ruthlessly undressed.

Patients, often in a passive subjection, in a reverential vulnerability, regress to infantile situations and feel small, like when Alice takes a wrong dose of the medicine and almost disappears in the white rabbit's hole. The logistical situation of some clinics, some professionals' jargon and tests put an already fragile and vulnerable sick person through an existential ordeal.

But is there a way we can escape this ordeal of facing an unwanted diagnosis, of being deprived in one's privacy and of being object of treatment? Some facts cannot be changed: a blood sample cannot be taken without a needle nor can a cancer diagnosis be hidden. Yet there are kinder ways of assisting a patient and more tactful ways to present facts to a patient. Much has to do with language: in healthcare professions, the cornerstone on which the relationship is built by gestures, sounds and words is called empathy. Empathy is often an overused word, taught through the slogan 'to be in another one's shoes': a utopian, impossible definition, in my opinion. The healthy person, still my opinion, will never be, never want to be and never can be in a sick person's shoes. So, what can we do? Let us dethrone this evangelical concept of empathy. As Atul Gawande teaches us in his book *Better: A Surgeon's Notes on Performance* (Gawande 2007), we need to try to discover the person with whom we are interacting by listening and observing them as much as possible so that we can affectionately support the person in finding himself/herself with a new way of living with disease. How can this be achieved?

The Lightness of a Wish

It is obvious that the wide use of the imperative mode in communicating with the patient actually restricts information to flow in one direction; hence, one of the first steps should be in finding a better way to express to the patient situations, actions or decisions to take. The classical Greek language used was called an 'optative' mode, a verbal mode used to express desire, potentialities and options. Although there is no direct equivalent in today's language, in global English, this mode would be the equivalent of expressing the concepts of wishing something happened *(if only the medication were taken or it would be desirable for you to take the medication)* and keeping options open to the possibilities that this may or may not happen (allows the patient's free decisions) in the future (opening to hope and optimism). Hence, before telling the patient *you must* or *you must not*, it may be appropriate to understand with whom we are talking, his/her values and beliefs, fears, resistances and passions. Professionals are there to take care, reinforce the patient's identity and support patients in difficult moments in which the patient feels guilty because he/she feels physically useless, a reject and a possible source of sufferance to those who love them.

The Lightness of Smile

Another step would be positive interaction, encouraging good mood and wellbeing. A smile is a good way to do this. Science has demonstrated that smiling and laughing increase the synthesis of endorphins (Pease and Pease 2006). Specifically, this effect on endorphins is mostly (85% of cases) evoked by a relationship, by the sense of the interconnection stimulating smiles and laughter and by jokes (15%). Recalling Berne's theories on the parent and child roles, we can see multiple roles: the ego states of two adults (the carer and the patient at the same level) as well as their two natural children, who play, for example, with the prescription, *follow my prescription and I'll take your recipe for....* We all have a secret recipe that gives pleasure: one for cooking and one for reading a good novel.

Positive acknowledgments produce smiles, which in turn produce endorphins: *You're looking great. That blue dress fits you nicely. Your nephews are sweethearts.* So why not use them as a good way to start off a meeting with the patient? A further step could be encouraging conversation asking *What would you like to do today?* Maybe the patient's wish is impossible, but expressing it to the carer allows more intimacy in the relationship. Open questions set the basis for empathy: *What brought you here*? instead of *Tell me your symptoms*. Curiosity is a flavoured ingredient to a satisfactory dialogue between patient and carers.

These are just proposals to develop an authentic empathic relationship and allow the production of endorphins both in patient and in carer: the professional will feel at ease, less rigid in his/her role, in a professional field complex and full of responsibilities. In the 1980s, some hospitals had the room of laughter (which perhaps still exists): a place where patients could relax, play and talk together or with their carers. This is a necessary moment of carnival before coming back to medicine's orders. Paediatric wards are full of Patch Adams, but there are too few, at least in Italy, for adult and older people: too often we think that they will face disease, exams and prescriptions with the right willingness thanks to the sense of duty.

There's another extraordinary finding regarding endorphins and language (Ripollés et al. 2014): the language takes care of itself to allow its own evolution. A Spanish and German research team found that learning a new language or inventing new words produces endorphins. Maybe this happens to facilitate both learning in childhood and the infinite evolution of language beyond the basic 65 words belonging to the NSM. It would be lovely to play with words, invent neologisms, look at other horizons of poetry and take time out from the verb 'must' that activates a regressive sense of guilt and inadequacy. With a feeling of joy, I found that the verb 'must' is not present in semantic primes, that universal language spoken by the entire world (Wierzbicka 1997). There are the verbs *to think, to want, to feel, to see* and *to do*. So, the word 'duty' is consequent to a social construction and not to the natural language. The philosophy of the duty is changed with the philosophy of the *Voluntas*, the wanting to do something, if possible good, for someone else and for one's self. The natural child wants to do something, without order, he/she simply wishes: everything related to command and to the sense of duty, even if appropriate, is an overconstruction.

Other Languages of Care: Music and Sound

Now, we shall enter into another realm of languages of care. No spoken language. No words. No sentences, neither oral nor written stories. No letters. Let us be taken by the mystery of the untold or unspeakable. Sometimes, there are no words to explain sorrow, joy or awe when they are so overwhelming. The true experience, the truth, in ancient Greek was called *aleziea*, i.e. 'something that finds no words', since it is not possible to put in words the nuances that we feel inside. Conversely, music and sounds can help one connect with one's inner self and understand what is happening inside. Maybe our language has to still develop accurate words that do not exist yet. Maybe, we cannot find the proper words to express particular situations of life and, even more, to write about them.

In this chapter, we explore the beauty of other languages of care, different ways able to produce that 'El Dorado' (the land of gold and silver, where people sued to live in peace and harmony) of neurotransmitters that we are looking for wellbeing. Serotonin helps in feeling the sense of acknowledgement and improves one's self-esteem; dopamine helps to develop resilience and project skills; oxytocin helps to feel loved; endorphins helps get rid of physical pain and mind sorrow (Breuning 2015). These neurotransmitters are the *El Dorado*, defined by some archaeologists as the golden man and by some others as the mythic land at the antipode, a sort of Eden, in which there are not only gold, silver and precious stones but also peace and harmony among all members of the tribe.

In this *treasure chest*, music, from classic one to pop, country to sacred style, is contemplated as the first precious stone—a *sapphire*. Music releases endorphins, and scientific literature has widely shown that it is extremely beneficial to many acute and chronic conditions: this is a physical impact of music. However, I quote June Boyce-Tillman, of whom we will read an interview from her book *Experiencing Music—Restoring the Spiritual, Music as Well-Being* (Tillman 2016): *At the end of the nineteenth century, Nietzsche declared God to be dead and the anima mundi became identified as aspects of culture which carries on today in the idea of memes. Chief among them, for Nietzsche, were the concepts of Apollonian and Dionysian. ...They were opposing elements. Nietzsche associated music with the Apollonian. However, I will argue that by rethinking the musical experience in its totality, it too has the capacity to integrate the Apollonian and Dionisian aspects—the personal and archetypal, mind and body—the mysterious and the rational.*

Beyond the physical impact of producing endorphins, music is a type of language which has an intrapersonal effect, such as evoking past memories, cheering up mood and softening harsh times of life, and interpersonal effect, such as developing empathy, interconnecting our minds and souls and evoking similar emotions, depending on our contextual environment and on our taste. *Music fills the vacuum of the Death of God*, quoting again Prof. Boyce-Tillman.

Music is known to support wellbeing in our bodies and minds, and maybe souls, if they exist. In this book, attention is given not only to words but also to voices, gestures, spaces, flavours, landscapes, mindscapes, sound and music. It is well established in scientific research that music produces endorphins in the brain that give us a feeling of excitement. They act on the same receptors on which analgesic drugs act and have the same effect of gymnastic, meditation and sex. They ease pain, stabilise the immune system and limit stress. Music can help perform better in sports, as shown by the fact that turning up your tunes can also increase the effort you exert during exercise. For pace-based exercises like running, music can help regulate the rhythm and signal to the brain when the body should move. This signal helps the body use energy more efficiently and delays the sense of exhaustion.

Amazing is the power of the lullabies: while encountering the work on lullabies made by Giuseppina Persico and her group, an Italian midwife who works in every part of the world, I was really fascinated, here below, the findings of her study called 'Maternal singing of lullabies during pregnancy and after birth: Effects on mother–infant bonding and on newborns' behaviour. Concurrent Cohort Study'. Here, the synthesis of this research, mother-infant bonding, is of great importance for the development and the wellbeing of the baby. The aim of this concurrent cohort study was to investigate the effects of mothers singing lullabies on bonding, newborns' behaviour and maternal stress. Eighty-three (singing cohort) and 85 (concurrent cohort) women were recruited at antenatal classes at 24 weeks of gestational age and followed up to 3 months after birth. The Prenatal Attachment Inventory (PAI) and the Mother-to-Infant Bonding Scale (MIBS) were used to assess maternal-foetal attachment and postnatal bonding. Results showed that no significant influence was found on prenatal attachment; by contrast, postnatal bonding was significantly greater (i.e. lower MIBS) in the singing group 3 months after birth (mean, 1.28 vs. 1.96; $p = 0.001$). In the same singing group, the incidence of neonatal crying episodes in the first month was significantly lower (18.5% vs. 28.2; $p < 0.0001$) as were the infantile colic (64.7% vs. 38.3%; $p = 0.003$) and perceived maternal stress (29.6% vs. 36.5%; $p < 0.05$). Infantile colic was reduced in the singing group, even in the second month after birth (22.8% vs. 36.5; $p = 0.002$). At the same time, a reduction was observed in the neonatal nightly awakening (1.5% vs. 4.7; $p < 0.0001$). In conclusion, mothers singing lullabies could improve maternal-infant bonding. It could also have positive effects on neonatal behaviour and maternal stress. The study was published by the Australian College of Midwives (Persico et al. 2017).

The event that struck me the most was the fact that this lullaby evidence-based story was published and presented by the Australian College of Midwives. I'm grateful to Australia because it is in this land that developed the NSM, the universal language spoken all over the world. I'm grateful to Australia because it is here that this lullaby study conducted by an Italian team was published: here, in the continent of the *songlines*. In his book *The Songlines*, written by Bruce Chatwin in Australia in 1984 and composed during a voyage in Australia, the author asserts that the language started as song and, in the aboriginal Dreamtime, sang the land into existence for the conscious mind and memory. As one sings, the land, the tree, the rock, the path and the singers are all one, in a oneness concept. The main scopes of the aboriginal tribes are to exchange the song and never let the melody fall, along their nomadic journeys from one cape onto Australia to the other one, playing as if this continent were just a gaming table onto which they walk (Chatwin 1984). Their nomadic enduring walking and their continuous singing produce the *songlines* which have the power to reconnect the individual self with the wholeness. This is the reason why they are holy.

Lullabies are the primordial *songlines*, and they are holy also because they can heal the bodies of both the child and the singers: as soon as a lullaby begins, a soothing sense of order infuses into the infantile consciousness. The swaying rhythm is close to the heartbeat, and the quiet melodious sounds are a blessed relief from the world's usual racket; the simple, repeating melody is also a source of comfort.

The evidence which in my opinion was the most interesting in the study of Persico is that, through the singing, there is no significant foetal bond to the biological mother, but this occurs only after the birth, when the mother is physically there. This changes the paradigm that things are almost fixed after conception and that a maternal-foetus line song is already in place. This expands the possibilities that other singers of lullabies, grandmothers, adoptive mothers, aunties, sisters, baby sitters- and this recalls me the concept of the tribe of people- may build their own bond with the baby, independently from the mere fact to be the biological mother. I have checked if, in the scientific literature, there is a male/female gender effect when singing lullaby, but nothing has been published yet, so this could be a next step for researches on the lullaby impact.

Tim Griffith, a neurologist of the Welcome Foundation, says that through lullabies: 'the emotional part of the brain is being stimulated by music. This decreases the arousal level, and that in turn is affecting babies, children, and I would add, adults, pain and stress levels' (Griffith 2013).

More than this, lullaby helps also premature babies: we have to move to another country, Iran, with a very interesting study in premature newborns risking their lives; in a study conducted by Fahrat Ahmadshah, the scope was to investigate the effect of lullaby music on the physiological response and weight gain of premature infants in Mashhad. Forty-four very low birth weight infants $\leq$34 weeks of gestational age that were admitted to the neonatal intensive care unit of Imam Reza Hospital in Mashhad, Iran, were enrolled. Infants were randomly assigned to one of two groups: the music group and the control group. Lullaby music was played through earphones for the music group. This continued for 8 days at 20 min per day. The control group received routine auditory stimulation. Neonates in the two groups were in stable condition and kept in their isolettes. Infants were monitored for 40 min: 10 min baseline, 20 min into the intervention and 10 min post intervention. Data measures were heart rate, respiration rate, oxygen saturation and body weight. Results showed that the two groups differed significantly in the respiratory rate ($p = 0.01$) and oxygen saturation ($p = 0.001$). There were no significant differences in the heart rate ($p = 0.24$) and weight gain ($p = 0.093$) between the two groups. It looked like preterm infants respond to lullaby music as evidenced by the changes in their respiratory rates and oxygen saturations. Although this study did not demonstrate an improvement in weight gain, further studies are recommended to examine the effect of music on other growth and developmental aspects (Ahmadshah et al. 2010). And technology can even help in neonatal intensive care with the recording of lullabies to be listened by tiny little babies through earphones.

If music and song produces a surplus of wellbeing when somebody is already fit, it is even more important to understand whether music modulates and enhances wellbeing in minds, bodies and souls of individuals who are experiencing illness.

To discuss the topic of therapeutic effects of music, I had the pleasure to interview Prof. June Boyce-Tillman, a theologian and expert in the use of music with vulnerable individuals.

MGM. Is music applicable to a care setting?

Prof. JBT. Yes, we can bring it inside hospitals, but we need to tailor the music appropriately. Music can play an important part in care settings. However, the most difficult aspect is understanding the kind of music that works for a specific patient. Music is not like standard pills or a pharmaceutical product. For some people, their chosen style is pop, for others, its jazz; for some, it will be Western classical music. Music plays an important part of human care. Some care institutions have sound systems that play music for their patients, but this is not always beneficial; it does not respect the personal tastes of the people being cared for, which can actually be harmful for the patients who cannot relate to the music being played.

It is very important to know when a person first heard a particular piece of music. I remember one woman with whom I was working, who enjoyed calming Baroque music. I played her Bach's famous Air on a G String. She became pale and screamed. It was the piece of music that was playing when she was abused. This is remarkable when most people would associate this piece with calm and tranquillity.

Music will revive memories, and certain pieces will have explicit meaning locked onto them by significant events in their lives as in the story above. This is the explicit meaning, and it overrides the implicit meaning in the music itself, which may be calming if soft and slow or exciting if loud and fast.

MGM. This is shocking: so how can a care provider choose appropriate music inside a care setting?

Prof. JBT. It is suggested that when people are diagnosed with dementia, they should prepare a list of their 50 favourite songs. These will reassure them of their identity when the memory loss progresses. This list will also help in choosing what to sing when a person is dying. Music causes a relaxation of the tensions and can enable people to relax enough to die. In the ancient Egyptian culture, music was believed to be a boat that carried the soul away.

The liking or disliking of music depends on the openness of the people who listen to it. Some people become more and more conservative as they get older. However, I think it is never too late to open up to a new kind of music, and this process helps to broaden the consciousness. It opens up different parts of the personality.

To investigate which music might be particularly meaningful for a certain person, we have to look at the narrative of the biography of this patient. A compass for orienteering might be given by knowing which music this person has listened to between the ages of 15 and 30 (the age in which musical tastes are formed often linked with strong and vivid memories) and also by their social standing. However, these cannot be used as fixed parameters to choose the music. For example, one might consider opera to be appropriate for a wealthy patient, but it actually can apply to other types of patients, given that nowadays opera has a broad diffusion through broadcasting and streaming and is appreciated by a much broader audience.

These favourite songs may also be sung when a person is dying by choirs called Threshold Choirs or by family members: I had a friend, who was already in comatose state, in a hospice where she was dying. In preparing for her funeral, she had given to me the list of the music she wanted to be used. All the family was there at the time of her passing. The family did not know what to do as she had criticised them earlier for talking too much. I suggested we sang these songs. It was a breath-taking moment for everybody—a really meaningful ritual.

Other musical practices in care contexts are bringing in instrumental groups and choirs to perform. Sometimes, the patients can be included in these, along with their family members or caregivers. These sometimes involve bringing younger people into the care contexts and bridging the gaps between generations.

MGM. Is there a universal sound that makes us feel better?

Prof. JBT. This varies from culture to culture. Some would see the *OM* as a basic sound of the universe. All meditation systems use particular sounds depending on the religion in which they are situated. Often these involve various vowel sounds in beautiful shapes, such as the Christian *Hallelujah.*

MGM. Is there a religious or spiritual music which can help in moments of illness?

Prof. JBT. For the older generation in the UK, hymns may have particular meaning. This will change in the next generation, brought up in a more secular age. There is a raft of songs developing that are broadly life-affirming—looking at nature, the cycle of life, building community and friendship. These are new narratives of healing.

MGM. What is the difference between the therapeutic use of music (your approach) and music therapy?

Prof. JBT. Music has been used therapeutically for much of human history. Music therapy has its roots back in the 1960s when the therapeutic use of music was professionalised in line with other developments of psychotherapy. It followed a particular practice, which was based on improvisation on the piano; this was to relate to the client's improvisation. The relationship is to be established through music (rather than the words of talking psychotherapy). The qualification involves a course in the areas of music and psychotherapy and also supervised practice. It is an expensive form of training and requires that the trainee therapist, in addition to attending lectures and the clinical supervision, be in therapy themselves. Music therapists practise privately or within the National Health Service (NHS); they have musical skills but not necessarily formal qualification in psychotherapy.

The use of music therapists in the NHS gradually increased from the 1970s; recently, there has been a move towards the meditative practice of mindfulness; this has sometimes replaced the art therapies in general. In my opinion, this limits the therapeutic techniques available. Mindfulness with its concentration on thoughts in the 'here and now' is beneficial to some patients, but it can be less beneficial when someone has lots of *unhelpful* thoughts. Music therapy with its concentration on expression, freedom and belonging may be more appropriate for some situations.

MGM. How do you envision the integration of narrative medicine and music?

Prof. JBT. I think that the collection of narratives, especially using the natural semantic metalanguage, is a wonderful way to get into a person's life. It would help discover a person's musical taste and also lead to the expression for their feelings and life experiences through music. Musical expression is a form of autobiography. It would be very good to collect narratives that reveal how people use music therapeutically in their lives. They would add a great deal to our understanding of what energises people and heals them.

Recently, Fondazione ISTUD conducted a survey to understand whether there could be some universal preferences for music as well as for language. We asked online to write down the playlist of ten favourite songs/melodies that the person would love to listen in a very delicate moment, such as the time of fragility, the times of 'troubled water' described by June Boyce-Tillman.

Here, we show the results of the playlist survey of the ten favourite music songs to listen in case of fragility (Fig. 6.1): *115 participants reported overall 1115 music composed by songs, classic and melodies reported by at least four generations of people.*

Participating countries: Italy, Switzerland, the UK, the USA, Chile and Israel

The English titles were left in English, while all the common words were translated from their original language (from Italian French and Spanish) into English:

With the microfragmentation of responses to the listening tastes of participants, this survey confirmed that what June Boyce-Tillman stated is very subjective. We did find very small clusters, recalling classical music, including Bach, Mozart and Beethoven, or rock and pop, Beatles and Pink Floyd, but there was a large divergence. Therefore, a forced playlist of music therapy, with a system of loud speakers in the places of care, goes against individual taste. Moreover, it can cause discomfort. We received some answers that mentioned the importance of silence, or passive and casual listening, with a greater pleasure of unexpectedly evoked emotions as possible 'therapy'.

Fig. 6.1 Results of the survey on favourite music songs listened in case of fragility reported as word cloud

However, the analysis of replies did in fact evidence some common trends. The most recurrent theme was YOU (second person) of the bond that becomes the main character of the music, while *I* (first person) was rarely mentioned, as if it covered a secondary role. Both *YOU* and I are core words of the NSM. The second most cited word was *love*, *amore*, *amor* and a*mour*, further confirming the importance of the emotional, passionate, emotional relationships in life especially in difficult moments. Differently from the pronouns you and I, *love* does not belong to the NSM. It can be, however, deconstructed to semantic atoms *I feel good with you. You feel good with me* regardless of the smallness or magnitude of this *you* (from the individual to the divine).

The third recurrent word was *life*, which is already a universal semantic present in all the languages of the world. There is the attachment to the word life and living in case of fragility; there is the wish to be in this world.

Therefore, regardless of the fact that *love* has been one of the most sung themes for centuries (with countless songs and melodies dedicated to love), the word 'life' appears to be more relevant as a driving force when fragility enters into one's lives.

Despite the small number of replies collected, the important message here is the potential of music in a patient's life. The listening, the narratives and individual musical taste could be used to tailor personalised music therapy to create a surrounding environment that could bring wellbeing to the patient.

Now let us deconstruct music into its basic sounds and rhythm alone with no particular complex 'Mozart' harmony behind? Is sound a language, and, if so, is it a part of this El Dorado we are talking about?

Sound belongs to the El Dorado as well, and the gemstones discovered in this land are rubies and diamonds. Allow me the analogy, but deconstructing music up to sounds reminds me of moving from complex languages to minimal language, so minimal as the NSM, which includes those kinds of word—a few—present in all the spoken languages of the world or from complex molecules to atoms or from complex numbers to the primes.

What is sound? Sound can be viewed as a wave motion in air or other elastic media. Sound is a stimulus. Sound can also be viewed as an excitation of the hearing mechanism that results in the perception of sound. In this case, sound is a sensation. Sound is a wave that spreads according to different frequencies called hertz. There are strong connections among the sounds that we listen and our brain waves. Our brain functions also produce waves: these can be the delta waves, with 0.5–3 Hz, occurring in the deepest sleep; beta waves, 25–100 Hz, which is in the arousal system (it does not mean necessary the awareness); and theta waves between 4 and 8 hertz, corresponding to light sleep and our REM (the dream phase) sleep. Gamma waves are the fastest of the brainwave frequencies and signify the highest state of focus possible. They are associated with peak concentration and the brain's optimal frequency for cognitive functioning. Sir Francis Crick, Nobel Prize winning scientist in 1962, hypothesised that the 40 Hz frequency could be the key to the act of cognition. Forty hertz is the window frequency used in all Brain Sync Gamma and Beta wave programmes. Moreover, alpha waves are from 8 to 12 Hz, and when you are caught up in their midst, you are likely to be paying attention to your inner experience rather than what's going on around you; therefore, these waves are related to an inner meditation, a concentration on the inside realm.

These are our El Dorado, the waves we are looking for: they are related to wellbeing state, those waves that we can achieve with mindfulness and with meditation. How can we accomplish this? Using external sounds able to trigger these alpha waves, focused on the 10 Hz.

Susan Evan Morris, a speech therapist, explained as follows: *research shows that different frequencies presented to each ear through stereo headphones… create a difference tone (or binaural beat) as the brain puts together the two tones it actually hears. The different can be identified through EEG monitoring as a change in the electrical pattern produced by the brain. For example, frequencies of 200 Hz and 210 Hz produce a binaural beat frequency of 10 Hz (the difference between 210 Hz and 200 Hz is 10 Hz). Monitoring of the brain's electricity (EEG) shows that the brain produces increased 10 Hz activity with equal frequency and amplitude of the wave form in both hemispheres of the brain (left and right hemisphere)* (Morris 1989).

These external sounds, with a hertz frequency included between 210 and 200, are those which can put our brain in meditation and peaceful state: more importantly, they can produce serotonin. A certified British Academy of Sound Therapy in the UK investigates the underlying mechanisms of many conditions such as 'tinnitus' and neurological diseases such as depression and dementia. Among the many interesting works, one of them is the creation of a validated questionnaire called the mystical experience questionnaire that can assess the sense of belonging, wholeness, self-esteem, oneness/wholeness and loneliness, spaceless and timeless concepts, sense of divine and sense of nature and interconnection among people in a qualitative/quantitative manner. This tool was set to investigate even the effects of psychedelic drugs or alcohol; it clarified that some 'short effect' not creating dependency are produced by sounds, dance, walking and doing pleasant activities. Well, coming back to sound, through this binaural frequencies—one per each ear, to be listened in headphones in the most complicated cases—the findings from this study on mystical experience result in an increase of awareness of inner quiet, peace, sense of wholeness and belonging in interconnection. All this can be summarised with one word: wellbeing. This is easy to carry out and apply in the setting of care as well as easy and available at a low cost. This could be an example of slow medicine.

Sound therapy 'believes that our bodies contain "energy frequencies" and that sonic frequencies can be used to tune these energies when they go off key. All you have to do is lie down and bask in the tuneful beauty of "pure" sound'.

Sound has been a tool for promoting the physical and emotional health of the body for as long as history can account for, deeply rooted in ancient cultures and civilisations. The ancient Egyptians used vowel sound chants in healing because they believed vowels were sacred. Tibetan monks still today use the sounds of singing bowls, which they believe to be 'a symbol of the unknowable' whose 'vibrations have been described as the sound of the universe's manifestation'. Furthermore, when some American Indian medicine men and women were called upon to heal an ailing tribe member, they would fast to receive a song in dream or vision instructing them on the cure.

Psychoacoustics is the scientific study of the perception of sound, and it has fuelled researchers' paths to better understand how it can be used as medicine. To understand the fundamentals of sound in healing, we must first understand our brain waves. The nucleus of our thoughts, emotions and behaviours is the communication between neurons. Brain waves are generated by way of electrical pulses working in unison from masses of neurons interacting with one another. Brain waves are divided into five different bandwidths that are thought to form a spectrum of human consciousness. The slowest of the waves are delta waves (5 to 3 Hz), which are the slowest brain waves and occur mostly during our deepest state of sleep. The fastest of the waves are gamma waves (25–100 Hz), which are associated with higher states of conscious perception. Alpha waves (8–12 Hz) occur when the brain is daydreaming or consciously practising mindfulness or meditation.

A series of experiments conducted by neuroelectric therapy engineer Dr. Margaret Patterson and Dr. Ifor Capel revealed how alpha brain waves boosted the production of serotonin. Dr. Capel explained as follows:

> *As far as we can tell, each brain centre generates impulses at a specific frequency based on the predominant neurotransmitter it secretes. In other words, the brain's internal communication system—its language, is based on frequency… Presumably, when we send in waves of electrical energy at, say, 10 Hz, certain cells in the lower brain stem will respond because they normally fire within that frequency range.* (McAuliffe 1983)

It's very intriguing to think that something as simple as sound, as music, which we have come to treat as utterly pleasurable entertainment, has not only been used to promote healing and wellbeing but has proven to work through research as well.

If your mental health is of concern, try listening to a binaural beat to generate alpha waves between 8 and 14 Hz to produce more serotonin. Another option is to take advantage of music that promotes a relaxed alpha state in the brain such as classical music.

An interesting study utilised a different method of sound therapy (Himalayan singing bowls, transitioning to gongs, transitioning to crystal singing bowls, transitioning to therapeutic percussion). It was delivered in two ways—by a live sound bath, where subjects lay on the floor and were exposed to approximately 35 min of live sound, and then to a digital recording of those same sounds. The focus of this research was to answer the following questions:

1. Is live sound more or less effective than digitally recorded and delivered sound? If so, across what domains?
2. What are the consciousness altering effects of this method and to what degree are the domains effected?
3. What are the therapeutic benefits of sound-induced altered states of consciousness (ASC)?

Data was analysed through a chi-square analysis to gauge significance. Statistically significant, highly significant and extremely significant data were produced in the domains of physical relaxation, imagery, ineffability, transcendence of time and space, positive mood, insightfulness, disembodiment and unity across both live and recorded studies. These findings have far-reaching implications for the use of sound therapy, specifically sound-induced ASC going forwards. The findings provide further understanding of the depth at which live therapeutic sound compared to a recording is experienced. Overall, the experience in a live studio seemed to be more emotionally moving, with participants being able to put their experience into words and experiencing joy. This may be due to the presence of the instruments and vibrations felt through the body, whereas the recorded sound seemed to create deeper introspection and a deeper ASC. This is like comparing being at a live concert and listening to an MP3 recording—the former is more rousing, and the latter is more immersive. Both groups seemed to benefit from the relaxing effect of the sound and lost their usual sense of time and space.

Perhaps, the spoken language has to evolve or regain their root meaning in which words were sacred. By synchronicity, just today, I stumbled into a poem, which has a very captive title for my thoughts and feelings: 'The Unwritten' by W. S. Merwin, who won the Pulitzer Prize for poetry.

The Unwritten

Inside this pencil
crouch words that have never been written
never been spoken
never been taught
they're hiding
they're awake in there
dark in the dark
hearing us
but they won't come out
not for love not for time not for fire

even when the dark has worn away
they'll still be there
hiding in the air
multitudes in days to come may walk through them
breathe them
be none the wiser

what script can it be
that they won't unroll
in what language
would I recognize it
would I be able to follow it
to make out the real names
of everything

maybe there aren't
many
it could be that there's only one word
and it's all we need
it's here in this pencil

every pencil in the world
is like this. (Merwin 1971)

Why not trying other pencils to find the right words?

I conclude coming back to poetry and smile, with Italo Calvino and his *Six Memos for the Next Millennium*: lightness, rapidity, exactness, visibility, multitude and coherence (O'Connor 2011). Among these values, I like lightness: *thoughtful lightness that can make appear frivolousness as heavy and opaque*. Expected jokes and cynical irony, they are lead trivialities. Calvino writes *Whenever humanity seems condemned to heaviness, I think I should fly like Perseus into a different space*. Perseus, the hero who wins Medusa, looking at her reflected and with detachment and with the winged sandals donated to him by Hermes, the god of language, he's capable to lightly fly over the horror of human affairs.

Now silence maybe the purest gemstone of the El Dorado.

Practice Time

Point of View of Healthcare Providers

Observe and listen to your colleagues (physicians, nurses, other healthcare providers) while talking to each other at the cafeteria or another informal place of the hospital and of other settings of care. How do they refer to their patients?

Observe and listen to patients, their family members and their friends at the cafeteria or another informal place of the hospital and of other settings of care. How do they refer to their healthcare providers?

How do you find their language? Easy, difficult, compassionate, harsh, empathetic, technical or all of these qualities? What else?

Point of View of Patients and Family Members

Observe and listen to your doctors, nurses and other therapists talking to each other at the cafeteria or another informal place of the hospital and of other settings of care. How do they refer to patients?

Observe and listen to your relatives, other patients with their relatives and friends talking to each other at the cafeteria or another informal place of the hospital and of other settings of care. How do they refer to the doctors, nurses and other therapists?

How do you find their language? Easy, difficult, compassionate, harsh, empathetic, technical or all of these qualities? What else?

Open questions are those introduced by an adverb why, what, when, how and where. Closed questions are those introduced by a verb do, were, did and had. Which power do you envision in open questions during a dialogue? Try to use only open questions for the first minutes when you have a conversation with anybody.

What are the things, people, places and time you love? Have you ever asked this question to the people around you, patients, colleagues, carers and friends? What about trying to discover their real passion as possible tools of care?

Try to estimate if your days are 'full' of I must do this or I want to do this (duty and willingness).

Music: have you decided your best favourite playlist? What do you think about asking to the people around, including patients, to prepare their playlist for vulnerable time?
Silence: quiet and stillness, what do they evoke in you during a conversation?
Sound: what do you think about this possible language of care? Have you ever tried binaural sound? Please, give it a try, you go to YouTube, you digit binaural music and feel the effects.
Would you suggest it also to your patients?

References

Ahmadshah F et al (2010) The effect of listening to lullaby music on physiologic response and weight gain of premature infants. J Neonatal-Perinatal Med 3(2):103–107

Banfi P, Cappuccio A, Latella ME, Reale L, Muscianisi E, Marini MG (2018) Narrative medicine to improve the management and quality of life of patients with COPD: the first experience applying parallel chart in Italy. Int J Chron Obstruct Pulmon Dis 13:287–297

Berne E (1972) What do you say after you say hallo? Time Book, New York

Breuning LG (2015) Habits of a happy brain: retrain your brain to boost your serotonin, dopamine, oxytocin, & endorphin levels. Adams Media Corporation, Avon, MA

Chatwin B (1984) The songlines. Penguin Edition, New York

Gawande A (2007) Better: a surgeon's notes on performance. Metropolitan, New York

Griffith T (2013) https://www.telegraph.co.uk/

Lacan J (1966) Écrits. First published by Éditions du Seuil

McAuliffe K (1983) Brain Tuner. Omni

Merwin WS (1971) The unwritten. The New Yorker

Morris S (1989) The Facilitation of Learning. Privately published manuscript, p. 15

Newberg A, Waldme MR (2012) Words can change your brain. Hudson Street Press, New York, NY

O'Connor Z (2011) Colour psychlogy and color therapy: caveat emptor. Color Res Appl 36(3):229–234

Pease A, Pease B (2006) The definitive book of body language: the hidden meaning behind people's gestures and expressions. Bantam Books, New York

Persico G et al (2017) Maternal singing of lullabies during pregnancy and after birth: effects on mother-infant bonding and on newborns' behaviour. Women Birth 30(4):e214–e220

Ripollés P et al (2014) The role of reward in word learning and its implications for language acquisition. Curr Biol 24(21):2606–2611

Skeat WW (1888) An etymological dictionary of the English language. Clarendon Press, Oxford

Tillman JB (2016) Experiencing music—restoring the spiritual, music as wellbeing. Oxford, Bern, Brussels, Frankfurt am Main. Peter Lang, New York. http://www.medicinanarrativa.eu/the-language-of-music-interview-with-june-boyce-tillman

Wierzbicka A (1997) Understanding cultures through their key words: English, Russian, Polish, German, and Japanese. Oxford University Press, New York

The Environment for Wellbeing: The Need for Therapeutic Places of Care and the Languages of Proportions and Colours

7

In ancient Greece, the concepts of beauty (*kalos*) and good (*agathos*) were considered as one: beauty implied goodness, and, vice versa, the individual virtue spreads charm. Ethics and aesthetics blend, and in the so-called *kalokagathia*, the ideal of the evolution of the human people could not be separated. Likewise, the term 'aesthetic', which comes from the word 'aesthesis'—sensorial perception—includes more than just the visual perception: it stands for a global perception with all given senses (Online Etymology Dictionary n.d.), encompassing the impression left by what is perceived. In the original meaning of the concept, tactile and visual perception constitutes a whole, together with hearing and feeling. Even scent is part of the aesthesis, as well discernment, which is part of the aesthetic experience. If we think about something very familiar to the medical world, we might refer to the 'anaesthesia', i.e. simply the blocking of the body's sensorial perception either at a general or a local level. As an oxymoron, anaesthesia seems quite to block the aesthesis, the aesthetic experience. We are definitely grateful to a group of researchers and physicians in Boston who discovered the anaesthetic gas in surgery at the end on the nineteenth century. They were not the first: probably, many centuries ago, anaesthetics herbs were used both for healing and for sacrifice. Calling in action the meaning of anaesthesia, I thought it to be powerful enough to explain deeply the roots of an aesthetic experience, something perceived by the whole body, and this something produces something good just by the fact of the engagement of our sensorial and logical system with the world around, the people around and the air around the body.

The beauty we want to address is not only that of persons around us but also of architectural spaces, nature and environment with which we continuously interact with. In a publication on Scientific American *How Room Design Affects your Work and Mood* (2009), Emily Anthes reported that in 1950, Jonas Salk, an award-winning doctor and a biologist, was working to find a therapy for polio in a subterranean laboratory in Pittsburgh. Advances were slow, so Salk decided to take a break and travel to Assisi to rest in a thirteenth-century monastery. This period of contemplation allowed him to see things from different points of view and eventually conceive the anti-polio vaccine. After that experience, Salk continued to

M. G. Marini, *Languages of Care in Narrative Medicine*,
https://doi.org/10.1007/978-3-319-94727-3_7

meditate on the influence of the architectural spaces of the monastery on him, which drove him to a collaboration with architect Louis Kahn in the construction of the Salk Institute in La Jolla, California.

The effects of spaces and colours in workplaces, living spaces and hospitals have been studied thoroughly. Many publications in scientific literature have been studied, and now several researches state that patients recover better and faster if treated in a beautiful place (Ulrich 2002; Sternberg 2009).

After all, we are talking about a revolution: let us think about workplaces as alienating open spaces and now in search of architectures integrated in the landscape. If we look at hospitals, we know that in Italy, many structures were built at the end of nineteenth century (and these, expect of dysfunctionality, maintain a certain style), and those more unaesthetic date back to the 1960s and 1970s wild overbuilding—the trend of single blocks. They may look like extraterrestrial spaceships as the Enterprise of Star Trek to admit patients in an alien place. Indoor gardens were forbidden; there are long corridors, with white walls and aluminium window fixtures.

However, time changes and accordingly narratives of spaces in healthcare places: I want to dedicate the next words to the Meyer Children's Hospital in Florence, a harmony between nature and architecture so beautiful to look at to become a model for the whole world. Before starting to describe the Meyer Hospital—a guided tour I sincerely recommend to and for those who work in healthcare and build hospital—I want to reflect again on the scientific discoveries that brought Salk to find how to develop a good anti-polio vaccine in an Italian monastery and not in his basement. Why do we recover faster in an aesthetically well-finished environment? Why we think better and produce more ideas?

Here comes into play the research by the team of Professor Rizzolatti of the University of Parma—the one that discovered the existence of mirror neurons, a population of visual-motor neurons identified in primates, some birds and humans (Rizzolatti and Craighero 2004). The activation of these neurons occurs both during the execution of actions and during the observation of the same actions made by others. In the observer, we can assist to a phenomenon of 'neuronal mirroring' of the behaviour of the person observed, as if—in other words—the first did the action made by the second.

Already in 1905, Henri Poincaré, a physicist, mathematician and philosopher of science, asserted that the spatial coordinates around our bodies, and our relationships with objects and people around us, involved the fundamental parts of our nervous system; therefore, the coordination with our 'outside' would be a conquest not by the individual but by species (Poincarè 1905).

What is more renowned is that mirror neurons have been localised near the Broca area, and they deal with language: researchers think that the skill of talking has evolved through information transmitted with gestural performances, and the mirror system has been able to comprehend and codify/decode (Rizzolatti and Craighero 2007). It has been confirmed that this system has the potential to give a comprehension mechanism of actions and for learning through imitation and simulation of the others' behaviour. In this sense, it is appropriate to repeat that the recognition does not happen only at the motor level but with the real recognition of the action, intended as a biophysical event.

However, this neuronal forest is not only involved with the importance of words of narrated language: neuroscientists of Parma identified that in this forest, there are some particular plants activating in the observation of other people's behaviour. If they are watered with clean water, i.e. positive gestures or beauty, mirror neurons activate positive behaviours. This is the relationship among neurons, beauty, arts and wellbeing (Di Dio et al. 2007). In Rizzolatti's words, *To understand the relationship between mirror neurons and art, we carried out some experiments on sculpture. We took in example ancient Greek artworks, and—with an algorithm done by some engineers—we slightly modified their measures. Then, we showed them to volunteer subjects, and we looked to what was happening in their brains using the functional magnetic resonance. We demonstrated that in the human brain there is a synchrony between action and observation. First of all, the original ancient Greek artworks activate the brain more than the modified ones, but the most interesting thing is that they activate the emotional area where there are mirror neurons of empathy (from the ancient Greek: to feel inside). So, the mechanisms that these Greek sculptors invented is not only the activation of the cerebral cortex with its neural circuits letting thousands of functions start, but also the moving of emotional center: in other words, the good artists succeed, in some way, in moving emotional centers by means of his artwork. Definitively, art reinforces the observer's empathy and activates some imitative processes, so that beauty creates further beauty.*

Ancient Greeks knew nothing about mirror neurons, but they found the golden section, the system of proportion that rules the world and we find in shell valves, in ionic capitals and in human figures, in the distance between our head and the navel and between navel and our feet. Let us recall the Discobolus of Myron or Botticelli's Venus. When we are in front of these proportions, we might calm ourselves; we feel as extraordinarily accepted by the figure we are observing: we are in empathy—sharing—with the environment, which is where also Poincaré's research comes in.

Rizzolatti with Professor Semir Zeki, at the Wellcome Laboratory of Neurobiology at University College London in the UK, and his colleague Dr. Tomohiro Ishizu discovered that the medial orbitofrontal cortex in human beings, what experts call the pleasure and reward centre of the brain, showed stronger activity in the brains of participants who listened to music or looked at a picture that they had already deemed beautiful (Zeki 1998; Ishizu and Zeki 2011; Chatterjee 2011). By examining MRI images of his subjects' brains, Zeki found that when people look at something they find beautiful, a portion in the front part of the brain called the medial orbitofrontal cortex 'lights up', i.e. there is increased blood flow in this area. He believes it is a near-universal response to beauty, and this is something aesthetic and ecstatic for me to discover while I am writing this book on the languages of care. It really tells us that seeking beauty puts us in the condition of 'feeling good', a universal thing; in some cases, there are universal ways to get to it. The brain pleasure centre is rewarded with the neurotransmitter dopamine, among the 'Eldorado' or good neurotransmitters. Zeki added that one thing that is novel about his study is that beauty as perceived through the eyes (e.g. visual art) and beauty you receive through the ears (e.g. music) are not routed to different parts of the brain; they both 'reward' the same place. The degree of activity in the medial orbitofrontal cortex correlates very strongly to the degree to which you find a thing attractive. He explained as follows: *The extent of activity in the medial frontal cortex is directly proportional to the declared intensity of beauty. So, if you experience something as very beautiful on a scale of 1–10 and you give it a 10, then the activity is going to be stronger than if you experience it as a 1 out of 10.* In contrast, Zeki said he found that when people see something that is aesthetically displeasing—something they find ugly—it lights up a completely different part of the brain: *It is another region of the brain, called the amygdyla, which is also active when you look at frightening stimuli, also active with fear and anger, as if the body is being mobilized, or prepared, or planning some kind of motor action to avoid what is ugly.* Now the challenge is to find out what objects stimulate the release of dopamine or the amygdala to foster these common patterns in the brain.

If we always need harmony, beauty and gently narrated words, this becomes truer when we are sick: for instance, if children fall ill in less illuminated schools, with walls in white monotony and neon lights, and in hospitals, where children and parents arrive with an only request or hope; cure, unfortunately, is not always but, in the most cases, possible. Care, instead, is always possible.

I let the architects of the Meyer Children Hospital in Florence speak: the concept of *therapeutic architecture*, adopted by the evidence-based design, leads the project from the entrance of the hospital, which constitutes the first stress factor of hospitalisation. At Meyer, the glass arbour that gradually leads into the hospital twists and turns in the park that, like a real care garden, contributes to the psychological wellbeing of little patients and their familiars. A comforting pathway in greenery leads to the spectacular entrance hall that constitutes a logical consequence of the planning value conferred to the contact with the surrounding nature. In fact, the hall is an innovative 'bioclimatic greenhouse that represents an excellent example of building integrated photovoltaic, which transforms sustainability in a language of materials, lights and colours. The convergence point of the wood pillars creates a fantastic atmosphere: they are a clear reference to the woods outside, as an ideal prosecution; the arches remind us of the ribs of the great whale in the Pinocchio tale, of which we find references in the design of other objects and technologies connoting interiors of the hospital ward' (Anshen and Allen, San Francisco) (Meyer Website n.d.).

In this hospital, personally, I met extraordinary professionals, full of energy and pride: I work at Meyer, and such a self-realisation is like a breath of spring in a healthcare system that has to strongly defense from lack of oxygen, due to lack of time and resources and humanistic competences. Beauty exists even in a public hospital. Burn out, compassion fatigue, trauma and risks of suicides by the physicians are remote, lowered by the beautiful environment which helps not only the children but also their proxies as well as the healthcare professionals.

When children are back on their feet, they have huge spaces in the game room, library and garden where they can play. They can also socialise with many volunteers (who consider it an honour to attend this hospital) and teachers who help them catch up with their school programme. Visiting hours are free, without curfew. Furthermore, the collaboration with the Fondazione Collodi made the Meyer Hospital an extraordinarily artistic exposition on Pinocchio. Artists have illustrated the narrative of one of the most known fairy tales in the world through the corridors and wards with sculptures, paintings and photos portraying Geppetto (the doctor or the father?), the Blue Fairy (the nurse or the doctor?), Mangiafuoco (the disease?) and the Belly of the Whale (as shown in Fig. 7.1) that is no longer frightening but joyful and bright. Then, with his growing up, and becoming a boy, but without strings—no strings, no intravenous, no ECG, no needles—let's go out. Maybe science will not tell you why, or maybe it will talk about another species of mirror neurons, but NM, always in search of meaning in a story we narrate to comprehend.

In this photo, the 'Belly of the Whale' at the Meyer Children's Hospital (WHO Website n.d.), with its tall glass ceiling, has been designed to transmit the universal perception of beauty to its young patients. The facility has also been awarded by the WHO.

In this Eldorado, utopic but real place, we would like also to fly over visual art: if visual art is music, we will focus on the 'sound' of visual art as the language of colours.

Neuroscientist Bevil Conway has studied colour for many years: he has studied vision and perception at Wellesley College and Harvard Medical School. Knowing that humans might also be hardwired for certain hues could be a gateway into understanding the neural properties of emotion (Conway 2012). Since researchers know that certain colours provoke strong feelings in people (blues and purples are more pleasant than yellows, for instance, while greens tend to be the most arousing), they might then work backwards to uncover the basic mechanisms for these feelings. If researchers can trace the neural circuitry that guides that distinction, they might enhance our understanding of how the brain categorises things more broadly—relevant or not relevant and left or right. From there, it is a short step to the architecture of human decision-making. Whatever brain activity leads us to prefer colour televisions might tell us a lot about rewards and non-verbal communication. In that sense, says Conway, colour could become 'a model system for something much more than colour'. Anyhow, key mediating variables in terms of the interface between colour and human response include an individual's personality, cultural experience and

Fig. 7.1 The Belly of the Whale at the Meyer Children Hospital in Florence

affective state (O'Connor 2011). Therefore, it is very important in different cultural context to know which colour is considered to be 'good' for obtaining certain results; in some cultures, red is associated with best performance, while its green in others. In some other context, 'green relieves the stress', and 'those who have a green work environment experience fewer stomach aches'. Even if this is totally subjective, what counts, at the end, is for everyone to find the colour that activates their wellbeing.

At the moment, we, at Fondazione ISTUD, are carrying out a pilot study to measure the effect of art therapy (colouring and drawing books) among patients with ostomy, mainly with colon cancer. The different colouring books were assigned by the enterostomist nurse to patients in random fashion. The study investigates the effects of colouring and drawing on patients' mood and wellbeing. Participants of the study received a colouring book and were asked to write about their experience (open plot of free narrative). Meanwhile, nurses were trained in the meaning of colour sand drawing traits to gain sensitivity to the meaning and power of artistic expression.

The data are still preliminary and refer to 35 patients (out of a total 100 who are still in process of providing feedback). Out of these 28 patients, 36% were men and 64% women, with a mean age of 47.3 years; 79% declared that colouring and drawing were a positive experience, 13% described it as neutral and 8% found it annoying. From the narratives of satisfied people, we quote as follows: *I became aware, at the end of my colouring, that I was feeling more relaxed and less stressful, It distracted me from thinking about my situation, I felt, through colours, a sense of freedom, I coloured with my child, I travelled with colours and I was no longer thinking about my illness, I found myself free as when I was a child.* However, there are also short narratives such as *I felt it like a waste of time, I could not finish any drawing since I have other thing to do, There are more stimulant visual arts as photography and cinema, I didn't feel it to be useful.*

Shortly, reflecting on these answers, colour and drawing may work for some people (likely the majority). People indeed can take care of themselves using different languages: from visual art up to routine daily activities that have the power to restore through different mechanisms.

To carry out this project, we interviewed the artist Rita Mangano, who has worked for many years in the field of art in healthcare environments (both acute and long-term settings). She has been and is still working in hospitals as a painter to make these places of care more beautiful.

This is an interview with Rita Mangano, a painter who is extremely sensitive to the world of health and wellbeing on art as a language for therapy in healthcare systems.

MGM. Who is Rita Mangano?

RM. I come from a long pedagogical experience with pre-schoolers in an era of experimentation and enthusiasm.

I am a painter and a self-taught artist. I have used this talent, built over the years, not only to create beauty in the surrounding environment (aesthetic function) but also to use beauty to achieve a state of better wellbeing (I am the first to use it).

I left the paediatric wards oncology to arrive then in the oncology for adult patients, Alzheimer's, residences for the elderly and hospices/palliative care that have different states of wellbeing.

My profession develops in two directions: the creation of paintings that I exhibit in my gallery on the Naviglio, Milan, and the production of works for healthcare settings. These works are the fruit of years of experience in pedagogy, psychology studies, courses on body language, emotions and non-verbal communication, having conducted painting workshops with women dealing with breast cancer and healthcare workers and, a determining factor, attention to the human being and love for nature.

I consider myself a real painter and an art therapist.

MGM. Could you tell us about colours?

RM. There are no universal readings on colour because every interpretation must be contextualised at the time and culture in which it is expressed.

An emblematic example is the use of the colour black, which in our Western culture is associated with mourning and death, while in cultures adhering to reincarnation, the colour of mourning is white.

There is no doubt that the warm colours, i.e. yellow, orange and red, are full of energy, while the cold colours return to interiority.

The colours, being carriers of emotions, are also language of non-verbal communication, and their symbolic meaning is ambivalent. For example, when I feel low and sluggish, I unconsciously choose to wear a dress or an accessory of red colour to charge me with the energy I am missing; yet, it is also true that when I do feel energetic I wear red because it is in tune with what I'm feeling inside. This refers to another significant variable with respect to the perception of colour, which changes according to our cultural heritage and our individual history. Fashion also imposes the use of colours, independently from moods or states of mind.

Our perception about colour may sometimes be misleading: in the past, I believed that red was not a suitable colour for patients, as they would associate it to wounds, withdrawals and suffering; so, I never used it. One day, I realised that some patients (such as depressed or traumatised patients) were actually attracted by red paintings.

I cite the example of a 40-year-old woman whom we call Carla who showed a strong aversion to green in clothing as well as both in the drawings she produced and those made by others. This woman almost hated green, but she did not know the reason why. After months of artistic practice, she realised that her mother, when she was small, was always wearing or having something green, and in the meanwhile, the mother kept on saying to her 'behave as a good girl'. After she had this sudden awareness, she reconciled with green and with her mother.

MGM. What about hospital facilities and colours?

RM. Some facility managements have understood the value of colour of the environment for patients' wellbeing and have made appropriate investments. In many other hospital facilities, colour is only used for direction lines for reaching the ward.

In some hospitals, colour is used heavily and completely fills the walls of hospital rooms and corridors: while it may positively impact a visitor's first approach, it might not be appropriate for patients and operators themselves. The perception of one colour compared to another considerably impacts the psychological and physical wellbeing of the people who come into contact with it.

For all these reasons, my work of pictorial decoration in the places of care, which I have been carrying out for more than 30 years, is specifically tailored upon age groups and type of disease.

MGM. What about colours in hospitals?

RM. In hospices, patients are often accompanied by relatives who live permanently in the ward for long periods of time. Luckily, in many cases, these facilities provide extra attention to the parental sphere: the kitchen area and the living room are furnished just as a home environment to make the space more welcoming. The paintings displayed are intended to decorate and make the space more welcoming, such as furniture, curtains, sofas and fabrics used.

People who bought my paintings told me that the paintings were not only aesthetically pleasant and soothing with their pastel colours but that the paintings also exerted a therapeutic effect on their health status. This happens in relation to the colours I use (saturated pastel colours) associated with subjects from nature.

Sometimes people I don't know (relatives who live in hospices) send me emails to thank me because the vision of my paintings helped them endure the tragic moment and high psychological stress that they were facing. I then placed small paintings in the hospice baths and in the changing rooms of the radiotherapy and oncology departments because they are private places, where you are alone with yourself and your burden of pain.

Not least, paintings, especially handmade ones, also represent an economic value added to the hospital facility and represent a visible sign of attention to the persons in hospital.

MGM. What if you had the magic wand to change settings of care?

RM. Any form of beauty in health resorts represents an added value if it brings along greater respect and humanity for people through a holistic vision towards the totality of the person. The hospital is anything but a warm and welcoming environment.

More attention should be paid to patients' quality of life and to provide them more domestic environment. Let us consider, for example, the hospital entrance leading on to the ward: the first impact is devastating. It would be nice if it were replaced by a more domestic entrance lighted by warm table lamps, carpets, wooden furniture and paintings gradually leading to the hospital room.

The rooms should also represent more intimate spaces. The forceful sharing of intimacy with strangers could be cushioned with functional screens rather than by shower curtains as I have seen in many departments or with sliding walls with appropriate decorations rather than doors (that appear as barriers). Bathrooms, in many cases, lack the minimum comfort features such as towel hook shelves for placing beauty cases or personal belongings and hangers for robes.

The choice of food is another issue. It would be nice to make the patient less passive by asking him or her to choose from a variety of options such as snacks. The patient should be asked at the entrance to the ward at the time of hospitalisation, what pictorial representation would he/she like in the room? From here, the choice of paintings through a photographic catalogue of hand-painted works is available and supplied and divided by subjects: marine environment, mountains, forests, tropical environment, animals, flowers, flowers, flowering trees, etc. In a nutshell, it would be useful to recover and enhance the residual capacity to make decisions and not only to be taxable persons of decisions that make decisions for others.

Communication should take place with a direct look in a gentle and polite way. In many care facilities, walls are covered with patient information that cover the walls, creating confusion of various messages. I would love to have hospitals or nursing homes that organise parties, cinema, theatre or musical events; there are some settings of care which are doing it, but patients barely attend them since they are not personally invited.

This is passive art for patients: if there were laboratories in the wards equipped with suitable staff, if there were music, musicians and artistic performances, gardens to care for and gardens to look after. It would be beneficial to have discussions on universal but pleasant themes, listen to the lives of others, enrich and enrich each other's non-health experiences and research and share joys and positivity in things.

Apart from artist and architects, is the environment something perceived as of importance by patients and relatives? To answer this, we present here some considerations of parents of premature children who are in the neonatal intensive care unit (Marini et al. 2017), where newborns may have to stay in the hospital for weeks, even months.

The environment gave me comfort with colorful drawings and decorations. I felt more at home than in a hospital.

I felt like I was on a spaceship. Everything was very updated. I did not understand anything about all those things attached to my child.

Despite the difficulty of creating a place to shelter small creatures who are often dealing with very problematic health problems, the department set many precautions to mitigate the impact with this reality, such as dim lights when possible, and decorations on the walls.

It was a clean place, where everything had order and meaning.

It was very cold place, with all that equipment, but fortunately the bed of F. facing a window with the view of a tree.

I will always remember the sound of the monitors. I hated the hospital from the first minute. The place very colorful but full of pain.

There was a lack of intimacy for the parents, I truly held back my tears so I would not pass on my sadness to the other parents.

On my right, in the dark, I found two small rooms, one next to the other, separated by a white wall. At the center of each of them is an incubator. I only saw the darkness, those incubators and monitors. I remember the smell of the department and the acre-sweetness of the hand. I remember the sound of the monitor every time one of my little ones had respiratory crises.

The department is nice new and comfortable for parents like me who spent the whole day next to the incubators.

The first impact was terrible... the department is in many respects obsolete—small and lacking in hygiene standards.

I still remember the smell of disinfectant characterizing that old structure.

A tiny place, full of bursting incubators, where an air of suspension was breathed. Time is suspended there, you go in there and it's like entering a bubble, a world apart, everything else is outside and will never realize how good it is to be out there.

In these parents' memoirs, the lights and dark are so vivid, as well as the sounds of the monitor and the idle time. However, the colours somehow mitigate the anxiety of the unknown destiny of their premature children. Intimacy is requested, a place to stay alone with the possibility to show the inner feeling, with tears, away from the other parents. A tree outside from the window is the natural presence in this artificial neonatal intensive care. More windows, more trees. When something hard is to face, the first gesture is to have the possibility to lift the eyes and look at a piece of sky.

In March 2018, we conducted an online survey asking, *If you had the magic wand, how would you imagine your place of care?* We collected 39 answers at the website www.NarrativeMedicine.eu, in a very short time. Preliminary feedback of these answers was represented into a wordcloud (Fig. 7.2).

You will see that we will not need 1000 answers: they are so much consistent in explaining what patients, doctors, nurses, psychotherapists, administrators, caregivers and citizen need. These include to have a nice reading: only one comment; nature above all in time, places and human relationship; art; healthy foods; and books. These also include trees of life everywhere as well as with sun and water.

Patients wish to have possibilities and not only rules. The place of care should give them possibilities, even to imagine a coloured and full of light inside space where to read, comfortable chairs and beds where to rest, a bar where to meet family

Fig. 7.2 Answers of the survey *If you had the magic wand, how would you imagine your place of care?* represented in a word cloud (Unpublished data, Fondazione Istud)

and nice people and an outside to breath fresh air in the green, facing the sea or a lake or where there is water.

Below are the excerpts from the tests:

- *Bright, in the middle of the mountains, with lots of green, with a large kitchen, where you can cook together hearty healthy and light dishes.*
- *A gym, with many machines, lots of indoor bikes, treadmills, and a beautiful spa to gratify one's effort and the end of the workout,*
- *Silent, with a beautiful garden around, bright rooms, common meeting halls*
- *Like a house: cosy, warm, furnished and with the ability to customize the environments with the hobbies of the pc, possibility to bring my furry friend with me, possibility to hear music, have privacy and the possibility to receive friends if I like. Yes, my ideal place of care is similar to a home.*
- A *place where professionalism and hospitality are guaranteed, human and logistic, a colourful place with green spaces and spaces where you can meet friends, family and pets. A place where you do not have the fear of going because it is aseptic and completely disconnected from your everyday life and above all where you can actively participate in your care path.*
- *I would like it to be a good environment with flowers, lights with delicate colours. With dedicated spaces for visits from relatives and friends.*
- *All painted cream and cherry wood surrounded by trees around. Immersed in the silence of the countryside.*
- *The most comfortable possible and the closest to a real home, while remaining operational needs.*
- *A Rainbow*
- *I would like to be in a place in which we have a library available, that in the rooms you can listen to music and the possibility that there are characters that make you laugh, as clowns.*

- *A place full of paintings with the colours of the sea and the green of spring, many plants placed in several corners.*
- *Relaxing music and cats free to move in space. Books, everywhere for everyone to read.*
- *An internal and external garden, where nature has Preponderant, because I believe in the possibility of taking care of nature.*
- *With murals of trees and the sound of a waterfall in the background.*
- *In my place of ideal care, the walls are not walls but they are trees, it is a wood. The noise of the nursery carts and the words of the operators are covered by the sound of a waterfall that spreads throughout the rooms.*
- *I would like to see an internal garden, because I think that when a person is sick, reconnection with nature is one of the elements that promote well-being. I imagine the people, the doctors, the nurses who touch my body with grace and safety, sure of what they do I suppose the needles can disappear... To give way to more and more refined imaging technologies... But if you have to do the injections, let's be pampered by a gentle language of the operators. I imagine common areas for family members, with kitchens where you can create a better lunch than a hurried sandwich at the bar. I imagine for children the possibility of having a playroom and a bed always present for the parent or an adult who cares for them. I imagine that doctors and nurses can be relieved of the control bureaucracy, and patients as well. No numbers like at the post office but be called by my name. I imagine that people do everything to stop the pain, not just the progression of the disease. I hope I do not have to wake up at 6 for my breakfast, but people let me sleep, because sleep is the best recovery. I imagine that there is no longer that slice of cooked ham, the apple purée and the chicken breast that is not known whether it is boiled or grilled. I would put more money on good food than on drugs. I imagine, a common space, or even more common spaces, where I can meet with others to listen to music, see a movie as in a pseudocinema, and paint and write. Hours of the larger visits, I know it is difficult to open 24 h a day, but at least 12 h a day yes… and I would like a bed near me, or a comfortable armchair for those who want to stay next to me to sleep.... I would like to have a room to meditate, without it being a fixed place of worship, And a small gym where I can train.... Clear indication and anyway, when I ask for information that people are kind and patient. And that the operators get along with each other.... If I see their harmony, I also feel in harmony.*
- *Coloured*
- *At my home with a hospital team*
- *Natural Light and Windows looking into a park and Lake... Like Swiss spas*
- *Bright and possibly surrounded by a garden with tall trees that are visible from the bed. The room should be painted in light colours, not white, perhaps with a green band. The maximum would be to have a round space, without edges, with a door that leads directly to the garden (maybe with a small pond in the centre like a Japanese garden).*
- *House and in the green*

- *Colour on the walls... Different colours. Many books, music... A laboratory space where to draw, sew, write, make art... Wooden floor to go ashore and walk barefoot, to dance. Large rooms, large luminous but with many light curtains, like veils, of those that move magically even with a bit of wind; but also niches, small nooks that are as comfortable and welcoming as burrows where they can gather between cushions. Scents, sounds, smell of wood and silent flowers but of coffee that grows noisy.*
- *A place of cordiality, kindness, understanding and choice with dignity.*
- *According to the polyvagal theory of Porges: safe and quiet.*
- *With a tearoom to converse not only among patients, family members, friends but also with health professionals. A meditation room and a small soundproof room to be able to yell and let out despair, anger, impotence but also happiness. Naturally the meditation and scream rooms are open to everyone.*
- *It would be a respectful space for the person and his family. I would like it spacious, cosy, possibly even a little colourful. It should not be a chamber of isolation from the world, but in relationship and contact with the world. With Internet and with the possibility of using one's own technological devices Open to visits (clearly compatible with pathologies and pathways of care). With quality food (also a sign of respect for the person). With refreshment areas for family members and with the possibility to have housing for caregivers close to the care facility. I would definitely like a place of acceptance and not rejection. Without forgetting the healthcare professionals who provide care. We should also think about them to ensure the best quality for their work.*
- *Bright, serene, with lots of nature and the possibility of being outdoors.*
- *A cosy room, where you can have a loved one beside me day and night, with kind and caring staff, ready to listen even the slightest doubt about my state of health.*
- *Pacific, with relaxing music, with the sea, heated by nature and then by the sun.*
- *Before all else I would like to stay in a big sunny room. Painted walls.*
- *Light blue colours. Quiet music, books and a big window to watch the sea and listen to it. Also with garden and different flowers.*
- *A large leafy tree, with the chirping of birds, a large window from which to access the tree, loving looks of the carers, attentive ears, a book or perhaps more.*
- *A large window open to the ocean, the sound of waves crashing on the beach, the sea breeze, the humming of seagulls, the sun warming your face.*
- *I would like a smile on the walls adorned with soft colours and windows from which the sky enters and lets me breathe.... A lilac blanket on the bed and a warmth in the skin... I would like to hear a music that makes my mind free and not no one's ears.*
- *A winter garden: every room is white and green, on the walls the drawings of plants and flowers and an embryo seedling in each room.*
- *No waiting especially if reserved appointment Special care for the elderly (they are so many in Western countries that they have no). Relaxing chairs, not the usual rigid metal ones. Provider Healthcare workers are listening to patient's needs. Improving communications skills that will allow appropriate language to patient literacy and origin. Involvement of patients in decision whenever the situ-*

ation in terms of understanding the clinical situation allows. Involvement of Caregivers

- *An element that could not be missing in my place of ideal care would certainly be nature: gardens with trees, flowers and above all ponds and streams. Better still if this place of care was located near the sea or a lake. I would also like the structure to be aesthetically pleasing to the eye and the architectural details and furnishings to be treated in detail (the image that springs to mind immediately is that of a liberty style villa with large windows and floral decorations). I would also like to have a pool environment because, as we have already noted, I am of the opinion that water and contact with it are already in itself exceptional therapeutic instruments. I would also like there to be a library, because reading can help to heal the mind and if my physical problem prevents me from making great journeys or journeys or living adventures, at least I can travel with the soul where I feel and do all that that I want. I would also like everyone who works in this place of care to never underestimate the value and the power of a kind smile, a gesture or a word and not only listen to the symptom or the results of the analysis, but first of all to the person who entrust him to his care.*
- *I do not want to live my place of care like a prison. Hospitals are often reclusion places from the outside world. It seems to enter a parallel reality, where an air of sickness and suffering dominates. In my opinion it would be appropriate to have architecturally harmonious spaces, because beauty makes you feel good. Finally, I believe that in an ideal place of health, there should also be some social activities to distract the patient from his illness.*
- *A house, overlooking the sea.*
- *It would be nice to live in a comic book... A world where one can enter and discover that everything is possible.*
- *Small building in the countryside with mountain views, meadows and silence; inside walls that are not white or blue but clad in wood, decorate with paintings, and with bookshelves.* (Unpublished data, Fondazione Istud)

According to Steven Kosslyn, the psychologist at Harvard University, our brain uses the same regions both for imagining a scene and actually viewing one (2005). Therefore, one could potentially benefit from looking at a painting of nature, imagining to be outdoors among trees, gardens, flowers and water. Taken together, nature has a pivotal role in the development of human beings, especially in moments of frailty when they yearn for a closer bond to their origins. This input should be a challenge for architects of the future, combining evolving technology mindscape with natural landscape.

Practice Time

Do you think that beauty is a language of care?

Did you know that proportioned objects reassure us and activate empathy? What do you think about it?

Did you know that 'ugly' things trigger the synthesis of neurotransmitters of fears by the amygdala theory? What is your opinion about this scientific discovery?
If you had the magic wand, how would you imagine your ideal place of care?
Going from fantasy to what you could really do, which are the things you would like to undertake to make your place of care more cosy and agreeable?
You read the 39 wishes of a nice place of care, do you think that there are some common trends? If so, which ones do you find out? If no, please explain the reason why.
Would you like to take some pictures or make some drawing to improve your place of care?
Any other thoughts?

References

Anthes E (2009) How room designs affect your work and mood—brain research can help us craft spaces that relax, inspire, awaken, comfort and heal. Scientific American Mind, Scientific American. http://shiverarchitects.com/resource/Room_Designs.pdf

Chatterjee A (2011) Neuroaesthetics: a coming of age story. J Cogn Neurosci 23(1):53–62

Conway BR (2012) Color consilience: color through the lens of art practice, history, philosophy, and neuroscience. Ann N Y Acad Sci 1251:77–94

Online Etymology Dictionary (n.d.) Definition of aesthetic. https://www.etymonline.com/word/aesthetic

Di Dio C, Macaluso E, Rizzolatti G (2007) The golden beauty: brain response to classical and renaissance sculptures. PLoS One 2(11):e1201

Poincarè H (1905) Space and geometry. Chapter 4 in science and hypothesis. Walter Scott Publishing, London, pp 51–71

Ishizu T, Zeki S (2011) Toward a brain-based theory of beauty. PLoS One 6(7):e21852

Kosslyn SM (2005) Mental images and the brain. Cogn Neuropsychol 22:3–4

Marini MG, Chesi P, Bruscagnin M, Ceccatelli M, Ruzzon E (2017) Digits and narratives of the experience of Italian families facing premature births. J Matern Fetal Neonatal Med 22:1–7

Meyer Website. http://www.meyer.it/index.php/en/hospital

O'Connor Z (2011) Colour psychology and color therapy: caveat emptor. Color Res Appl 36(3):229–234

Rizzolatti G, Craighero L (2004) The mirror-neuron system. Annu Rev Neurosci 27:169–192

Rizzolatti G, Craighero L (2007) Language and mirror neurons. In: Gareth Gaskell M (ed) The Oxford handbook of psycholinguistics. Oxford University Press, Oxford

Sternberg EM (2009) Healing spaces: the science of place and well-being. Belknap Press of Harvard University Press, Cambridge, MA

Ulrich RS (2002) Health Benefits of Gardens in Hospitals. Paper for conference, Plants for People—International Exhibition Floriade

WHO Website. http://www.euro.who.int/en/countries/italy/news/news/2015/01/bridging-the-gap-between-hospital-and-school-an-initiative-of-meyer-childrens-hospital

Zeki S (1998) Art and the brain. Daedalus 127(2):71–103

8 Trauma and Coping Activation of Patients and Curers: Learning from Humanities Mythology (Odysseus and the Minotaur) and Fairy Tales (the Beauty and the Beast), Suicides and Recovery Practice

The topic of trauma and coping is a complex one. In this chapter, we approach them starting from a broader context of symbolisms and patients' narratives and then discuss them in light of current clinical evidence. Specifically, we start by analysing the myth of the Minotaur in the Labyrinth and the Beauty and the Beast as examples of diverse patient journeys. The first represents the patient's approach to illness passing through the maze of healthcare, with its closed ends, tortuous paths and eventually its exit; the second represents the patient's coping with the beast of illness.

The Minotaur in the Labyrinth

The Minotaur is a beast, half man, half bull, which eats the flesh of youth, seven boys and seven girls, a given holocaust from Athens. The Minotaur is imprisoned in a Labyrinth, without any chance of escaping (Rouse 1957). This myth belongs to the Bronze Greek age, dated around 1500 BC, and calls into action a 'beauty', Ariadne, daughter of Minos, King of Crete and a hero, Theseus, son of the King of Athens, Aegeus, who wish to cease this sacrifice of the best of youth of his city. How does this myth of the Minotaur as the Beast connect to NM? In the setting of medical illness, the terms 'beast' or 'monster' and their synonyms are recurrently used in patients' narratives in reference to their disease—for example, talking about their life with multiple sclerosis, cancer, psoriasis and even in the fragility of the ageing process. This occurs especially when the person exhibits poor coping strategies, the ability to master 'something unwanted, disruptive and unforeseeable'.

In a study on 123 patients with multiple sclerosis (Fondazione ISTUD 2015), the word 'beast' was mentioned at diagnosis by approximately 7% and by 40% patients who were not able to cope with the trauma brought by the disease in their life.

In fact, if there is no chance of creating and finding any possible solution to afford the change of life with the disease, the monster is always there as a Minotaur

M. G. Marini, *Languages of Care in Narrative Medicine*,
https://doi.org/10.1007/978-3-319-94727-3_8

that the patients will eventually encounter constrained in the Labyrinth. By analogy, the maze symbolises the setting in which care is carried out which can either be the home, hospitals, nursing homes and practices. All these places of care change according to where each patient is, at a given time, according to the severity of the illness: he/she might be in a hospital bed, or at home or at the workplace. A patient therefore 'travels' around different places of care: thus, it is called 'patient's journey'. Its formal definition is 'the sequence of care events which a patient follows from an entry point into the system of care triggered by a certain illness, until the patient is discharged from hospital to his or her home, care home, hospice or due to death' (Trebble et al. 2010).

How is this patient's journey? Is it linear? Is it circular? Does it have an exit point? Is it a Labyrinth? Complexity increases. In these situations, the patient's journey is similar to the maze, which people and carers find themselves in, and this is often what they declare both in the diagnostic phase, when it is difficult to give a name to their disease, and in finding the carer most suitable for the patient's dreams and needs.

As the Latin etymology of word Labyrinth recalls *labor intus*, the fatigue put into each step (either physical or metaphorical) to find the way out, we are facing two big dangers related to the healthcare setting: the first is getting lost in the pathway of care, and the second is being eaten by the disease, the Minotaur. Here, there is no possibility to tame the beast, but there is only one chance to get rid of it: being brave as Theseus who first killed the Minotaur through the help of the sword given by Ariadne and then found the way out from the Labyrinth using the thread from a ball of yarn to keep track of his path and avoid him getting lost. This thread could be associated to the rational mind, which opposes itself to the naïve thoughts of the youth who instead are going to perish in sacrifice.

By analogy with the maze, the pathways of care translate into algorithm of care, where one patient may follow the branch where there are good carers and another patient might end up in the branch with an extreme medicalisation due to improper listening. As most of us experienced, often after being referred to a simple diagnostic test, we are later recommended more that, in some cases, we will not perform. However, there are many people who torture themselves, also in a hypochondriac way, by the idea that they have to undergo from test to test, from physician to physician. They draw a Labyrinth as their patient's journey, without giving themselves any possibility to get out from the maze with the 'thread' of the rational mind. Theseus was able to overcome this Labyrinth only holding the thread given by the beautiful Ariadne, the Mistress of the Labyrinth, and by being able not to be in panic in front of the Beast. Insane passions, too strong emotions and fear among all, are not the right attitudes to get out from the space of the Labyrinth, a space that is an archetype into the humankind realm; it is able to represent the life of every person, as soon as launched in our earthly dimension, with its degree of unforeseeable events. Theseus went to Crete to kill the Minotaur with the clear scope to eradicate the sacrifice of 14 Athenians; from the myth, it is not clear whether he even cheated Ariadne, letting her hope in his love, leaving her abandoned in Naxos. He will pay for being so superficial, forgetting to change the black sails of his ship with the white sails, which would have been the signal for King Aegeus that the Minotaur was defeated. King Aegeus, looking at the back sails, thought that his son was dead. He suicides, throwing himself in the sea; it will be named from this action the Aegean Sea.

Patients get lost not only when they are diagnosed a disease by a physician but also when they self-diagnose a disease through the Labyrinth of the web: they lose certainties, becoming fragile, with no clear map given (Anwar and Khan 2013). A saver, external or internal, as Ariadne, is warranted not only to fight the disease but also to find good therapists.

Patients, as the innocent young people, after getting lost in the Labyrinth are forced to live in a chaos attitude (Frank 1995), with no possibility of escaping from the end which might be caused by the beast itself or by starving to death in a hidden branch of the maze. Even the hero Theseus, who is able to fight the monster with the thread, is in a chaos, forgetting to change the sails of his ship.

He kills the Beast (because this Beast has to be killed and there are objectively situations in which no pity should be there for the Beasts, even if we are living in a politically correct world), but he does not gain any teaching from the disease, if not the memory of a terrible trauma. He totally lacks empathy and cannot perceive the true love of Ariadne and of his father Aegeus. He escapes the Labyrinth, though with an open wound.

This is the opening scenario of the post-traumatic stress disorders. In Chap. 2, we have seen how the term 'trauma' can be de-structured using the NSM. Let us easily go through this once more:

(a) Something very bad happens to someone for some time.
(b) At this time, this someone thinks like this.
(c) I want these bad things not to be happening.
(d) I want to do something because of this.
(e) I know that I can't do anything.
(f) Because of this, after this, this someone feels something very bad for a long time.
(g) This someone can't say anything of this to other people for a long time.
(h) This someone does not want to think about it for a long time.
(i) Because of all of these things, this someone is not like this someone was before.
(j) Because of all these things, this someone can't feel many good things like this someone could before.

I quote the article written on the Chronicle of Narrative Medicine Journal by Prof. Delia Duccoli, a philosopher and psychoanalyst (Duccoli 2017):

> *Insomnia, physic symptoms without an organic base, dependences, ruminations, general anxiety, activation and dissolution of the emotions or emotive distance sometimes are the only signals of traumas suffered in the course of life, and never understood.*
>
> *There are different kind of traumas, small ones, called trauma with a lowercase 't' and big Traumas, with the capital 'T'. The great disasters like earthquakes, like fire, like suffering an abuse, diseases, or invasive surgical interventions are traumas. The word Trauma can*

also be referred to a series of adverse events or periods of carelessness, as in some Traumas of the 'addictive attachment' happened during childhood where no explicit memory is conserved.

We can also have the Vicarial Trauma, a trauma experienced by whom is close to person who experiences the Trauma: relatives, partners, friends, caregivers who take care of the traumatised person, sometimes suffering the same reactions.

Which adverse event will turn into a trauma, with the lowercase or upper-case letter, also depends by the individual and by the subjective experience that the person perceives. Not everybody that is exposed to a trauma is being traumatized, a lot depends by the actions that someone could use to defend oneself, react and assimilate the event in their existence.

Indeed, Trauma is defined by WHO and by international literature like a unique individual experience of an event or a group of events which the person is unable to assimilate in their emotional experience: this is the ability of gaining awareness, understanding what is happening, assimilate emotions and give a meaning to the experience.

A traumatic situation is the one that had been detected like a threat to one's safety or survival and stimulates the animal subcortical defensive responses of fight or flight and of freezing until reaching an apparent death and fostering the hyper or hypo arousal, an excessive activation or a freezing of the physiological activation. The perception of the threat came not only through a cognitive judgement, a rational and objective decision, but also through physical and physiological feelings and impulses. Physical feelings and impulses actually anticipate the cognitive and emotive perception.

The body remembers old traumas and it's like if the feeling of threat tends to persist in a modified and exaggerated mode long after the real threat has gone. The body reactivates the defences in reaction to signals that appear to be distant from the traumatic situation, when a sound or a noise is heard, when gestures and innocuous behaviours are seen. Even if sometimes the memory is vague and archived, the implicit memories, like the somatic, the sensorial and the emotive ones keep tracks on what has happened.

Body and mind continually interact, they are like 'intertwined' in the human organism and the comprehension of how all our experience is registered in the body allows us to communicate with the conscious and unconscious mind through corporeal experiences, integrating top-down ways (from thoughts to the emotions to the body) with bottom up ways (from corporeal feelings to the emotions to the thoughts).

When the body is evaluated like a source of intelligence, of memories, of data, we can find in any significant corporeal experiences a mental emotive and spiritual element.

Past studies have shown evidence of PTSD symptoms among people who have been treated for cancer, heart attacks and stroke as well as organ transplant patients. Migrants, veterans, soldiers and refugees suffer from PTSD too. However, PTSD may go unrecognised in many people, and they have sometimes a slow recovery from a critical illness and induce an associated mental illness.

Here is some evidence of coming back from the trauma of the Labyrinth, being with hidden memory still in the Labyrinth:

- Heart attack. According to researchers who analysed data from 24 PTSD studies that included 2383 heart patients, one out of eight persons who had a heart attack or other acute coronary emergency develops PTSD symptoms. The analysis, published in June 2012 by *PLOS One*, noted that heart patients with PTSD have a twofold risk of having a second heart attack or dying within the next 3 years (Edmondson et al. 2012).
- Eighteen per cent of stroke and mini-stroke survivors reported symptoms of PTSD in a study published online in January 2013 by the *British Journal of*

Health Psychology. Sixty-five per cent of those patients with PTSD symptoms were less likely to follow their drug regimen—perhaps because it reminded them of their stroke—putting them at risk for another stroke (Edmondson et al. 2013).
- Breast cancer. A study published online in February 2013 by the *Journal of the National Cancer Institute* indicated that nearly one in four women with breast cancer developed PTSD symptoms within the first 2–3 months after diagnosis. Symptoms were most common in African American and Asian women and women under 50 years of age (Vin-Raviv 2013).
- Spine surgery. In a study on 73 patients who underwent elective lumbar spinal fusion surgery—a procedure that fuses together two or more vertebrae—nearly one in five had PTSD symptoms within 1 year of surgery. Patients who had pre-surgery depression or anxiety were most likely to develop PTSD (Oregon Health and Science University 2012).
- Hospitalisation in an ICU. According to a recent meta-analysis conducted by Johns Hopkins and published online in March 2013 by *Psychological Medicine*, one in three patients admitted to an ICU with an acute lung injury and connected to a ventilator to aid in breathing had PTSD symptoms up to 2 years after their stay. The Hopkins doctors suspect that PTSD is common among other ICU patients as well (Johns Hopkins Medicine 2013).
- PTSD does not only deal with clinical conditions but also with social situations such as migration: *We must openly question our practices with regard to refugees: always insisting that more be done for people in immediate need to reduce physical and psychological trauma, but always remembering that medicine and humanitarian aid can also contribute to longer term problems for people who do not simply have 'needs' in order to stay alive but ambitions to live fully* (Van Tulleken and Hamlyn 2016).

What do we learn from this scientific literature? If there is no change of attitude from *chaos* to *quest* (Frank 1995) (that is to say, no lesson learned from this experience and, moreover, the opening to empathetic feelings towards the helpers), trauma will persist and will become bigger than the disease itself.

The space of Labyrinth has a secret order, however, not fully acknowledgeable to human sense: it generates chaos, and when we are fragile during a disease, we need somewhat some few certainties, not only the eternal living in the idea to be lost.

The PTSD Migrants and the Odysseus Syndrome

In the cultural context document of WHO on narrative research (Greenhalgh 2016), one case is dedicated to migrants and PTSD. The researcher, Roberto Beneduce, expressed concern that one unintended consequence of the psychiatric assessment is that these metanarratives become obscured by the medical diagnosis. While migrants' symptoms often bear cultural hallmarks of suffering, they also reveal images of a traumatic history, which resurface in moments of danger, uncertainty and crisis. Trauma symptoms keep returning to a collective past and can be considered to be a particular form of historical consciousness. Psychiatric diagnoses may obscure these counter-memories. In particular, the diagnostic category of PTSD that is commonly attached to traumatic experiences in current clinical practice recognises the truth of individual traumatic events; at the same time, it contributes to concealing the political, racial and historical roots of suffering. Some authors have used a more radical, semi-fictional approach to convey sufferers' experiences: Dr. Joseph Achotegui, professor of psychopathology at the University of Barcelona, has described a new syndrome, the Ulysses syndrome, which he defines as a combination of both physical symptoms (e.g. insomnia, headaches and tiredness) and psychological ones (e.g. hallucinations, irritability and anxiety) experienced by migrants facing multiple stressors (Achotegui 2005). This is not an accepted mental health disorder under WHO's 'Classification of mental and behavioural disorders' as PTSD, for example. Rather, Achotegui suggests that it is an extreme form of migratory mourning and a holistic disorder of wellbeing generated by the extremes of context and is better studied with reference to myth and meta-narrative than to medical disease manuals.

The condition is named after Homer's Greek hero Odysseus who spent 10 years through a long and exceptionally harrowing sea journey to return to his home; far from his loved ones, he spent days 'sitting on the rocks, at the edge of the sea, staring the barren sea and crying inconsolably'. The syndrome has been described in the following way: the Ulysses syndrome takes place at the extreme level of stressors. The complex migration context may include factors causing high levels of stress such as forced separation, dangers of the migratory journey, social isolation, absence of opportunities, sense of failure of the migratory goals, drop in social status, extreme struggle for survival and discriminatory attitudes in the receiving country. The migrant's identity is so affected by the ordeal, just as Odysseus who states, 'You ask me my name. I shall tell you. My name is nobody and nobody is what everyone calls me'.

In my previous book, *Narrative Medicine: Bridging the Gap Between Evidence Based Medicine and Medical Humanities* (Marini 2016), I wrote about Odysseus and his need to tell his whole journey's narrative to the Phaeaces before having access to his homeland. Myth can help in explaining complex situations as the adventures of life. However, what comes out is that the DSM, with easy labels of the language, might be dangerous: there are situations, as we have written already for depression, which might be much better expressed by simple words, *I don't want to live*. Furthermore, 'nobody' is a composition given by the NSM, and 'everyone calls me as nobody' can be translated in simple NSM like 'everybody says about me, I am nobody'. Here, the myth of Odysseus and the atoms of language are connecting to display a true that is better defined as in the DSM.

The NSM de-structuring of the word trauma indicates 'this somebody does not want to talk about the bad things happened', and narrating about the trauma might be the right remedy. Hence, in waiting for that person to feel ready to tell their story, other activities or forms of expressions could provide some benefit, such as activities that trigger positive physical sensations, stimulating sensorial activities and artistic expressions like the theatre, music, dance, painting and sculpture. These are only some of the protective ways that facilitate the integration of emotions, the regulation of physiological activation and the ability to focus on the here and now, eventually leading to the breaking of the silence and to a better feeling.

The Point of View of Neurosciences on Trauma

Studies in literature have suggested that PTSD might cause chronic modifications in the brain. Recently, researchers from the Queen College Oxford University were able to show the brain of people living with PTSD after shocking condition as war or disaster, with group of controls who were put in simulation of a traumatic situation, without having the PTSD. Authors state as follows (Stark et al. 2015): *Stress affects brain function and may lead to PTSD. Considerable empirical data for the neurobiology of PTSD has been derived from neuroimaging studies, although findings have proven inconsistent. We used an activation likelihood estimation analysis to explore differences in brain activity between adults with and without PTSD in response to affective stimuli. We separated studies by type of control group: trauma-exposed and trauma-naïve. This revealed distinct patterns of differences in functional activity. Compared to trauma-exposed controls, regions of the brain basal ganglia were differentially active in PTSD; whereas the comparison with trauma-naïve controls revealed differential involvement in the right anterior insula, precuneus, cingulate and orbitofrontal cortices known to be involved in emotional regulation. Changes in activity in the amygdala and parahippocampal cortex distinguished PTSD from both control groups. Results suggest that trauma has a measurable, enduring effect upon the functional dynamics of the brain, even in individuals who experience trauma but do not develop PTSD. These findings contribute to the understanding of whole-brain network activity following trauma, and its transition to clinical PTSD.*

Prof. Kringelbach, the chief coordinator, commented these results as follows: *This research suggests that there may be a spectrum of traumatic effects on the brain, where people who have experienced trauma may not meet the threshold for a diagnosis of PTSD but may have similar changes within the brain. This could make them more susceptible to PTSD if they experience a subsequent trauma. While PTSD is often seen and portrayed as an issue for war veterans, it can affect other groups, including emergency service workers and refugees from conflict or disaster. By understanding how the brain is changed, we may be better placed to prevent the effects of trauma developing into clinical PTSD.*

For decades, neuroscience claimed that the hardware of the brain is fixed from birth; however, recent pioneering experiments in the field of neuroplasticity reveal that the brain is capable not only of altering its structure but also of generating new neurons, even in older age. The brain can adapt, heal, renew itself after trauma and compensate for disability. This brain plasticity and neural plasticity are the ability of the brain to change throughout an individual's life, e.g. brain activity associated with a given function can be transferred to a different location, and synapses may strengthen or weaken over time.

From static to plastic: research in the latter half of the twentieth century showed that many aspects of the brain can be altered even through adulthood. This notion is totally in contrast with the previous scientific consensus that the brain develops during a critical period in early childhood and then remains relatively unchanged. This contrast is a possible reason why this discovery was not revealed earlier (Pascual-Leone et al. 2005).

Neuroplasticity can be observed at multiple scales, from microscopic changes in individual neurons to larger-scale changes such as cortical remapping in response to injury. Behaviour, environmental stimuli, thought and emotions may also cause neuroplastic change through activity-dependent plasticity, which has significant implications for healthy development, learning, memory and recovery from brain damage.

The science writer Sharon Begley documents neuroplasticity in her book *The Plastic Mind* (Begley 2009), in which she describes that the fundamental paradigm shift is transforming both our understanding of the human mind and our approach to deep-seated emotional, cognitive and behavioural problems: she explores through documented research how to reset our happiness metre, regain of course partially the use of limbs disabled by stroke, train the mind to break cycles of depression and OCD and reverse age-related changes in the brain. I read the book, which has the preface by the Dalai Lama and Daniel Goleman: I suggested this reading to many people, especially persons who have had ordinary or extraordinary trauma coming from life. I think that for most of people, it might be a good tool and a wonderful journey inside brain research.

Let us continue with humanities to learn how to cope with trauma. Perhaps, while reading these lines, our neurons will discover new patterns of connection.

The Beauty and the Beast

The Beauty and the Beast is a fairy tale, which probably has its roots in the Greek age, or earlier in Bronze Age, 4000 BC (Graça da Silva and Tehrani 2017). Fairy stories, as mythologies, often have themes common to humankind throughout the world and through all ages, such as family, betrayal, violence and survival. However, fairy tales, differently from mythology, are characterised by a happy ending since they were and still are nourishment for positive thinking.

The Beauty and the Beast fairy tale has a positive happy ending, which shows that even scaring figures can be 'tamed' and 'transformed through love'. In this story, another Beauty is the main character, the daughter of a merchant who gets in a forest during a storm. Seeking shelter, he enters a dazzling palace. A hidden figure opens the giant doors and silently invites him in. As the merchant is about to leave, he sees a rose garden and recalls that Beauty had desired a rose before his leaving. Upon picking the rose, the merchant is confronted by a hideous 'Beast', which tells him that for taking his most precious possession after accepting his hospitality, the merchant must die. The merchant begs to be set free, arguing that he had only picked the rose as a gift for his youngest daughter. The Beast agrees to let him give the rose to Beauty but only if the merchant or one of his daughters will return.

The merchant accepts this condition. Beauty accepts responsibility for her actions and willingly goes to the Beast's Castle. The Beast receives her graciously and informs her that she is now the mistress of the Castle. He gives her lavish clothing and food and carries on lengthy conversations with her. For several months, Beauty lives a life of luxury at the Beast's palace, with no end of riches to amuse her and an endless supply of exquisite finery to wear. Eventually, she becomes homesick and begs the Beast to allow her to go see her family. He allows it on the condition that she returns exactly a week later. However, Beauty stays at her father's home longer than a week, and while staying there, she begins to feel guilty about breaking her promise to the Beast and decides to go back to the Castle. She is horrified to discover that the Beast is lying half-dead from heartbreak and the Beauty weeps over the Beast. This true authentic love finally broke curse and made him return to be the beautiful prince.

As the analogy of 'the Beauty and the Beast' is put into the context of illness, who or what does the 'Beauty' embody? Is there a way to induce a metamorphosis of a 'Beast disease' into a less threatening situation? The 'Beauty' could be the care, as well as the patient's coping factors as agreeableness, extroversion, openness, optimism and consciousness inborn to humankind, which might lead to the acceptance of the 'Beast'. It is nice to consider that even in the ancient time, this optimistic view on surviving the most cumbersome situation was there.

When someone has to face a disease, a new space-temporal condition is there. Time might seem longer and unbearable as ever, looking forward to receiving the results of the test or the access to a new cure or an innovative treatment. The mental space of a patient is invaded by the Beast, which takes the control of the whole body or of the whole context in which the ill person lives. However, in this tale, if at the beginning, the Beauty is shocked by the Beast and his ugliness, as time goes by, she discovers that he has some kind manners: even if he looks scary, he does everything to try to calm down the Beauty, going from nice presents up to talking with her, being capable to create a dialogue.

Ariadne is used by a man and then left abandoned on a desert island: on the contrary, the Beauty is able to find her inner resources to go back on her own willingness to the Castle and to stay with the monster. Culture helped her. Neuroplasticity helped her. She is a woman with empathetic skills, not falling immediately in a passionate love for a hero but discovering on a more intimate ordinary life, a way to cope with the Beast, even reaching the 'absurd' position of loving the Beast itself. The fact is that the Castle is not a Labyrinth, with only one way of getting in and out, but it is an easier place to go in and to get out representing a wider freedom.

The Beast is scaring at the beginning but gave Beauty all the entertainment she wanted and also the ultimate chance: freedom to go back to her relatives and to her beloved father. If Aegeus dies because of his son's post-traumatic chaotic mind, who misses to change the sails, in this fairy tale, a father keeps his life through the empathetic point of view of the Beauty. Curiosity saves her and her father, as well as with compassion, whereas Theseus' courage is not enough to prevent fatal events.

The Beauty has chosen to live in a 'quest' attitude (Frank 1995), knowing that a Beast, which belongs to the danger, is always behind; however, only good manners, empathy, fascination for the oddity and inclusion skills might be the trigger factors not for defeating the Beast but for controlling and accepting it.

While the Labyrinth is an architecture, which has ground in the soil, the Castle is a building, which elevates itself towards the sky, above the Labyrinth of the ordinary lives. Its walls are able to let people in and out, protecting them during the attacks. Castle is a fascinating architecture since there is almost no fairy tales without such a palace.

The Castle, although in dark time might become a prison—think to the cellars—is something beloved by people and gives protection and security: with no need of thread, one just can try to accomplish with it. If it is too high and isolated, there is a close village where people can go and have a chat in a bar, or in open air, or can open it to give a party, with the roses of the gardens as decorations. The trauma, if not totally vanished, is in the background, but with much less power than before is gone, by reflecting upon it; by living with it, through the open talking of the fears—as Odysseus did with the Phaeaces before reaching Ithaca—the living and doing arts and music; and by committing to do something personally meaningful and important every day.

Writing down the traumatic experiences, as NM teaches, is a helpful tool which through Beauty is able to tell and write a story. As the patients with multiple sclerosis have taught us through their stories (Fondazione ISTUD 2015), many showed to be able to cope with the beast by finding something new and beautiful every single day in their lives. Indeed, many narratives showed the 'quest' attitude of many patients who were able to find the inner resources to cope with disease—or rather 'the beast'—as many patients identify it at the beginning of their illness and which over time transforms to become considered as 'a part of myself', 'an invasive event' and up to a 'mate, even if an uncomfortable one'. It is considered a roommate, a live mate, a mate and a person who mirrors you, and, if taken with the proper rhythm, entertainment, words, gestures and right distance can bring also peace in this war.

In the Labyrinth, there are no decorations; in the Castles, the roses that the Beast had sown when he was alone, waiting for somebody to scare and to stand by at the same time, are in blossom.

The Beauty wins because of her optimism, openness and extroversion, to mention the three factors of Carver for a good coping. If people with multiple sclerosis are still in a Labyrinth, keeping in naming the disease as the beast to 'stab', they are often introvert, lonely and not willing to share their thoughts and feelings with other people. Who helps the Beauty? The Beast itself, allowing to see the good inside, the hidden prince, what it looks evil. Hopefully, in this case, there is a good inside: at least the Beast has plastic neurons.

Far Inside the Trauma: 'To Want to Live' and 'to Want to Die' (Where Are We in the Society?)

To live and *to die* are two words of the NSM and, hence, are universal thoughts. Along with these words, there are also two universal words that are 'to want' and 'don't want', which we can then place near the first two primes: *want to live*, *do not want to die*, *do not want to live* and *want to die*.

Perhaps, human existence unfolds or rather the quintessence of medical humanities on these four quadrants.

To Want to Live

In the first case, the wish to live is the blossom of the joy of living, the nature of spring that rises after the dead winter, the project, the light after the tunnel and the creation of the new. It is easy to create new things when someone is a child and is amazed at every new discovery. It is more difficult to find this vital force late in the years, when much has been seen, much has been done and the traumas, however big or small, have penetrated into our tree bark and inside our brain cortex.

Thinking that sometimes it is even harder finding the strength for going on when an illness occurs may be a stereotype: from the patients' narratives, we read joy for life and attachment to everyday life as well as a planning phase that can only be triggered when a person is able to find a new way of living with their disease. It is like saying that healthy subjects have less appreciation of life and that ill people begin to have the capacity of feeling good again once they have overcome the first initial impact of their disease. With a Proust's attitude, in pursuing the life gone, many seek out the lost time, that precise one in which everything could be done, the degrees of freedom were many, much more than the current ones and then are keen to remember. However, many patients move on and cope and learn to enjoy from the little things that happen in their daily life.

Marina was ill of a rare form of bone cancer since the age of 22 years and lived with this disease for 10 years. During this time, she wrote a beautiful diary *A black spot in the immense blue of sea* (Neri 2011), which I read after her death. In her diary, there is no 'lost time search' because there is no old age beyond: there is an extraordinary will and desire to live despite it all; there is no search for oblivion but a basic wisdom in knowing how to appreciate, for example, a dove that comes to the window of her hospital room. She wanted to fly to visit art exhibitions in all parts of the world, and she understood that cutting unnecessary ties strengthened new healthy bonds and support.

My gratitude and admiration also go to Pilar Lorente, a Spanish woman, whose story contains the desire to live. Pilar did not write a book but did much to coexist with a tumour. At first, she discovered she had nasal polyps and then that cancer invaded the back of the eye bulb. The only thing the doctors could do for her after a standard cycle of chemotherapy and radiotherapy was to take the eye out and partially rebuilt her nose. Despite this, this young woman, Pilar, chose to live amidst design and beauty: an architect, so is naturally attracted by an innate aesthetic natural sentiment. After eye surgery 7 years ago, she decided not to take any further action to put a fake eye on but preferred to open a nice bakery in the centre of Madrid. Given the economic crisis, business did not go well, so she began drawing jewelry, which she now sells on the web. She recently wrote to me telling that she enrolled in a master course on the ancient Mediterranean culture and wants to take advantage of this second opportunity that life has given her to study the Greek beauty and thought and feel alive and happy. She adds, *I've never felt the loss of my eye as a loss, for me it was the Door to Life. It is my medal, I feel very proud to be able to show that life deserves to be lived.*

It is a surprise to me and for many of us too: a trusted faith in the things that happen across the watershed between life and death has given her and continues to give her energy and vitality.

Do Not Want to Die

The second molecule of meaning *don't want to die* is something more attenuated in its vitality: if in *to want to live*, there is in fact 'the vital force', where 'vital' also means essential, in the sense that it is the only way for survival, the *do not want to die* involves a denial, a departure, 'get away from me this cup'; in this chess game with death, some are saved how and when they want, while others live with greater passivity.

In patients' narratives, we read about how to learn to live day after day in 'extreme' conditions, but it is very rarely said 'I do not want to die'. The fear of dying is much more explicit, the fear that something 'ugly' happens. In the trauma of communicating the diagnosis of serious illness, patients 'feel the world falling down', 'feel the ground quacking under their feet' or say 'I am afraid of dying'. While 'to want to live' is dictated by a prospective desire and a survival instinct challenged by fear, but patient is able to overcome it, the 'don't want to die' attitude is related not only by fear but also by anger, rebellion and a passive submission to something more powerful and ineluctable. It is a weak cry of strength against an immense power, that one of life or death.

In the Mahabharata (Slavitt and Carrigan 2015), a part of the poem is related to the beauty of mankind's thinking that 'removes' the idea of death, erasing this concept, while knowing the inevitability entangled by a vital spirit that puts it into a daily oblivion: if every moment we had the 'memento mori', the remembering of dying, we would be so paralysed by failing in our life project. This point is denied by the stories of the patients but also of the elderly who just because they have the 'memento mori', after a first panic attack, then they take back all their left resources to struggle, finding their own art form to be vital until the end. Moreover, in the Mahabharata, there is a dialogue between the hero, Yudishtira and an ordinary boy during death: the hero is afraid of dying and tells the boy that even gods make sacrifices for not having to die. The boy replies, '… I tell you that death is negligence and ignorance, and that vigilance is immortality. Death is a tiger swirling in the bushes. We have children for death, but death cannot devour who shook his life as dust. Death does not have power over eternity. The wind and life flow from infinity. The moon drinks the breath of life. The sun drinks the moon and infinity drinks the sun. The wise man hovers among the worlds'.

Hindu philosophy therefore reveals the importance of not overestimating the issue between life and death—the wise man moves through the air among the worlds. Yet, something must not be under evaluated: knowledge, understanding or better awareness. Death is negligence, ignorance, deception and deathlessness and therefore far more than one life alone, but immortality is wakefulness and understanding.

When I read the narrative of an old lady who knows very well that her husband is living his last few months and still organises a 20-mile trip from home so that they can spend happy days in a vacation spot, but with the necessary places of care nearby, here I feel for a wise woman who moves through the air among the worlds.

Do Not Want to Live

In the third and fourth quadrants, there are the other two possible universal 'do not want to live' and 'want to die'. Here, I help myself with a text published on the *Right to Die–The death treatment–When should people be affected by a non-terminal illness?* (Aviv 2015).

I thought I was a free person, disseminating what it is written in the Article 13 of the Italian Constitution which states 'personal freedom is inviolable'. The freedom of choice between extremes of living and dying is sanctioned and accepted by our constitution. I am glad to see that the Italian government has finally approved the *biological will* at the end 2017, including also the concept of not wanting to live anymore, in extreme desperate conditions.

I do not want to live is the semantic molecule—the third quadrant. In Belgium, the Distelmans Clinic offers the so-called death treatment, which helps people to die; the treatment is not only for sick people on palliative care but for depressed people as well. (I knew nothing about this, and it represents a totally unknown world to me.)

We know depressed people commit suicide because they no longer want to live, but, personally, I was not informed of the help given by doctors to realise the *unwillingness to live*. Wim Distelmans is an oncologist. As such, considering the background of these specialists, they often are related to end-of-life care and concerned with ensuring 'sweet death', i.e. euthanasia for patients with advanced cancers who are no longer curable and who desire not to prolong their life longer.

To this point, everything is part of the normal debate, surely intrigued by moral dilemma, whether to slowly but irreversibly lead a person to the 'eternal sleep' in the last days of life or rather to give a much faster death through the use of higher doses of hypnoinductive. In 2017, there was a great debate around the episode wherein Dr. Distelmans provided euthanasia to a 17-year-old boy affected by cancer. Although an arguable situation, I think that it may fall into the possible range of interventions of a conscientious oncologist who 'overcomes the hypocrisy' of the 6-month legal age to wait for the major age and to act in concordance on the desire of the minor.

However, by getting to know who goes to Distelmans, we discover that not only cancer patients are going but also patients who have 'terrible lives' go to him asking for assisted suicide. The oncologist, who is neither a psychiatrist nor a psychotherapist, after a series of early visits, succeeds in assisting them in the suicide to make them achieve the 'not wanting to live' state. This action, not only protected by the Belgian government in the name of the highest expression of freedom of the person, has become an icon of the utmost expression of freedom.

People who go to Wim Distelmans to ask for death are often 'labelled' depressed, but if we read in their writings, they are sick of loneliness and abandonment by children and partners.

In a narrative of an Italian anaesthesiologist who mourns a patient who had recently died, what struck me was the network of bonds on one side (sister, carer), with many lost people on the other; in particular, it was the case of an old woman who had poor relations with her adopted son, who was practically waiting for his mother to pass away to get the inheritance. A huge loneliness is triggered by the abandonment of her son, perhaps the most important link in her life: children no longer assist their parents, creating a devastating feeling of exclusion not only in this old lady but in elderly people.

The article *The Death Treatment* in the *New York Times* (Aviv 2015) focuses on a patient who asked Distelmans for assisted 'suicide'. Godelieva, at the age of 19 years, wanted to graduate in history, while her father imposed her to study medicine. This seems to be the origin of the trauma, or at least of the whole narrative. A good counsellor/psychotherapist or another person would ask, *But do you really want to graduate in history? You're young, you can do it! Or you can study history on your own! Or you can join a study group! Or is it just an alibi?* or many more open questions finding a creative solution to the problem.

My feeling, drawn from the article, is that of an 'old-fashioned' psychoanalysis, too quick in accusing parents and too reluctant to solve issues: there is no perfect family and no perfect parent. All of us have suffered more or less being conditioned, even when they told us 'do whatever you want to': we had the unconditional freedom to manage all its consequences. The analysis is a useful tool if it then leads to action—however small it might be—but if it stops in the past, the bottomless pit from which it is difficult to get out might become harmful.

Godelieva's life goes on after the suicide of her first husband, her black tunnel of depression, two children who always saw her sad: at a certain point of their life, she lives a second spring with a new partner, but again she is left abandoned. She is now in menopause, she is sad, she wants to see her children, but the children are projected on their careers and their own children. The trauma is deep, true and unquantifiable: here, I can see the failure of a social system and its relationships of help and the ability to create vitality.

The article also gives another clue: it seems that the escalation of suicides in Belgium is due to secularisation, i.e. the lack of faith in God. Whoever believes in God does not commit suicide. Those who do not believe in God are more committed to suicide. This is the meaning assigned to the Christian religion, a very reductive and, perhaps, offensive dichotomy for secular ethics, which is made up of love, relationships, bonds, help, support and preciousness for life. The over simplification that those who do not believe in a 'world beyond' have less power to try to live here a good life in 'this world' is really shocking, and at least to see it written in 2015.

The oncologist Distelmans, with his Life End Information Forum (LEIF Website n.d.; Wesemael et al. 2009), promotes informative sessions on the right to die with primary school children (age of the listeners, 9 years) with the approval of the Belgian government. We know that children are like sponges: what they hear at that age will mark them for a long time, maybe forever. Going to talk to them about the right to death when they are in the fullness of their bloom, curiosity, vitality and playfulness is, in my opinion, an act of perversion, and by the term 'perversion', I suppose an act against nature.

Furthermore, Distelmans brings doctors and students to discover the real sorrow and pain in the concentration camps of the Jews. He therefore wants to explain to doctors and future researchers the difference of how to die in a 'horrible' way and how to 'die gently': pleonastic to say that the people who complained the most about this gesture were the Jews who claimed that Auschwitz has to be a symbol for life and not for teaching to kill in whatever way.

Children come to know about the death of their parents by receiving a letter by Dr. Distelmans' clinic, telling them that 'the last will of their parent of "dying" has been accomplished'. This leaves the monstrous guilty feeling for not realising their parent's loneliness sooner. However, there are still ways to come out from this sudden trauma. For instance, in the case of Tom, Godelieva's son, this is shown in strong activism against euthanasia with religious associations. It is a shame that 'wanting to live' is cherished as well almost always in religious institutions and not enough in secular associations as a spiritual good.

The third quadrant is 'do not want to live' where despair is so great and life so meaningless that refuses it, where we are not in the degree to see it a small shade of light in a black abyss. Later, after the fourth quadrant, there will be the interview with Pamela Wible, who will talk about the *not want to live* of the American physicians.

To Want to Die

In the fourth quadrant, *to wish to die*, two atoms of meaning that united together seem to leave a total desperation. However, we can admit that this happens in the great mythologies of the travels of the heroes, the martyrs, the saints and those who fight for an ideal worth of their life. The death epic is glorified in military songs, in monuments to the fallen soldiers and in national hymns. However, this attitude to *wanting to die* is quite different, with respect to *do not want to live* people … 'Heroes Are All Young and Beautiful'.

The annoying part for me is the 'not wanting to live' as something that keeps repeating, and in our narratives of elderly people, the most profound cause of sorrow is Lady of Solitude, when there is nobody with whom talking about beautiful things and little traumas. That is the big trauma: our postmodern society which is much more than 'liquid', where '*panta rei*', everything flows, everything is distorted, dispersed, vanquished and disappears. Faced with a parallel chart of a doctor who writes about a patient, 'she no longer wanted to live but she wanted to continue smoking', one remains ashamed: as if the worst problem for this doctor to settle is the fight against smoking. The despair of the patient was not seen, heard or understood.

The Case of *to Not Want to Live* in Doctors

As Pamela Wible writes in her October blog and on the *Washington Post*, suicide among physicians in the USA has accounted for a shocking 757 deaths over approximately less than 7 years (Wible 2018—Washington Post Website). When dedicating this chapter to trauma and the will of dying, it is astonishing to find these figures in people who should, on the contrary, spread wellbeing and reinforce, giving hopes, being genuinely positive thinkers. It is called 'the hidden epidemic of doctors' suicide'. The reason why? Dr. Wible, who directly launched a series of activities for the wellbeing of the carers, writes, 'Patient deaths hurt doctors. A lot. Even when there's no medical error, doctors may never forgive themselves for losing a patient'. Suicide is the ultimate self-punishment. In several cases, the death of a patient seemed to be the key factor in pushing them over the edge. Malpractice suits can be devastating. Humans make mistakes. Yet, when doctors make mistakes, they are publicly shamed in court, on TV and in newspapers (that live online forever). Many continue to suffer the agony of harming someone else—unintentionally—for the rest of our lives. Academic distress kills medical students' dreams. Failing medical board exams and not getting a post-medical school assignment in a specialty of choice has led to suicides. Doctors can be shattered if they fail to gain a residency.

Dr. Wible is a family physician born into a family of physicians. Despite her parents' warning not to pursue medicine, Pamela followed her heart to discover 1 day that before healing her patients, she first needed to heal her profession. Fed up with 'assembly-line medicine', Dr. Wible held town hall meetings where she invited citizens to design their ideal clinic. Open since 2005, Wible's innovative model has sparked a populist movement that has inspired Americans to create ideal clinics and hospitals nationwide. When she is not treating patients, Pamela devotes her time to medical student and physician suicide prevention. She was nominated as the 2015 Women Leader in Medicine. With Dr. Wible, I want to discover more about the 'I don't want to live anymore' by physicians. She is very clear in writing that if they commit suicide, it is because they want to end their pain. For me, it is exactly the same conclusion: when people literally want to die, as we have already said, they can do it driven by a specific cause, like martyrs of an ideology or an ideal: when they do not want to live anymore, the cause is generally unbearable pain and sorrow.

MGM. Dr. Wible, the suicide rates among physicians in the USA is called the hidden epidemic.

Now thanks to your extraordinary work it is no longer 'hidden'. Which are the main causes for this epidemic?

PW. Well, as I describe in my work *What I've learned from 757 doctor suicides* (Wible 2018—Washington Post Website), there are many reasons.

Patient deaths hurt doctors a lot. Even when there's no medical error, doctors may never forgive themselves for losing a patient. Suicide is the ultimate self-punishment.

Malpractice suits kill doctors. Humans make mistakes. Yet when doctors make mistakes, they're publicly shamed in court on TV and in newspapers (that live online forever). We continue to suffer the agony of harming someone else—unintentionally—for the rest of our lives.

Doctors who do illegal things kill themselves. Medicare fraud and sex with a patient may lead to loss of medical license, prison time and suicide.

Doctors have personal problems—like everyone else. We get divorced, have custody battles, infidelity, disabled children and deaths in our families. Working 100+ h per week immersed in our patients' pain, we've got no time to deal with our own pain. (Spending so much time at work actually leads to divorce and completely dysfunctional personal lives).

Bullying, hazing and sleep deprivation increase suicide risk. Medical training is rampant with human right violations illegal in all other industries.

Sleep deprivation is a (deadly) torture technique. Physicians have suffered hallucinations, life-threatening seizures, depression and suicide solely related to sleep deprivation. Sleep-deprived doctors disclose hospital horrors that kill or injure patients. Others die in fatigue-related car crashes after long shifts. Resident physicians are now 'capped' at 28-h shifts and 80-h weeks. If they 'violate' work hours (by caring for patients), they are forced to lie on their time cards or be written up as 'inefficient' and are sent to a psychiatrist for stimulant medications. Some doctors kill themselves for fear of harming a patient from extreme sleep deprivation.

Blaming doctors increases suicides. Words like 'burnout' and 'resilience' are often employed by medical institutions as psychological warfare to blame and shame doctors while deflecting attention from inhumane working conditions. When doctors are punished for occupationally induced mental health conditions (while underlying human rights violations are not addressed), they become even more hopeless and desperate.

Sweet, sensitive souls are at highest risk. Some of the most caring, compassionate and intelligent doctors choose suicide rather than continuing to work in such callous, uncaring and ruthlessly greedy medical corporations.

Doctors can't get confidential mental healthcare. So they drive out of town, pay cash and use fake names to hide from state medical boards, hospitals and insurance plans that ask doctors about their mental healthcare and may then exclude them from state licensure, hospital privileges and health plan participation.

Doctors have trouble caring for doctors. Doctors treat physician patients differently by downplaying psychiatric issues to protect physicians from medical board mental health investigations. Untreated mental health conditions may lead to suicide.

Doctors' family members are at high risk of suicide. One physician died using the same gun his son used to kill himself. Kaitlyn Elkins, a star third-year medical student, chose suicide by helium inhalation. One year later, her mother Rhonda killed herself the same way. At Rhonda's funeral, I asked her husband if he thought his wife and daughter would still be alive had Kaitlyn not pursued medicine. He replied, 'Yes. Medical school has killed half my family'.

MGM. Do you think that the private and insurance system that you have in USA, in comparison to a functioning public system, might be a risk factor for this?

PW. Yes, only because it adds another onerous and dysfunctional layer of bureaucracy on top of a failing medical model. Some of the way that the for-profit system works here is in withholding care from those who need it.

Assembly-line medicine kills doctors. Brilliant, compassionate people can't care for complex patients in 10-min slots. When punished or fired for 'inefficiency' or 'low productivity', doctors may choose suicide. Pressure from insurance companies and government mandates further crush the souls of these talented people who just want to help their patients. Many doctors cite inhumane working conditions in their suicide notes.

Medical board investigations increase suicide risk. One doctor hanged himself from a tree outside the Florida medical board office after being denied his license. He was told to 'come back in a year and we will reinstate your license'. Meanwhile, he lost everything and was living in a halfway house.

MGM. Therefore, we have to keep on defending an eco-friendly health care service, with proper paces and work load and time to establish nurturing relationship with patients, their caregivers and all carers. In the UK which has a public NHS, there is a publication) in which it is reported that the people who work in health care have a faster access to lethal drugs, and therefore can commit suicide in an easier way (Csete et al. 2016). *Do you believe in this explanation?*

PW. Yes, especially with anaesthesiologists, as here in United States, male anaesthesiologists are at highest risk. They die most by overdose. Many are found dead in hospital call rooms.

MGM. So, look out for anaesthesiologists as a possible category at risk of fragility. In Italy as well, where there is a public health care system, however with huge cut of resources and an average mean age of the physicians' class of 51 years, we do have an alarming situation on suicide, with a double rate of self-inflicted death than among the average population. Dr. Wible, do you think that some factors are universals, such as being in touch with pain, the sorrow and the death of the patients?

PW. Yes. Vicarious trauma and PTSD - Post Traumatic Stress Disorder, are reality for doctors. This is something that I think every emergency physician and neonatologist and surgeon have probably experienced. I consider myself fortunate to be born in a family of physicians. I don't feel that I've had much of this. However, a neonatology fellow recently called me wondering if it was normal for her to have like panic attacks and start crying in the middle of the night. Then, I asked her about her job. Well she's flying around in a helicopter, picking up half-dead babies... I think that would cause anyone on the planet to be having panic attacks. This is occupationally induced PTSD, vicarious trauma and there's no help. … This is why, these people are crying to me on the phone at midnight wondering if they're normal. It's a normal reaction to have panic attacks if you've seen that much trauma.

MGM. Do you think that there is a bias in teaching in our academies of Medicine and Nursing, teaching the possibility to save everybody, not talking enough of the natural cycle between life and death and no longer considering death as a limit? Like a superhomistic approach in which death of the patient becomes a Taboo (with so much enabling technology available)?

PW. Yes, academic distress kills medical students' dreams. Failing board exams and being unmatched into a specialty of choice has led to suicides. There is really is a lack of leadership in medicine. What's happening is you have the old guard just preparing people to do it the same way we've always done it because that's how we've always done it. The world is not what it was 20, 30, 40 years ago. There are so many things that have changed in medicine. To have this knee-jerk reaction to lock medical students back into this regurgitation-memorisation cycle when we can obviously access things at our fingertips. We need to have the joy of learning. We need to stop pushing people to continue in a system that's obviously failing and imploding, right? We need new thinking. We need new ways of training physicians. We need to stop terrorising them and violating their human rights.

Whole classes of people they're going to call little snowflakes. People don't make it into medical school without determination, intelligence, compassion and to beat this out of them—a love of learning and a love for humanity—is absolutely the wrong way to train people. I'm going to give some examples of two people who've written to me here lately.

One says, 'I had married the year before residency, and for the first 2 years, I was either at work or asleep, so I didn't see my wife. It was the start of the erosion of the relationship that led to divorce years later. I also suffered permanent health problems, some extreme sleep deprivation. Prior to residency, I slept fine 8 h a night and had regular bowel movements. Since my internship, I developed lifelong severe insomnia and went for decades on 4–5 h of sleep per night as well as severe constipation using the toilet about every 5 days'.

MGM. Dr. Wible provides a lot of commentary of harsh pressure, difficult exams, bullyish situation in academy: beyond this, in my opinion lessons are overwhelmed by a technocracy and humanities, including empathy and self awareness, are left out from the teaching and this might be one of the possible cause of this depersonalisation, alienation which could lead to suicide. Dr. Wible, in your website you mention Ideal medical care. Could you explain the basic concept of this Ideal Medical care? Does it have to do with the services to patients and physicians, as well to architecture of setting of care?

PW. Simplifying the delivery of healthcare by removing the no-value added intermediaries and allowing patients and doctors to design their ideal medical clinics and hospitals is essential. In hospital, there should be a ball room, one could smell scents, colours should be everywhere. There should be a silent room to comfort the pain and the sorrow. The food should be good (Idealmedicalcare Website n.d.).

At this point, I ask our readers to imagine and write down 'If I had the magic wand, how would I wish my ideal place of care to be like'. We did it already for the very first time in 2004 and 2005 in an oncology department, where we asked patients, their family members and doctors to design their hospital room, write the rules they wanted and they did not want and the best strategies for living together in the so-called constellation, patient, family and healthcare professional. Please, reader, leave your voice about your ideal world of care.

MGM. Dr. Wible, you have organized retreats for physicians and for other health care workers. I think that this might be a wonderful support and help also physicians and nurses of other countries: how are they organised?

PW. By myself. Bi-annually and open to anyone in the world who wishes to come. More here: Physician Retreat: Live Your Dream. I also offer smaller monthly retreats for individuals and small groups. The topics include how to rediscover the joy of being a doctor, how to build the ideal place of care, how to get rid of bureaucracy and being paid for, how to be paid as a doctor for being a doctor, how to get rid of the stress, with no digital social network, and learn to recover.

I feel that some points can fit into the Italian healthcare services; some other like the fact to be paid is different, because in Italy, doctors are well paid and money is not the main reason for suicide. I love the idea to ask more money for any useless bureaucracy to fill in. I love the idea to talk about joy in the caring profession. Furthermore, I cherish the courage to stay offline for 5 days, to do a washout period from overwhelming social and digital society, a little bit, like to get rid of potential most severe addiction of our age.

MGM. Dr. Wible, I have been observing your continuous honouring the suicides of your colleagues, keeping their memory alive. It's a great sign of respect. Which are the effects of this behaviour in your colleagues and in the public opinion?

PW. I think others are now starting to realise that we have an epidemic and that this is truly a public health crisis. Cultural taboos reinforce secrecy, and suicide is a sin in many religions. Islam and Christian families have asked that I hide the suicides of family members. Indian families often claim a suicide is a homicide or an accident, even when it's obviously self-inflicted.

Media offers incomplete coverage of suspicious deaths. Articles about doctors found dead in hospital call rooms claim 'no foul play'. No follow-up stories.

Medical schools and hospitals lie (or omit the truth) to cover up suicides—even when media and family report cause of death. Medical student Ari Frosch stood in front of a train, yet his school reported he died at home with his family.

Though the family of psychiatrist Christine Petrich shared that she bought a gun and killed herself (just after getting her hair done and planning a surprise trip to Lego Land and Disney for her kids) on their GoFundMe page (https://www.gofundme.com/), her employer wrote she 'passed away'. Shouldn't the department of psychiatry take a more active interest in physician suicide?

Euphemisms cover up doctor suicides. Suicide is omitted from obituaries, funerals, clinics, hospitals and medical schools. Instead, we hear 'passed away unexpectedly in her sleep' and 'he went to be with the Lord'. Secrets will not save us. We're unlikely to make a medical breakthrough on a hidden medical condition.

I've been shunned for speaking about doctor suicide. After being invited by the American Medical Association (AMA) to deliver my TEDMED talk, I was disinvited shortly before the event because they were 'uncomfortable' with the topic on physicians' suicide. Ignoring doctor suicides leads to more doctor suicides.

MGM. Thank you so much for having shared with us your knowledge and your opinion. Personally, I had spoken of this issue of suicide in UK and Italy providing the statistics in USA, in class this February with different kinds of healthcare operators. Yes, Dr. Wible, you are right: talking of this topic causes uneasiness, and people attending the class at the beginning where saying: but these data refer to the United States a country that has a completely different system. Then, when I presented the Italian data with a double rate of suicides among physicians compared to the averages, well, people remained in silence, and they immediately wanted to change the topic. As a sort of protection, but silence has to be broken, and a serious reflection should start to make better, our healthcare service and to improve lives of all people who dedicate their life days and night to our wellbeing.

Therefore, also the doctors are facing their Minotaur but without knowing the possible evilness of the Beast or without knowing how to get out from the over complex structure of the Labyrinth of study, career and emotions. However, above all, the trauma of seeing and living with daily possible death is something which goes beyond any possible role and reminds to the universal of humankind, 'to live' or 'to die'. NM may help these physicians who often wear the masks of 'everything is fine' in letting them express their feeling, including their pain for the loss of the patients, without the ambition to be God and to cure all possible patients. These guilty feelings due to the death of the patients, in my opinion, are generated also by a 'super homism thought', in which natural laws, including the cycle of life and death, are the basic rules and are dis-learnt in scientific faculties. Technologies sell the illusion to make as immortals. Thus, it is useful and beautiful to see death as the limit of life, and these come from many spiritual and Eastern philosophy. Subsequently, we will learn to master, in a better way, emotions beyond big events as life and death.

Chapter 11 of the Book of Tao (Laozi (4th century BC) n.d.) can be somehow of enlightening regarding this dichotomy between 'life/fullness/owning' and 'death/emptiness/loss':

> *Thirty spokes unite around one hub to make a wheel.*
> *It is the presence of the empty space that gives the function of a vehicle.*
> *Clay is molded into a vase.*
> *It is the empty space that gives the function of a vase.*
> *Doors and windows are chisel out to make a room.*
> *It is the empty space in the room that gives its function.*
> *Therefore, something substantial can be beneficial.*
> *While the emptiness of void is what can be utilized.*

Meditating on TAO, or other spiritual and philosophical consideration about our human nature, included in a cosmic environment (i.e. the Sky and the Earth) produces happiness and calm and peace. This could be a great and low-cost practice to teach future doctors when they are at the university and to carers who are traumatised by daily contact with pain. *Medice, cura te ipsum* (Gospel according to Luke 4:23—The Holy Bible: King James Version 2004) indicates 'healthcare provider take care of yourself' not only from physical diseases but also from mental illness, starting with getting rid of guilty feelings and poor love towards mainly 'themselves'.

This not only holds true for carers but for everybody who desire good books for meditation and relaxing beyond the strong semantic words as life and death: The Way of Tao, The Mahabharata, The Bible, Homer, Platos' Dialogues, Dante, Shakespeare, Virginia Wolff, William Blake, Emily Dickinson, Walter Witman and so many writers have faced these existential issues.

The following is the letter of the Greek philosopher Epicurus to his friend Menoeceus, explaining his reflection upon life and death:

> *Let no one be slow to seek wisdom when he is young nor weary in the search of it when he has grown old. For no age is too early or too late for the health of the soul. And to say that the season for studying philosophy has not yet come, or that it is past and gone, is like saying that the season for happiness is not yet or that it is now no more. Therefore, both old and young alike ought to seek wisdom, the former in order that, as age comes over him, he may be young in good things because of the grace of what has been, and the latter in order that, while he is young, he may at the same time be old, because he has no fear of the things which are to come. So, we must exercise ourselves in the things which bring happiness, since, if that be present, we have everything, and, if that be absent, all our actions are directed towards attaining it.*
>
> *Those things which without ceasing I have declared unto you, do them, and exercise yourself in them, holding them to be the elements of right life. First believe that God is a living being immortal and blessed, according to the notion of a god indicated by the common sense of mankind; and so, believing, you shall not affirm of him anything that is foreign to his immortality or that is repugnant to his blessedness. Believe about him whatever may uphold both his blessedness and his immortality. For there are gods, and the knowledge of them is manifest; but they are not such as the multitude believe, seeing that men do not steadfastly maintain the notions they form respecting them. Not the man who denies the gods worshipped by the multitude, but he who affirms of the gods what the multitude believes about them is truly impious. For the utterances of the multitude about the gods are*

not true preconceptions but false assumptions; hence it is that the greatest evils happen to the wicked and the greatest blessings happen to the good from the hand of the gods, seeing that they are always favourable to their own good qualities and take pleasure in men like themselves, but reject as alien whatever is not of their kind.

Accustom yourself to believing that death is nothing to us, for good and evil imply the capacity for sensation, and death is the privation of all sentience; therefore, a correct understanding that death is nothing to us makes the mortality of life enjoyable, not by adding to life a limitless time, but by taking away the yearning after immortality. For life has no terrors for him who has thoroughly understood that there are no terrors for him in ceasing to live. Foolish, therefore, is the man who says that he fears death, not because it will hurt when it comes, but because it hurts in the prospect. Death, therefore, the most awful of evils, is nothing to us, seeing that, when we are, death is not come, and, when death has come, we are no longer. It is nothing, then, either to the living or to the dead, for with the living it is not and the dead exist no longer.

But in the world, at one-time men shun death as the greatest of all evils, and at another time choose it as a break from the evils in life. The wise man does not deprecate life nor does he fear the cessation of life. The thought of life is no offense to him, nor is the cessation of life regarded as an evil. And even as men choose of food not merely and simply the larger portion, but the more pleasant, so the wise seek to enjoy the time which is most pleasant and not merely that which is longest. And he who admonishes the young to live well and the old to make a good end speaks foolishly, not merely because of the desirability of life, but because the same exercise at once teaches to live well and to die well. Much worse is he who says that it were good not to be born, but when once one is born to pass quickly through the gates of Hades. For if he truly believes this, why does he not depart from life? It would be easy for him to do so once he were firmly convinced. If he speaks only in jest, his words are foolishness as those who hear him do not believe.

We must remember that the future is neither wholly ours nor wholly not ours, so that neither must we count upon it as quite certain to come nor despair of it as quite certain not to come.

We must also reflect that of desires some are natural, others are groundless; and that of the natural some are necessary as well as natural, and some natural only. And of the necessary desires some are necessary if we are to be happy, some if the body is to be rid of uneasiness, some if we are even to live. He who has a clear and certain understanding of these things will direct every preference and aversion toward securing health of body and tranquillity of mind, seeing that this is the sum and end of a blessed life. For the end of all our actions is to be free from pain and fear, and, when once we have attained all this, the tempest of the soul is laid; seeing that the living creature has no need to go in search of something that is lacking, nor to look for anything else by which the good of the soul and of the body will be fulfilled. When we are pained because of the absence of pleasure, then, and then only, do we feel the need of pleasure. Wherefore we call pleasure the alpha and omega of a blessed life. Pleasure is our first and kindred good. It is the starting-point of every choice and of every aversion, and to it we come back, inasmuch as we make feeling the rule by which to judge of every good thing.

And since pleasure is our first and native good, for that reason we do not choose every pleasure whatsoever, but will often pass over many pleasures when a greater annoyance ensues from them. And often we consider pains superior to pleasures when submission to the pains for a long time brings us as a consequence a greater pleasure. While therefore all pleasure because it is naturally akin to us is good, not all pleasure is should be chosen, just as all pain is an evil and yet not all pain is to be shunned. It is, however, by measuring one against another, and by looking at the conveniences and inconveniences, that all these matters must be judged. Sometimes we treat the good as an evil, and the evil, on the contrary, as a good.

Again, we regard independence of outward things as a great good, not so as in all cases to use little, but so as to be contented with little if we have not much, being honestly persuaded that they have the sweetest enjoyment of luxury who stand least in need of it, and that whatever is natural is easily procured and only the vain and worthless hard to win. Plain fare gives as much pleasure as a costly diet, when once the pain of want has been removed, while bread and water confer the highest possible pleasure when they are brought to hungry lips. To habituate one's self, therefore, to simple and inexpensive diet supplies all that is needful for health and enables a man to meet the necessary requirements of life without shrinking, and it places us in a better condition when we approach at intervals a costly fare and renders us fearless of fortune.

When we say, then, that pleasure is the end and aim, we do not mean the pleasures of the prodigal or the pleasures of sensuality, as we are understood to do by some through ignorance, prejudice, or wilful misrepresentation. By pleasure we mean the absence of pain in the body and of trouble in the soul. It is not an unbroken succession of drinking-bouts and of revelry, not sexual lust, not the enjoyment of the fish and other delicacies of a luxurious table, which produce a pleasant life; it is sober reasoning, searching out the grounds of every choice and avoidance, and banishing those beliefs through which the greatest tumults take possession of the soul. Of all this the beginning and the greatest good is wisdom. Therefore, wisdom is a more precious thing even than philosophy; from it spring all the other virtues, for it teaches that we cannot live pleasantly without living wisely, honourably, and justly; nor live wisely, honourably, and justly without living pleasantly. For the virtues have grown into one with a pleasant life, and a pleasant life is inseparable from them.

Who, then, is superior in your judgment to such a man? He holds a holy belief concerning the gods and is altogether free from the fear of death. He has diligently considered the end fixed by nature and understands how easily the limit of good things can be reached and attained, and how either the duration or the intensity of evils is but slight. Fate, which some introduce as sovereign over all things, he scorns, affirming rather that some things happen of necessity, others by chance, others through our own agency. For he sees that necessity destroys responsibility and that chance is inconstant; whereas our own actions are autonomous, and it is to them that praise and blame naturally attach. It were better, indeed, to accept the legends of the gods than to bow beneath that yoke of destiny which the natural philosophers have imposed. The one holds out some faint hope that we may escape if we honour the gods, while the necessity of the naturalists is deaf to all entreaties. Nor does he hold chance to be a god, as the world in general does, for in the acts of a god there is no disorder; nor to be a cause, though an uncertain one, for he believes that no good or evil is dispensed by chance to men so as to make life blessed, though it supplies the starting-point of great good and great evil. He believes that the misfortune of the wise is better than the prosperity of the fool. It is better, in short, that what is well judged in action should not owe its successful issue to the aid of chance.

Exercise yourself in these and related precepts day and night, both by yourself and with one who is like-minded; then never, either in waking or in dream, will you be disturbed, but will live as a god among men. For man loses all semblance of mortality by living in the midst of immortal blessings (Epicurus (341–270 BC) n.d.).

Practice Time

How do you consider your patient's journey? As a labyrinth or as a castle? Are there enemies? If so, who are they?

Have you ever tried to give another name to the disease? A personal name, a metaphoric name? Do you think that this name can vary during the phase of *being ill*? Do you think that this name is personal?

As far as trauma is concerned, would you like to try to write yourself about your little or big trauma?

Would you like to share this with somebody who you really trust? Do you think that there might be preparatory exercises before writing about the trauma?

Have you ever written about traumas of somebody else, for instance, a patient's trauma?

Have you ever tried to speak about some possible traumas with your patients? If so, how did it go? What can you do for improving it? If not, why? Would you like to try?

What do you think about neuroplasticity? Do you think that by some practice exercise, someone can refocus on the here and now?

Suicides and doctors: were you aware of these numbers? Do you have some possible explanations?

Finding the joy in your profession of carer…

Finding the joy in being a patient…

Finding the joy in being a person…

Finding the joy to be in this world…

References

Achotegui J (2005) Emigration in hard conditions: the Immigrant Syndrome with chronic and multiple stress—Ulysses' Syndrome. Vertex 16(60):105–113

Anwar S, Khan S (2013) Risks of online self-diagnosing: cyberchondriacs. BCMJ 55(2):72

Aviv R (2015) The death treatment—when should people with a non-terminal illness be helped to die? The New Yorker. https://www.newyorker.com/magazine/2015/06/22/the-death-treatment

Begley S (2009) The Plastic Mind. Constable

Csete J et al (2016) Report of the Johns Hopkins—Lancet Commission on Drug Policy and Health. Public Health and International Drug Policy. Lancet 387(10026):1427–1480

Duccoli D (2017), The Trauma and the Body, Chronicles of Narrative Medicine, https://www.narrativemedicine.eu

Edmondson D, Horowitz CR, Goldfinger JZ, Fei K, Kronish IM (2013) Concerns about medications mediate the association of posttraumatic stress disorder with adherence to medication in stroke survivors. Br J Health Psychol 18(4):799–813

Edmondson D, Richardson S, Falzon L, Davidson KW, Mills MA, Neria Y (2012) Posttraumatic stress disorder prevalence and risk of recurrence in acute coronary syndrome patients: a meta-analytic review. PLoS One 7(6):e38915

Epicurus (341–270 BC). Letter to Menoeceus

Fondazione ISTUD (2015) Storie luminose. Esperienze di straordinaria quotidianità nei racconti delle persone che vivono con la sclerosi multipla. 24 Ore Cultura

Frank AW (1995) The wounded storyteller: body, illness, and ethics. University of Chicago Press, Chicago

Gospel according to Luke 4:23—the Holy Bible: King James version (2004). Brown Books Publishing, Dallas, TX

Graça da Silva S, Tehrani JJ (2017) Comparative phylogenetic analyses uncover the ancient roots of Indo-European folktales. R Soc Open Sci 3(1):150645

Greenhalgh T (2016) Cultural contexts of health: the use of narrative research in the health sector Copenhagen: WHO Regional Office for Europe; Health Evidence Network synthesis report 49, viii + 54p. http://www.euro.who.int/en/publications/abstracts/cultural-contexts-of-health-the-use-of-narrative-research-in-the-health-sector-2016

Idealmedicalcare Website. http://www.idealmedicalcare.org/blog/wp-content/uploads/docs/Optimism-Anthology.pdf

Johns Hopkins Medicine (2013) PTSD symptoms common among ICU survivors. ScienceDaily. www.sciencedaily.com/releases/2013/02/130226081238.htm
Laozi (4th century BC). Tao Te Ching. (The book of Tao)
LEIF Website. http://leif.be/home/
Marini MG (2016) Narrative medicine: bridging the gap between evidence-based care and medical humanities. Springer, Cham
Neri M (2011) Un punto nero nell'immenso azzurro del mare. UR Editore
Oregon Health & Science University (2012) One-fifth of spine surgery patients develop PTSD symptoms. ScienceDaily. www.sciencedaily.com/releases/2012/09/120928103800.htm
Pascual-Leone A, Amedi A, Fregni F, Merabet LB (2005) The plastic human brain cortex. Annu Rev Neurosci 28:377–401
Rouse WHD (1957) Gods, heroes and men of ancient Greece. The New American Library, New York
Slavitt DR, Carrigan HL (2015) Mahabharata (6th ed)
Stark E et al (2015) Post-traumatic stress influences the brain even in the absence of symptoms: a systematic, quantitative meta-analysis of neuroimaging studies. Neurosci Biobehav Rev 56:207–221
Trebble TM et al (2010) Process mapping the patient's journey through healthcare: an introduction. BMJ 341:c4078
Tulleken V, Hamlyn H (2016) Refugee crisis presents a humanitarian paradox. BMJ 355:i5412
Vin-Raviv N (2013) Racial disparities in posttraumatic stress after diagnosis of localized breast cancer: the BQUAL study. J Natl Cancer Inst 105(8):563–572
Wesemael YV et al (2009) Role and involvement of life end information forum physicians in euthanasia and other end-of-life care decisions in Flanders, Belgium. Health Serv Res 44(6):2180–2192
Wible P (2018) Washington post website. https://www.washingtonpost.com/national/health-science/what-ive-learned-from-my-tally-of-757-doctor-suicides/2018/01/12/b0ea9126-eb50-11e7-9f92-10a2203f6c8d_story.html?utm_term=.4d790d8f9e33

9 Language of Emotions, with a Focus on Shame to Be Defeated: The Flower of Emotions and Their Role in a Post-contemporary Society

Shame is a soul eating emotion

—Carl Gustav Jung

Emotions are debated daily in scientific and social literature, social media and media in general. In the narrative turn, described by John Launer (2007) in our postmodern age, emotions are playing a dominant role. This is illustrated in *Inside Out*, a movie produced by Disney Pixar in 2015, which aimed at familiarising young children, teenagers, parents and relatives regarding the functioning and importance of emotions beyond our 'decision free will' based on reason (Dacher and Paul 2015). The main characters are five emotions, joy, sadness, disgust, anger and fear that live in the minds (somewhere in imaginary control stations) of a family who recently moved from Minnesota to San Francisco. In this family, the adventures of Riley, a girl aged 11 years, in coping with the difficulty of the new environment are demonstrated. Inside Out had the expert input of the psychologist Dacher Keltner, Berkeley University, California, who says that emotions are really critical as to how we look at the world—our perception, our attention, our memories and our judgement.

Emotions guide us in our handling of really important life circumstances, like moves and developmental changes, and emotions shape us in the way we relate to other people. Furthermore, we may think that our memories are a factual representation of events, but in fact, we lose a lot of information. Memory is imperfect, and emotions are part of the reconstruction of the past. The movie has oversimplified the emotions, their numbers, and, in my opinion, did not give almost any room to free will, letting the people understand that emotions are the dominant part of the brain. The most robust part of the movie, or at least the part I appreciated the most, is that positive thinking alone, with basic sentences like 'be happy', 'whatever it is, smile', was banned in the plot of this movie. Only letting go of sadness, along with disgust, fear and anger in past memories, will joy come back again eventually in Riley? Will she cope with the new house, new school, new food and new friends?

M. G. Marini, *Languages of Care in Narrative Medicine*,
https://doi.org/10.1007/978-3-319-94727-3_9

Almost daily, a book on emotions is published; however, before speaking about sick or ill patients who feel ashamed, we have to choose a system of categorisation. In *Inside Out*, shame is already considered by disgust and fear. However, before going to examine shame, I will introduce the system that we use when we listen to patients' and carers' dialogues, and we read their written narrative as well.

Classification of Emotions According to Robert Plutchik

Robert Plutchik, a psychologist and professor emeritus at the Albert Einstein College of Medicine, developed a classification system known as the 'wheel of emotions' (Plutchik 1980a, 1991). Plutchik proposed that eight 'basic' emotions are biologically primitive joy, fear, anger, disgust, sadness, (the same as Inside Out) plus trust, surprise and anticipation. By the way, Prof. Wierzbicka thinks the same about NSM applied to the human kind: the very first 65 words, the primes, belong to our evolution. These emotions have evolved to increase the reproductive fitness of the animal. Plutchik argued for the primacy of these emotions by showing each to be the trigger of behaviour with high survival value, such as the way fear inspires the fight-or-flight response.

Plutchik's psychoevolutionary theory of basic emotions has ten postulates:

1. The concept of emotion is applicable to all evolutionary levels and applies to all animals, including humans.
2. Emotions have an evolutionary history and have evolved various forms of expression in different species.
3. Emotions served an adaptive role in helping organisms deal with key survival issues posed by the environment.
4. Despite different forms of expression of emotions in different species, there are certain common elements, or prototype patterns, which can be identified.
5. There are a small number of basic, primary or prototype emotions.
6. All other emotions are mixed or derivative states; that is, they occur as combinations, mixtures or compounds of the primary emotions.
7. Primary emotions are hypothetical constructs or idealised states whose properties and characteristics can only be inferred from various kinds of evidence.
8. Primary emotions can be conceptualised in terms of pairs of polar opposites.
9. All emotions vary in their degree of similarity to one another.
10. Each emotion can exist in varying degrees of intensity or levels of arousal (Plutchik 1980b).

This model demonstrated how different emotions can be combined or mixed together, similar to a way in which an artist mixes primary colours to create other colours. Plutchik first suggested eight primary bipolar emotions (as reported in Fig. 9.1): joy versus sadness, anger versus fear, trust versus disgust and surprise versus anticipation.

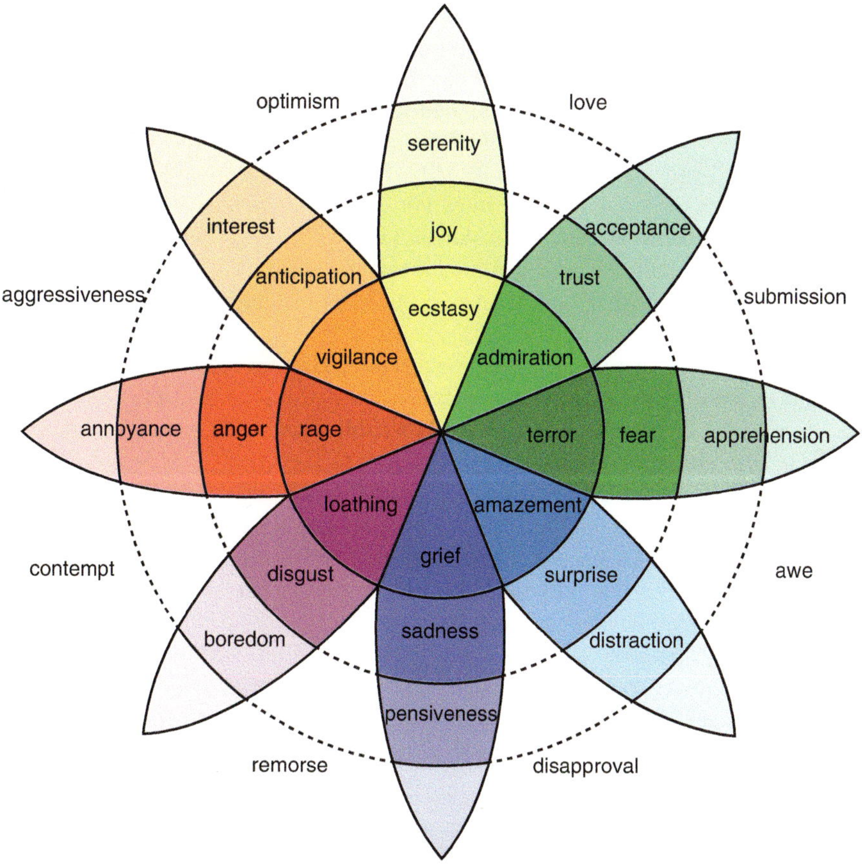

Fig. 9.1 The wheel of emotions, which shows Plutchik's eight primary emotions

If we think with regard to NSM, we do have some opposite words: DO, a term in the anticipation realm, is balanced by HAPPEN, in the surprise realm. FEEL GOOD, in the joy realm, is opposed by FEEL BAD, in the sadness realm. Disgust has something to deal with 'this someone or something, people make me FEEL BAD IN THE BODY and THINK BAD. I don't want to be with this someone by my side'. On the contrary, trust could be roughly explained using the semantic primes by 'this someone or something makes me FEEL GOOD IN THE BODY and THINK GOOD. I want to be with this someone or something by my side'. Let us try to use these semantic primes: for fear, it is 'this someone or something makes me FEEL BAD IN THE BODY and THINK BAD. I move very far from this someone or something', and this explains the flight situation. For anger, it is 'this someone or something, makes me FEEL BAD IN THE BODY and THINK BAD. I want to do something bad to this someone or something'. According to NSM, all emotions described by these basic words are universal: however, it is up to us how to manage them and how to live with them. Thus, I started this chapter with something which might not seem serious enough, a cartoon: emotions should be learned, self-diagnosed and mastered since we are children.

Plutchik's basic emotions can then be combined in a variety of ways (as shown in Fig. 9.2). For example, happiness and anticipation might combine to create excitement. From there, Plutchik identified more advanced emotions based on their differences in intensities. There are actually dyads, listed below, which arise from the combination of core/basic emotions. For example, when we combine joy and trust, we experience what Plutchik would call love.

The names originate from the combinations of the dyads. This wheel of emotions as well as the table of the dyad was an eye opener for me, with the same importance of NSM.

In the narratives, we observe and register the movement of emotions from the initial position of possible patient's apprehension and fear at the time of knowing the diagnosis, and, if the doctor-patient relationship works well, patients migrate to trust and admiration for their carers.

Alternatively, if the doctor and nurse mainly show interest at the beginning, mixed with anticipation, this can lead eventually to trust and to patient's admiration and to reciprocal joy. This is if the situation is easy and smooth: in some other cases, patients are so scared that they might become angry and the doctors become predominant and do not pay enough interest to the words of the patients. This indifference showed by doctors to the patients can lead to rebellion, activating the unwanted dyad of fear and anger. Our study (SOUND in press) showed that doctors are able to deal with fear of the patients by reassuring them and are able to cope with sadness

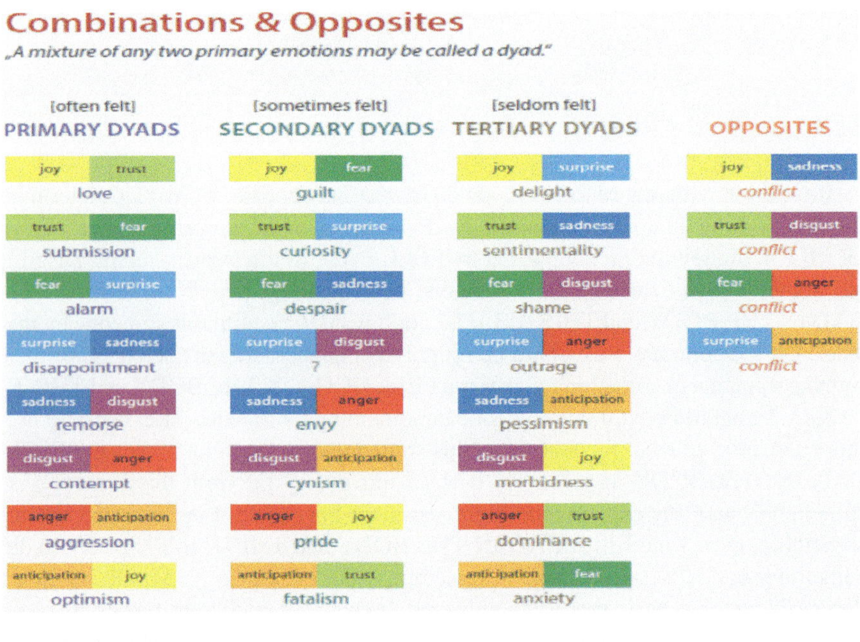

Fig. 9.2 Plutchik's emotional dyads

by comforting them; however, they are not yet skilled in managing anger, which generate fear in doctors and reciprocal anger, which leads to a vicious cycle hard to break.

Shame: An Undesired Emotion Not Enough Rewarded and Respected

Shame is a told or rather mainly an untold feeling which relates to the illness of the patients and the inclusion or discrimination by the outer world. Shame has to do with humiliation, inadequacy, disgrace and inferiority. To experience the feeling of being ashamed, there will always be someone else, 'the else', who is judging and criticising both verbally and non-verbally. In my opinion, of the many types of emotions, shame is the most social one: when one is angry or happy, other emotions may or may not be present, but in the majority of cases, shame has to do with a tertiary point of view, which could be the microcosm or macrocosm of the society it belongs to. The microcosm is family, work, school and friends; the macrocosm is the wider community, the city and the country of belonging internationally or globally.

Before going into the healthcare world, let us examine the word 'shame' and its Italian counterpart *vergogna*. In Italian, the word *vergogna* comes from Latin *vereri* (Online Etymology Dictionary n.d.) and has a slightly different meaning from the English word. It means to feel pain and humiliating perturbation inside; it is like to feel ashamed and is very much related to the word *verecondia* concerned with a proper way of behaving and respect for others, generally among upper classes, nobles and in the relationship between men and women. *Verecondia* was a virtue for women, the opposite of arrogance and not related to 'humiliation' but instead for respect towards men. Although not my mother tongue, I understand from my studies that the word 'shame' comes from *skam*, a proto-German word with a very strong impact, related to a committed sin: the expression 'shame on you' is almost like cursing (Online Etymology Dictionary n.d.).

When considering these nuances of interpretation, we move between these different historical derivations of *vergogna* and *shame*. The Italian word has to do with the noble sentiment of *humbleness*, which is not totally or exclusively humiliation. Symbolically, it is the ritual of village people removing their hats in front of knights or nobles or of the peasants who concealed their dirty hands because they were feeling inadequate. These are just a few examples to explain why *vergogna* or shame has to do with social class, beliefs and roles.

Robert Plutchik says that this feeling is originated by two primary emotions as disgust and fear. Their combination results in shame and embarrassment and humiliation (Plutchik 1991).

If we consider the classical definition of Arthur Kleinman, we know that with the word 'disease', we call into action the biomedical model, the body/mind as a broken machine to repair; with the word 'illness', it is the inner living of a patient with a disease, and with the word 'sickness', it is the way a disease is considered by society (Kleinman 1988). Therefore, the word 'shame' falls more into the definition of sickness with a constant impact on the illness, the 'inside' of the patient. What strikes a chord is the relation between patient and social context: in this case, even with ups and downs, the predominant emotions and behaviours are inclusiveness, attention, compassion, shared fears and shared rage, if any. There is a dynamic alignment between the ill person and others, which changes hand in hand with the development of the disease.

When there is no tuning between the realm of the ill person and the realm of the others outside, sharing is very hard to achieve and eventually exclusion and loneliness are consequences on both sides: shame or vergogna could be the 'culprit' of discrimination.

When is shame present in sickness? When does the disease undermine the body's aesthetics? When does the disease affect functionality? When does something odd start to appear, the 'irregular outlier'? All of these could be valid, but their predominance is very different according to the environment within which the ill person resides.

Shame is a very difficult emotion to uncover because when someone feels embarrassed, they are not willing to speak about the reasons for these feelings. It is precisely this type of situation where NM can be of help: patients, in the comfort zone of anonymity, can finally be empowered through writing, with openness and intimacy. While the oral interview with patients often does not allow the expression of the feeling of humiliation, the words 'shame' and 'feeling ashamed and embarrassed' are recorded more easily by the written word.

In the research on shame carried out by Luna Dolezal and Barry Lyons, there is a useful information which help us in understanding the benefits in containing and fighting this emotion (Lyons and Dolezal 2017). Shame is the primary 'emotion of politics and conformity', particularly 'for those who have the *wrong* bodies or the *wrong* desires'. Those who deviate from entrenched social norms are frequently subjected to stigma, 'a social process, experienced or anticipated, characterised by exclusion, rejection, blame or devaluation that results from experience, perception or reasonable anticipation of an adverse social judgement about a person or group'. The impact of social exclusion contributes substantially to the burden of illness, to the extent that in highly stigmatised disorders the suffering brought on by the disease process may be outweighed by the impact of stigma-induced social rejection. Gilbert proposed that shame represents a major threat to human wellbeing as it increases vulnerability to illness, undermines physical and mental healing and reduces help seeking (Gilbert 2017). Shame affects medical help seeking, disclosure, truthfulness and willingness to engage in treatment as well as ceases health-affecting behaviours or return for further consultations. Furthermore, the pervasive use of shaming of *deviant* bodies and behaviours in contemporary medical culture can inform how we view ourselves and lead to the pernicious and damaging state of chronic shame.

Patients' Narratives on Shame and Coping

In our Western world, skin diseases which impact the aesthetics of the face and the body, such as acne, psoriasis, atopic dermatitis and hives, can cause people to live in shame. Using NSM, affected people find it easier to express shame for diseases which impact their outlook: *I think I am not good in my body or a part of my body. I don't want you to see me. I don't want the people to see me.* The verb mainly involved by shame is 'to see', with the willingness of 'not to be seen', that is, to 'hide'. The hiding procedure is very much present in patients and people affected by skin diseases.

Below are some verbatim statements from narratives of patients affected by psoriasis (Unpublished data, Fondazione Istud):

> *Removing my clothes was a cause of shame, and looking at myself in the mirror was traumatic. Today, I have overcome my problems; phototherapy makes me feel good. I feel that I have not lost anything because of my psoriasis. I do not have to feel down …* there are fare worse illnesses.
>
> *They said there was nothing that could be done to help. I just had to relax and be less nervous. But how do you do that? There were times that I did not leave home, because of the shame of how I looked, all crusted and because the people and family around me were commenting on how I looked I was ashamed that they were ashamed of me. Psoriasis has taught me that we should never judge people by appearances, that everybody of us suffers from something and that we must go beyond, listen and become good and sensible.*
>
> *I felt ashamed at work and with my friends when I started suffering from psoriasis. It was impossible for me to dress up, and looking in the mirror was not a nice thing to do. I have a bad image of psoriasis, but there are worse illnesses in life. Today I'm resigned.*

In the three written narratives on psoriasis above, the words *vergogna* and *vergognarsi* were automatically translated into or linked with 'shame' and 'feeling ashamed'.

Skin diseases evoke a strong feeling of shame; from our narratives, this is much more prevalent among people who are ill than among the regular population. There is a cruel, critical, inner judgement when it comes to aesthetics associated with skin disease, which shows no compassion for the disease. However, despite this inward persecution, we learned the three main factors for coping from the narratives: first, rationalise that there are worse diseases. For the young, it is being helped by their partners who love and accept them unconditionally. Finally, learn to approach the illness more sensibly and therefore help others to respond in a similar way.

If we recall our research on neuroesthetics in Chap. 7 and the research by Semir Zeki, as far as we know, what we consider 'ugly' is something which activates the amygdala of the brain, together with fear (Ishizu and Zeki 2011). The researcher Dolan found that the amygdala and the fusiform gyrus area of the temporal lobe respond to the image of a face regardless of the emotion being displayed and regardless of whether the image is perceived consciously or unconsciously (Morris et al. 1996). In a similar vein, using PET imaging studies, Dolan found that when people view faces that express either fear or happiness, seeing progressively more fearful faces increases activity in the amygdala, whereas seeing increasingly happy faces decreases activity. Perhaps, there is something ancestral and archetypal in front of something which does not fall into the frames of beauty and the golden section, something that has proportions different from what we are ordinary able to see. An education should be supported to see something different, to get out from a concept of beauty which is dictated by fashion and trends, and art, in particular art of the last century, for which painters were the first to 'de-compose' the beauty in the face of women and men: thinking to

Lucien Freud, the artist who made the first revolution on the portrait, able to transform ugliness into the beauty of art (Theartstory Website n.d.).

In a short novel *Liking What You See: A Documentary* written by Ted Chiang, a science fiction novelist, as a final story of his wonderful book *Stories of Your Life and Others*, there is a technology called the *kalli*, again from the Greek word *kalos* which means beautiful, which allows people to turn off their ability to see beauty in others, thereby making the ugly and the beautiful all look basically the same (Chiang 2002). This novel tackles the uncommon prejudice due to the way the people look. The story is written as a form of interviews for students and professors in a college, and all of them give different answers to the pros and the cons in getting free of the *kalli*, which means able to explore the inside of the people, despite their beauty. Reading this novel made me reflect so much on the possibility of building relationships among people without this connatural need of beauty: this novel hits the point of the 'selfie' age and 'beauty cam' and covers social dynamics related to the shame of being 'not good looking enough'.

As a last message from the narratives of patients with skin disease, we learn that their shame is exaggerated in comparison to the acceptance by the society. If not all people can embrace the oddity of 'the bad outlook', real loving and caring people will stay close to the person and help them to find inner resources to fight the disease and to accept it.

Shame and Cancer

However, there are other diseases, considered in common belief (personally, I don't want to provide any ranking on the severity of illness but prefer to respect every disease as it is) as more severe, cancer, for instance. Cancer has to do with survival, with the fear of dying, with invasive and 'cruel' drugs and tests: however, the most common things considered by patients, even before the chance of survival? *Doctor, will I lose my hair?* The loss of hair has to do with identity, with aesthetics and the social code of our society (Rosman 2004). Recently, there have been many campaigns which promote bald men and women after chemotherapy, such as the Bald Mona Lisa, to educate people and build patients' self-esteem (Edwards 2013). However, the shame, especially for a woman, in appearing bald, is still there. Hair seems more powerful than the life wish: something which may have to do with heritages of the past where women accused of witchery had their hair cut off, something still witnessed in August 2017 at Agra in India (Ray 2017). How to cope with hair loss? Strategies for women coping with hair loss are narrated through the use of beautiful silk and cotton scarves, something which is becoming more popular than the use of wigs which seem too artificial.

Moving on with shame, there are striking cases of embarrassment when dealing with patients who have undergone an ostomy and the consequent use of pouches for ileum and colon cancer. We have collected their narratives (Reale et al. 2017) both in Italy and in Australia, and in only a few cases is the word 'shame' clearly mentioned, but it is clearly identified between the lines: *I don't want to look at myself, I don't want to touch the pouch and even more extremely, I have a disgust of it.* Here, there is a mutilated body with an external bag collecting their faeces. Shame is definitely there; however, the miracle of life comes to at least half of these patients and teaches patients sharing their illness with relatives and healthcare providers that the feeling of humiliation can be overcome. Patients' associations count for a lot and help at a peer level for people who live with a stoma. Following a good coping strategy, the outcome is a sort of pacification or 'coming to terms with' the traumatised body: *after surgery, I'm happy to wear a bikini, and I go to swim regularly*; this is the happy ending of the narrative of a girl. The goal of being able to show one's body again, wearing less visible pouches, is a recurrent theme of a coping activity for people with stomas: also, in this case, an intense rationalisation was carried out. *I'm alive, thanks to the ostomy, and the stoma is now a part of me.* Giving a name to one's stoma is a sign as to whether the patient is coping or whether they still feel shame. Below are the four clusters of reaction to a stoma (Fig. 9.3): emotional acceptance, technical acceptance, passive (resignation) mode and difficulty, which is the furthest away from coping. Names are important, and if we see that a first name was given to the stoma, we might think that acceptance strategies are underway. On the contrary, if asking the patients to name the stoma, the result is *something disgusting*; we realise that there is still a long way to go to accepting the stoma, if any acceptance at all.

However, there are many people when questioned who will not dare to give the stoma a name: shame is too much, and the stoma is still a taboo. On social media, one is allowed to write up on colon cancer prevention and treatment but not about living with a stoma. Stigma, for this condition, is among the highest level ever met.

Fig. 9.3 The clusters of the names given by patients to their ostomy

I strongly believe that if the collection of these narratives from patients with stoma were not anonymous, the embarrassment and difficulty of living with shame would not have emerged through purely oral investigation.

Another extreme case where the body image is involved and where shame is often seen is in the narratives of elderly people: in this case, this feeling is not associated with a particular disease but with the natural ageing of the human mind and body over the years. Here, shame is even more difficult to decode because it is not often clearly expressed by old people. The continuous complaints of elderly people about their doctors, the places they visit, the food they eat and the constant looking at the past, 'When I was young…' as the *golden age*, when the body was strong and the mind was faster (perhaps less sharp), could be a signal of shame.

An old woman, who is very dear to me, was complaining for a period of days and then started to cry, expressing her fears of discrimination for not being able to use technology: *I am shameful of my heart which is not beating at the right pace, and I am afraid of being put in a nursing home. Furthermore, I'm a disaster with the Internet, and everything now goes through that technology.* Nobody around her suspected this because she appears outwardly to be a very active and proactive woman. The shame was silent, difficult to unmask and was hidden by complaints and nostalgic feelings. The good news is that after sharing this with friends and relatives and the clear request for help, shame melted away like snow exposed to sunlight for this lady. In some cases, shame is 'put into words', written and reported, as in the narratives of people with skin diseases. But in many cases, this feeling is often masked to others. Since shame has to do with showing oneself in public, the untold here is very present, and even with good coping skills, it will take time before this emotion is revealed. It is shameful even to feel ashamed. However, as we know, the first step to begin coping is being aware of the emotions being felt.

Shame and the Healthcare Providers

In a study carried out in Italy, narratives from paediatricians on children and adolescents affected by severe asthma were analysed to see if this writing approach allowed fine-tuning for both patients' and physicians' cultural construction, including emotions and values of the illness and the pathways to care (Cappuccio et al. 2017). Out of 68 parallel charts, the full narrative of a clinical case, including the attention to the illness, the sickness and the quality of the relationship, the most frequent risk factors for difficult relationships were physicians' moral judgement (73%) and patients' anger (50%). A patient's expression of anger is often attributable to a sense of feeling ashamed for something that should not have occurred. For example, keeping an animal at home or continuing to smoke as a parent or the feeling of being judged by the practitioner for how they are dressed or in the manner in which they speak and behave. Indeed, there are comments in their writing on poor or excessive parenting style of the mothers of the children. Sometimes, doctors are evaluators of the qualities of being a good parent, and they can be deeply judgemental where they see possible shortfalls in these skills. *The girl should go to live with the father because the mother is totally inadequate, lacking of empathy.* All of this, if not related to shame, does create an embarrassing relationship between the doctor and patient, which has led to a refusal to change therapy in half of the cases (50%) and to a lower rate of restored activities. Feelings of being humiliated and judged by a physician create the desire to leave the care of the physician and the suggested treatments to choose a less judgemental practitioner. Physicians who are able to control their judgemental attitude can master listening and patients' emotions of fear and sadness and provide reassurance and comfort. This behaviour improved the alliance with patients and the effectiveness of treatments.

Whenever possible, a good carer should restrain from falling into the trap of moral judgement, verbally; otherwise, this will prevent feelings of inadequacy and inferiority that contribute to shame and lead patients to a passive attitude or an aggressive reaction, both of them ineffective in the pathways of care. Kindness is the antidote to moral judgement, and that is both rational (intelligent) and emotional (compassionate).

Medicine in Contemporary Society

The contemporary healthcare system typically focuses on lab tests, investigations and images but tends to neglect the presence of the body and the soul, putting emphasis on the mind and rational technology. It would appear that society generally assists in promoting a schizoid separation, on one hand, the disembodied medicine, with no flesh, no bones, no blood and no entire body but mainly microsurgery and laser techniques and invisible receptors and neurotransmitters and, on the other hand, the body and the soul in their wholeness of the human being. Changes to the body and in the mind, because of illness and old age, and other possible events, will forever exist for the individual and society. Belonging to the history of the humankind, we all bear the list of emotions including shame.

Therefore, trying to answer the question of how to cope with shame, we have learned from reading patients' and doctors' narratives: some of the Carver's factors are still there, agreeableness (looking for loving relationship, practising kindness), extroversion (sharing the burden with others), consciousness (starting to cure the illness, ranking the illness with a responsible attitude towards more severe diseases) and getting away from obsessive thoughts of shame by doing something else, as a creative activity (Carver and Connor-Smith 2010).

Beyond the conventional, pride might be an interesting antidote to shame; if shame originates from fear and disgust, pride, according to Plutchik, is a secondary emotion born from 'mother joy' and 'father anger' (Plutchik 1991):

> *'I've never felt the loss of my eye as a loss, for me it was the Door to Life. It is my medal, I feel very proud to be able to show that life deserves to be lived'.*

As we have seen, shame may prevent a person from having a normal social life. A balance of anger and joy would allow one to cope with shame. I am writing this because I learned it personally from the medal of the lady with the lost eye and from women who dare to show their breasts after a mastectomy, with no plastic surgery, only scars decorated with tattoos.

In Japan, there is an art called kintsugi: when a pot is broken into pieces, they do not use invisible glue, and they do not throw away the pot. With kintsugi, they put gold all along the broken pieces and rebuild the pot again (Gopnik 2009). They will have a new pot, in which every break is prominent in its golden coating. Scars are all there and visible: the more scars there are, the more precious the pot.

When you make a hole in your dress, don't repair it with invisible mending, but sew laces and embroidery to make it even more beautiful (Italian anonymous saying).

Practice Time

What do you think and feel about the Plutchik wheel?

Would you like to see while you're reading these pages? Which emotions are calling for your attention?

What are the basic primary emotions? Do you think there are more?

What is the dyadic composition of the emotions? Do you think that they cover the rainbow of the emotions?

Try, if you wish to take an emotion and apply NSM. Do you think that is useful to go the core of the feeling?

Shame: if you deal with patients, doctors, nurses or colleagues, is something that we can address? You wish to address, but you cannot? You never tried to address but you would like to talk about it?

What do you think about giving a nickname to a condition and a disease to understand the level of coping engagement or disengagement?

There is a website called the 'Dictionary of Obscure Sorrows' created by John Koenig (www.dictionaryofobscuresorrows.com/), in which rare and strange or normal emotions are defined by neologisms. Here is an example: *exulansis, n., the tendency to give up trying to talk about an experience because people are unable to relate to it—whether through envy or pity or simple foreignness—which allows it to drift away from the rest of your life story, until the memory itself feels out of place, almost mythical, wandering restlessly in the fog, no longer even looking for a place to land.*

Would you like to try to invent neologisms to define emotions, thoughts and facts?

References

Cappuccio A, Latella M, Pelaia G, Menzella F, Pellegrini G, Marini MG (2017) Narrative medicine to evaluate the relationship between clinicians and patients living with severe asthma. Eur Respir J 50:PA2779

Carver C, Connor-Smith J (2010) Personality and coping. Annu Rev Psychol 61:679–704

Chiang T (2002) liking what you see: a documentary. Tor, New York

Dacher K, Paul E (2015) The science of inside out. The New York Times

Edwards C (2013) Mona Lisa goes bald in fight against cancer. https://www.thelocal.it/20131118/mona-lisa-goes-bald-in-fight-against-cancer

Gilbert P (2017) Shame and the vulnerable self in medical contexts: the compassionate solution. Med Humanit 43(4):211–217

Gopnik B (2009) Golden Seams: The Japanese Art of Mending Ceramics. Washington Post. http://www.washingtonpost.com/wp-dyn/content/article/2009/03/02/AR2009030202723.html

Ishizu T, Zeki S (2011) Toward a brain-based theory of beauty. PLoS One 6(7):e21852

Kleinman A (1988) The illness narratives: suffering, healing, and the human condition. Basic Books, New York

Launer J (2007) How not to be a doctor and other essays. Royal Society of Medicine Press, London

Lyons B, Dolezal L (2017) Shame, stigma and medicine. Med Humanit 43(4):208–210

Morris JS, Frith CD, Perrett DI et al (1996) A differential neural response in the human amygdala to fearful and happy facial expressions. Nature 383:812–815

Online Etymology Dictionary (n.d.) Vergogna. https://www.etimo.it/; shame: https://www.etymonline.com/word/shame

Plutchik R (1980a) A general psychoevolutionary theory of emotion. Academic, New York

Plutchik R (1980b) Emotion: theory, research, and experience, Theories of emotion 1, vol 1. Academic, New York

Plutchik R (1991) The Emotions. University Press of America, New York

Ray S (2017) A 'phantom barber' in India is stealing women's hair while they sleep. http://nationalpost.com/news/world/a-phantom-barber-in-india-is-stealing-womens-hair-while-they-sleep

Reale R, Marini MG, Gatti V (2017) Narrare il dolore per guarire. Il Sole 24 Ore Sanità

Rosman S (2004) Cancer and stigma: experience of patients with chemotherapy-induced alopecia. Patient Educ Couns 52(3):333–339

Theartstory Website. http://www.theartstory.org/artist-freud-lucian.htm

The Language of Spirituality in the Pathway of Care. Hope, Good Relationships, Setting Priority, Inner Space and Divine Space, If Any. Patients' Beliefs as a Starting Point to Engage in the Pathway of Care, Kindness and Compassion

10

As we know, NM, or better narrative healthcare, focuses on the interaction between patients and healthcare professionals, especially across moments of disease starting from when the disease first manifested. It gives voice and meanings to the way the patient lives the disease, how the disease and the patient are treated and to critical aspects that might suggest unmet needs in healthcare pathways (Greenhalgh and Hurwitz 1999). Narratives can be collected either through reflective writing (which itself elicits a therapeutic effect on the person writing) or through verbal testimony. The narratives we collect are authentic and do not belong to the fiction or literature. The aim of NM is to create an aligned relationship between carers and patients to allow patients to find the factors for coping, i.e. to master the stress induced by the disease, the rupture of a previous status of wellbeing, with its partial loss.

In over a decade of research at Fondazione ISTUD, our group has collected approximately 7000 narratives written by patients, family members, physicians and nurses: a collection of unique, authentic and precious testimonies of their personal inner experiences. Narratives can be presented in many ways, yet they can be mainly categorised under one of three categories: *chaotic*, when the patient is unaware of his/her situation and can be overwhelmed by feelings such as fear, anger, shame and sorrow; *restitution*, when the patient behaves similarly to a soldier submitting himself/herself to all medical prescription and is rewarded with the healing; and the *quest*, unfolding just as a hero's journey (Frank 1995). Patients have to overcome the hurdles brought by physical and mental illnesses to win a new style for living with the illness. Moreover, most stories follow a chronological narrating sequence starting with the 'becoming ill' phase, 'being ill' phase and then either as the 'getting worse' or 'getting better' phase, provided that the happy ending could be the resolution of a profound sorrow despite the serious body impairment might still be present.

We collect illness stories mainly through an *illness script*, using the universal, simple terms of NSM (Chap. 3) to express the prompts for narration. Avoiding the use of difficult words reduces misunderstanding of the prompts as well as

M. G. Marini, *Languages of Care in Narrative Medicine*,
https://doi.org/10.1007/978-3-319-94727-3_10

influencing what or how the person might narrate their story. To illustrate how this might occur, let us see a sample dialogue between a patient and an interviewer.

- Patient: 'They told me I had a cancer'.
- Interviewer: 'This must be a shock for you'.

In this case, despite the empathic interaction by the interviewer, there is an evident bias influencing the future contents of the patient's narration and the methodological design of what should have been a free/open-pattern interview.

The NSM evocative words as *think*, *feel*, *do* and *want* are powerful enough to explore the coping factors and the patient's spirituality realm. This is the last chapter, closing the book with a discussion and reflection on spirituality. My wish is to shift from a biomedical model to a biopsychosocial model and eventually to a biopsychosocial spiritual philosophy for an eco-friendly healthcare ecosystem. However, before approaching spirituality, as a step towards this 'intangible' asset, using the economist jargon, we do have to spend some words on coping. Inside coping, hidden there, someone can find a well-developed spirituality.

The Coping Factors

Another common classification of narratives is based on the evidence of any coping mechanisms, i.e. the mastering of a stressful event as an illness. In this chapter, we will see how many coping factors are woven also by the spirituality loom in a tapestry of wellbeing. Let us start from examining the main features which enable coping, with a zoom on consciousness, moving later to narrative spirituality, with a step-by-step approach.

As described by Carver, one main reference name on the study of coping, coping is generally enhanced when in the presence of five variables, agreeableness, openness, consciousness, extroversion and optimism, whereas denial, isolation and obsessive thought are generally associated to lack of coping (Carver et al. 1989). In performing field analysis of narrations, these aspects are the first to be sought for and are generally assessed by two independent blinded researchers. Direct experience has, however, taught us that coping after trauma of a disease is multifactorial and goes far beyond these elements and that many adaptation modes fall into religious and spiritual features.

Let us focus on some words of what consciousness is: the other factors can be easier to grasp. Consciousness, according to the neurologist Ramachandran, is composed of seven elements which are strongly interconnected.

1. Unity: Despite the millions of diversities of sensorial perception, we feel like one person. I am an individual, you are an individual, so not fractionable.
2. Continuity: it is related to the sense of time, we were children, now growing up, we have memories. Most of us live diachronically, and this is why our illness plot is structured from a past to a present and to a future.

3. Embodiment: Our home is our body. Body is a prime word of NSM. Generally, we do not perceive our body when it is ill, but we immediately perceive when something starts to ache, to give pain.
4. Privacy: Despite mirror neurons, I can feel compassion for your pain, but I cannot ever experience the same level of pain. That is, there is and will always be a divide between healthy people and sick people, and even among sick people, they can 'understand' the pain of the other person, but the privacy of the body does not allow to share the intensity of a mental of physical impairment.
5. Social embedding: We are all hardwired into a social context, entangled with the people of our family met during our life. This interaction is at the basis of the emotions and thoughts of the belonging, the boundaries, the inclusion and the exclusion in our microcosms and macrocosms.
6. Free will: We can decide among alternative courses of action, and we have brain area dedicated to the decision-making. Here is also the responsibility of choosing.
7. Self-awareness: A self that is not aware is an oxymoron. I am what I am, you are what you are (Ramachandran 2012).

Provocatively, even in the so-called craziness, when someone might feel to be 'Jesus Christ' or 'Julius Caesar', this is also a self-awareness, which, according to what Oliver Sacks has written in *Hallucination* (2013), has to be embraced and respected and not rejected and labelled.

These are the seven factors of consciousness: it is very interesting to discover how wide the meaning of this world is. Probably, there are more factors to define the infinity of consciousness.

Religion and Spirituality as Coping Factors for Recovery in Illness Time

Catholic religion is deeply rooted in daily life of Italian society despite an increasing detachment from religious tradition of younger generations towards 'free' spirituality.

Such religious and spiritual feeling often finds renewed momentum in times of adverse health conditions with mental distress. The investigation of religion and spirituality of patients' narratives provides semantic insight, yielding useful elements for building coping strategies (Carver 2010) to overcome trauma of diseases such as cancer or physical disability.

Spirituality and religiosity are common across illness. Some narratives feature more 'folkloristic' Catholic sentiment, invoking supernatural help from 'above' (blessings from God or local saints) to tread the care pathways (metaphorically described as biblical sufferings, e.g. the Passion of Christ) and receive the strength to overcome the fear of illness. Recurrent themes are also self-discipline in praying, therapeutic compliance and other duties (adoration of images) in hope of a restitution of physical or spiritual (earthy or afterlife) healing. Younger patients instead manifest spirituality expressing appreciation to others, enjoying the 'seize the day', freedom from worldly matters and living in a quest attitude towards the illness.

Religion

The use of religion from the narratives that we have analysed is based on two main topics: on one hand, the mind equation is 'disease as a passion of Christ'; on the other hand, it is a 'total unconditioned trust in the willing of God, where human power is not so much contemplated'.

The diagnostic path and the treatments are often mentioned in patients' narratives affected by serious disease as a 'Via Crucis' as a 'calvary' or as a cross to carry. For the psychological sorrow and the physical body pain, there is like a mirroring with the pain assigned to the last earthy journey to the figure of Jesus. Hence, patients use these metaphors to communicate the process they are going through, with the aim of being accepted and understood by the others, by family members or carers.

We analysed narratives of patients with cancer and religion in one cancer hospital of Northern Italy, and here are the results: 45% patients refer to religion; in particular they have indicated faith and prayer as a fundamental support in dealing with the illness *the Lord is my shepherd, I lack nothing… He is my support and my walking stick. I will not be afraid of the assault of even one thousand enemies*. Results from narratives show that, there is no need for healing (e.g. miracle), but there is an unconditioned trust to whatever will be is the will of God, *without finding any answer one accepts what our Lord has planned*, but God is also seen as the creator, the one whom we must be thankful for the gifts of life that are tasted daily, *my prayer, because I am a believer, a Catholic, and I realise the value of life, the Greatness of God, creator and redeemer.* Cancer led many patients to a rediscovery of faith and prayer, both as a guide in moments of difficulty and as a value to convey: *Thanks to you, cancer, I rediscovered, indeed enriched my faith; even in times of discomfort I know there is someone above, Prayer gives me so much serenity and peace*. A percentage of patients also *rediscover the cult of the ancestors* as protectors of their people: *To come to you and to talk to you maybe is what gives me a sense of tranquillity, peace, it only lasts when I'm next to you and it makes me feel a bit better.*

Perhaps this was an isolated cluster, belonging to a context which is basically quite rural and traditional: the use in these narratives of rituals such as prayers and the description of their saint images was very much present. Also, in another study, in patients with prostatic cancer, from their narratives religion comes to be 'an intangible asset'. One patient writes that he was before the altar dedicated to Saint Rita and in that moment *I heard a voice which was telling me I was not alone. In that moment, I decided to undergo the surgery.* One patient wrote *I cannot tell this to anybody because I'd be teased but on my mobile phone I've an APP with daily reading of the gospel and prayers.*

This evidences the fact that religion is, from a scientific, professional point of view and cultural point of view, considered to be a belief for poor and less instructed people. Even the most knowledgeable people sometimes have to hide their beliefs or desire of believing, in the name of a ratio barely capable of explaining the basic existential question of life and death. Religion, however, is a coping factor, embedded in optimism and consciousness with the free will component to choose whether to be or not to be a believer and the social embedding, which shows the beliefs with which we are in acquaintance since we are children.

The opposite reaction is to abandon religion when a serious disease occurs, especially in people who have been always practising the rituals and going to masses: reasons might be in the feeling betrayed by beliefs and rituals.

Spirituality

Spirituality is less controversial than Catholic religion (faith in a transcendental God) in Italy and is much more widely accepted and nourished.

In the UK, spirituality is an 'art/discipline/topic' within the NHS. We do not have anything similar in Italy; there is no official institution on spirituality in case of mental and physical impairment by our NHS, and I would add most of private healthcare services. Here, spirituality is left to the initiative of the individual, to patient associations, hospices and, alarmingly, to branches of complementary medicine very far from the current clinical settings and daily practice.

However, the need for spirituality in clinical setting is fundamental: we finally move beyond the biopsychosocial model to embrace the biopsychosocial spiritual philosophy. Some years ago, the European research on cancer and treatment came up with a questionnaire on spirituality. It failed. Why? I think it was in the structure itself; there was a question with a rating scale ranging from 1 to 5 which was asking patients *How much do you believe in a supreme force*? which I believe is not the right kind of question to investigating properly spirituality.

What is spirituality? As I said, I like to call it, a little ironically as an *intangible asset*. Words might be redundant or not adequate to explain it; however, narratives might be the key factors for endorsing spirituality. It can refer to those invisible but real qualities which shape a person or community, such as love, hope, peace and truth. In the NHS in the UK, everything has to be evidence-based, as well as in Italy: therefore, since religion looked and still is considered to be even more intangible by the scientific community, with the mystery of miracles and rituals, perhaps, spirituality was a smoother and less dogmatic 'tool' which entered in the places of care around the 1950s and 1960s. By doing this, some veiled beliefs on which religions are based, and banished by the scientific societies, are still brought in the hospitals.

In the figure, we see the flower of spirituality (Fig. 10.1), developed by the Durham University *spirituality and recovery* conference (Durham University Website n.d.) and adopted by the National Healthcare Service, in the UK.

The flower of spirituality depicted in the figure is not to be intended as a univocal definition and can be used for different purposes. At a first level, it can be used as a poster as food for thought to stimulate reflection among patients, carers and people, as well as establishing a common language. At a second level, it can be used to

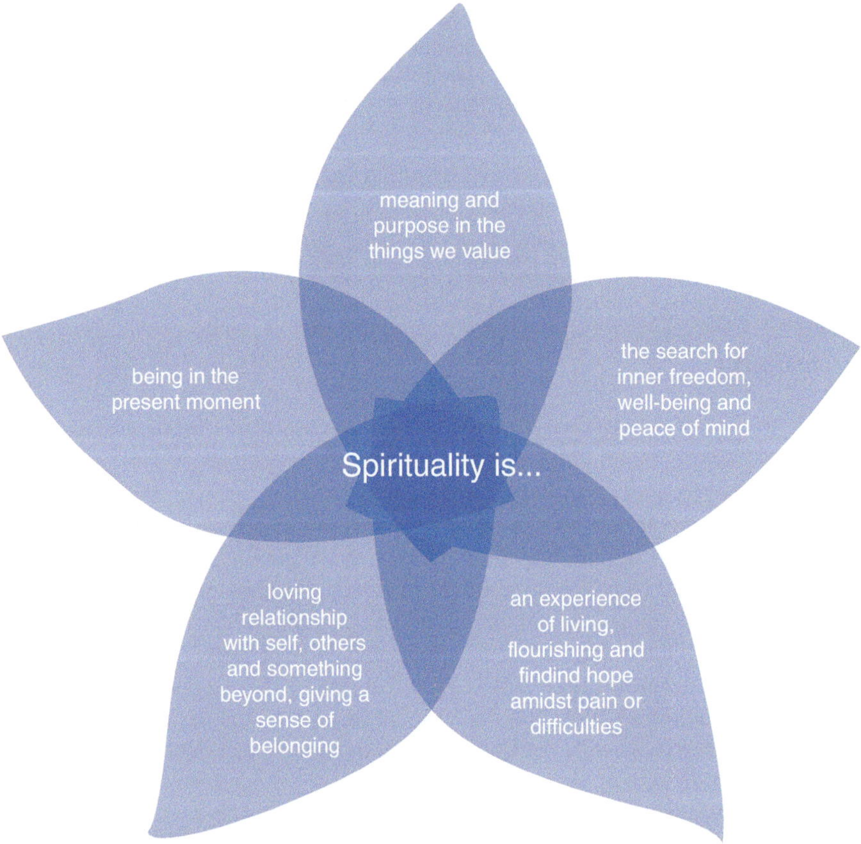

Fig. 10.1 The Spirituality Flower, used as a way to explore spiritual or religious needs

reflect on the single petals and definitions in search of one's own answer. There is a third level of action: the flower is empty so that everyone is able to fill in the five petals with the characteristics of human being.

First Petal: Loving Relationship

In Italy, spirituality is very much associated to the petal of *loving relationships* and their quality: the surrounding family is something 'sacred', much more than in other cultures. In the experience of NM, this clearly emerged from a recent Italian-Australian study on patients affected by colon cancer and who underwent ostomy surgery (Reale et al. 2017). When participants were asked 'The people you would like at your side…', 80% of Italian patients (out of 152 Italian patients) answered family members, while 80% (out of 76) of the Australian patients mentioned 'nobody' or 'healthcare professionals'. Even if these data are not significant, they are evidence of the cultural feeling of belonging to the family among Italian people as well as a scarce independence and huge interdependency.

In agreement with this cultural imprint, a study on 123 patients affected by multiple sclerosis evidenced that those who had a solid family to support them or who were able to develop ties in a new family or building new friendship were also those who were able to achieve a better quality of life and live a partial serene life.

The patients' associations are an incredible meeting point to donate hope and to take hope and to exchange experience, even in a light mood. Many narratives of patients were very 'romantic', much dedicated to protect the other *healthy* people so that they do not have to suffer for the disease of the one who is ill. There are indeed narratives of caregivers who write about protection and love as main reason for staying close to the patients. On the other hand, stories also tell about tiredness and rage of the family members, evident because they feel somewhat powerless in front of the illness.

Second Petal: Being in the Present Moment

From these patients, we learn also the importance of being able to enjoy the small things of the here and now daily life, as *seizing the day, a smile, a gesture of kindness, are so important, before the illness I was not able to notice them, but I do now, being able to do a flight of stairs, learning to listen to the limits of my body*. The future is not given for granted. Having the skills to stay in the here and now makes patients happier and less worried in the future.

From a patient with COPD, we learn: *I cannot walk as fast as the others. I enjoy the landscape, moment by moment, as I have never seen it so beautiful before when I was always in a rush.*

Third Petal: Meaning and Purpose of the Things We Value

Setting or discovering new values is something very important in all patients who are coping: it is like moving from the same old styles and beliefs to something more meaningful and important: *before I was taken by the commitment to my job and by so many small things that risked drifting me away from the people I love*. Here, we are talking about discovering, identifying and fixing new priorities once an illness or a new condition has entered in our life.

An example of reorganising priorities that are meaningful can be seen in narratives of women in fertile age who were diagnosed with cancer and who were offered the possibility to preserve their fertility by cryoconservation of their oocytes to become mother in the future before undergoing traditional protocols of chemotherapy and radiotherapy.

"After the surprise in seeing ovarian function tests heavily altered, I have been busy finding a way to" run to shelter *"in the hope of having a pregnancy in the future"; "Protect my dream... The joy of being a mother... Have finally something*

eternal. Love for a Son"; "I was 34 years old and we were hoping for a baby… instead we found the tumor, strongly hormonal, which therefore required long-term care that involved chemical menopause for 5 years".

Maternity for me is the meaning of life. A woman encloses everything in her baby. Love, strength, values. Everything. And a part of themselves. The hope is that when I try motherhood, everything will be good, that the ovaries react well to fertilisation and then the embryo will survive. Obviously, I'm scared to think something can go wrong but I'll try to be afraid of them;

To be honest, before diagnosis, maternity was something that made me anxious, and I had put it in "a closet" and I was surprised to want to open that closet, not wanting to give up the chance to give birth, not wanting to allow the cancer sweep this joy away.

'Having a child is not a fancy, and I decided that running the risk was worth it.

Through these lines, we become aware of how the preservation of fertility is meaningful for these women. Moreover, the future perspective of having a baby, in most of the cases, became a key element for enduring throughout the burden of anticancer treatments.

The importance of maternity and paternity also emerges from a study of families going through the experience of a premature birth (Marini et al. 2017) and the risk their little, new born could not survive.

During neonatal intensive therapy, *I remember living in a strange state of mind, like in a limbo where everything was flowing around, but it did not touch me, I had to go to my girls, I was out of the hospital; Pain, fear, sadness, anxiety. You do not know if you'll see your daughter. You don't know why access to the room is closed: is there a problem with your child or with someone else? You live with fear; Everyone had trouble dealing with me: I was not reacting, I was always crying, I was sad, I was afraid I'd lose my little girl, my partner never left me alone, while others around tried to give me comforting words, but during those days I was not able to accept them.*

I was overwhelmed by sorrow, it surrounded me like a tornado and dragged me away, spinning my thoughts and emotions. It's not right, it should not go this way. I should be the one attached to those machines, with all those needles, not you, so small, why do you have to suffer so much, why it is so difficult for us to become a family, why are we put through this further test.

As we can see from these recurrences in narratives, there is a huge despair, no faith and a huge depression often due to guilty feeling of being not capable to become a good mother. However, as time goes by, the recovery comes:

After the first 40 days, we began to believe that we could make it. We could bring our baby back home. The hope of improvements slowly grew on us day by day; I started to feel better… in the sense of being more… when my daughter finally started to stick to her breast …and it all started to look more "normal";

What we experienced has certainly made me stronger, and I really feel that way. I've learned that sometimes you just have to wait and it's all over…; I learned so much: my life has become enriched, I grew up, matured. I'm happy, I learned what's important in life and what's not; I learned to give the right weight to things, I received so much affection

Partners are facing together the risk of death of their babies, not left alone but supported by wonderful clinicians who try to do their very best with poor resources: here, spirituality lies in the bonds between healthcare providers and the parents. After such experience, full of sorrow and pain as we have seen, women and men come out, in most of the cases, stronger and happier.

Fourth Petal: Inner Freedom and Wellbeing and Peace

Another consideration to spirituality is left to this 'difficult' petal of the flower of spirituality: *inner freedom and wellbeing.* While the three petals of above were very much present in the narratives, there is a poor attitude to dedicate to oneself, to find an inner peace and freedom. Personally, I was quite stunned from the results of the analysis the narratives under this profile. Probably in Italy, there is a huge devotion to family, boundaries, babies, children, partners, quite in a romantic way.

However, the fourth petal, which might come from contemplation, concentration, self-dialogue towards a peace of mind, is still rare and to be empowered. There is a lack of culture on this in our country. Only spot practices are spread to bring relief, mainly in patients who live with cancer and are terminally ill in hospices.

However, let's try to get out some voices of patients… who are moving searching for wellbeing and peace… here is the statement of a girl with a cancer who underwent in the fertility program:

I am much stronger and aware of my strength, my emotional resources. I want to be comfortable and surround myself with positive people. Despite the therapeutic path, I carry out a normal life, I go out more than before and I have much more appreciation for happy moments and people who support and surround me;

It is a life still to discover and build a piece at a time, but with a smile and courage in the DNA. I need normality and equanimity that for too long I didn't have, I need to meditate and to feel good about myself and who I'm close to;

Fifth Petal: Flourishing and Finding Hope

Here, there is an intertwined approach between religion and spirituality. Since hope is 'to think, to feel that something good can happen in a short time or in a long time (Oxforddictionaries Website n.d.), well, of these words belongs to NSM, psychologists define this emotion as belonging to all humankind, albeit is very much related to the context of living.

Optimism is more related to rational thought, to cognitive process than to a deep inspired emotion. In the philosophical literature, it has been suggested that hope may mediate major life events, as illness and main human relationships, while optimism may mediate more routine or minor problems. Perhaps more hopeful individuals, as compared to optimists, can cope better with more stressful life events and are thus less susceptible to illness.

When patients are seriously ill, it is self-evident that hope becomes a tool for a better coping with the current condition of the disease, as well as optimism which is indicated by Carver being one of the five key factors for coping together with agreeableness, openness, responsibility and awareness (Carver et al. 1989). While responsibility and awareness are 'virtues' in the mainstream of our modern society, being kind to others and agreeableness have only been investigated in recent years (Ballatt and Campling 2011) and associated to better health outcomes.

Optimism can be very much related to hope since it has to do with a positive emotion, based on 'trust of the future': however, hope does not count on probabilities but on an unconditioned trust (Kalnbach and Lantz 1997).

Clinicians have quite an ambiguous reaction about the possibility of giving or not hope to patients. On one hand, their duty is to clearly inform patients about their conditions and even about their survival times. In some countries, this is regulated by laws and represents an achievement of 'civilised society' which review the paternalistic role of the doctor of when the physician perhaps omitted the truth to the patient in the sake of the patient's own good).

On the other, in the attempt of being very straight and sincere with their patients basing prognosis on scientific evidence, doctors may take out hope of a longer survival and interfere with the patient's coping mechanisms and free will of consciousness. In fact, EBM is based on averages in a given population and does not predict individual outcome; as some narrations testify, it is not rare to read about patients with advanced-stage cancer who 'surprise' their doctors and live longer beyond the statistical forecasts.

Hope is very important to coping needed to support one's inner resources. As written in one of the narratives we received, one day a cancer patient returning to the hospital was welcomed by a young doctor with the very awkward statement *So, you're still alive!*. The sentence pronounced by this physician was considered similar to a capital execution and felt like a cold shower indeed for the patient. The patient was so stunned that he did not even reply. Instead, he wrote to us *she wanted to see me buried, already in the grave*. In his narrative, he writes that he fell in depression, having no more energy to fight the illness. He was pushed far away from the coping attitude. Words can be poison or medicine; here, the words of this young lady doctor killed the patient's hope.

However, before blaming this deed, let us try to consider why she, along with other doctors, was so much surprised to see this patient still alive: based on figures of EBM, he was an outlier, an oddity: this patient caused a 'black swan effect' as well explained by Nicholas Thaleb, essayist, scholar, philosopher and statistician. What is a 'black swan effect'? It means the extreme impact of certain kinds of rare and unpredictable events, the outliers related to the human tendency, to retrospectively find simplistic explanations for these events (Thaleb 2007). The term 'black swan' comes from a Latin expression: its oldest reference is by the poet Juvenal that *a good person is as rare as a black swan* (*rara avis in terris nigroque simillima cygno*) (Juvenal, 2nd-century AD n.d.)). It is a statement that describes the impossibility of the existence of a black swan, deriving from the old-world presumption that 'all swans must be white' because all historical records of swans reported that they had white feathers. No hope for a black swan however there are many much, especially in the Austral hemisphere. Back to the clinic, the mistake lies in the professional education of some doctors who consider EBM as a dogma, which provides undeniable trues, *all the swans are white*, whereas, EBM can only provide probabilities, and Thaleb knows it because he is not only a philosopher but a statistician as well, which do not cover the opacity of the real world. Some patients can be black swans as hopefully for our 'long-term survivor' who was welcomed by the sentence *So, you're still alive*.

Hopefully, there are very competent doctors who are able to inform patients about their objective situations, providing them, without lying, the probabilities of a possible healing or becoming chronic or dying which belong—most often—to population data and not to the single case: and, furthermore, they are able also to say that, by the way, hope is always there, because just on the next day a new technology might be discovered or some other deus ex machina can come down from the sky, with the proper solution to the real problem.

Hope is essential for people who are coping with serious and prolonged psychological stress; however, hope is not a perpetually self-renewing resource because it has ups and downs, and therefore, it has to be empowered by the system in which the patients live. Family members, carers are called to provide this feeling that has the tremendous power to manage uncertainties, the oddities, and it is proven that it produces better health outcomes.

NM is a basic tool for searching the presence of hope and other coping factors for establishing a trustful and positive relationship with the patients, curers and family members.

"*Since the greatest hope, when embarking on this path, is to be able, in the end, to resume normal life…*" Patients' hope sometimes falls into the trap of 'resuming a normal life, the life as it was before'. The real adventure is the hope, to be able to change the lifestyle when living with a chronic disease in a quest mode, so to broaden that inner freedom and peace of the fourth petal. This, forgetting the absolute basic need of being 'normal'.

While you read this page, I ask you to go to YouTube and listen to a song that speaks about the impossibility of catching the future: *Que sera sera, whatever will be, will be*.

Here the lyrics of this song:

When I was just a little girl
I asked my mother
What will I be
Will I be pretty
Will I be rich
Here's what she said to me
Que sera, sera
Whatever will be, will be
The future's not ours to see
Que sera, sera
What will be, will be

When I grew up and fell in love
I asked my sweetheart
What lies ahead
Will we have rainbows
Day after day
Here's what my sweetheart said
Que sera, sera
Whatever will be, will be
The future's not ours to see
Que sera, sera
What will be, will be
Now I have Children of my own
They ask their mother
What will I be
Will I be handsome
Will I be rich
I tell them tenderly
Que sera, sera
Whatever will be, will be
The future's not ours to see
Que sera, sera
What will be, will be
Que Sera, Sera

A very spiritual coping factor is agreeableness, kindness, that I consider mainly embedded in the first petal of the blue flower of loving/caring relationship. I was very pleased to learn that there were managers and consultants for the healthcare service but also for the private companies who were teaching the art of kindness and that there is a difference between intelligent and study kindness as well. Here, an etymological help: kind—which is a prime of the natural semantic metalanguage—comes from kinship, which means brotherhood, belonging to, and recalls the concept of cooperation. We have a similarity in Italian for which 'gentilezza'—kindness, which comes from the Latin 'gens' (Online Etymology Dictionary n.d.), the 'ancestry' or also the 'family'. It means the ties to a group of people. To be kind means to belong to a clan.

Think Kind: Intelligent Kindness—Interview to John Ballatt

We host an interview to John Ballatt, author of the book *Intelligent Kindness: Reforming the Culture of Healthcare*, with Penelope Campling (Ballatt and Campling 2011).

John began his career in democratic therapeutic communities and then moved on to training and managing social workers, becoming a senior manager in the UK NHS. He was in charge of managing services and leading strategic organisational change. He now works independently to support individuals, teams and organisations in health and social care.

MGM. How did you get to rediscover the concept of kindness, which somehow reminds us of 'an ancient forgotten style'?

JB. It's a bit complicated. Several years ago, there were a number of scandals showing shocking neglect and abuse in a number of settings in the UK NHS. Penelope Campling (co-author of *Intelligent Kindness: Reforming the Culture of Healthcare*) and I were concerned about the understandable reaction. Calls to improve systems, to demand compassion from staff, to ensure cultures of compassion, seemed to us to fail to think about what such cultures entailed and what is needed to sustain compassion. In particular, there was a dangerous failure to think about the nature of, and factors influencing, clinician-patient and clinician-clinician relationships, especially factors relating to the dynamics of human groups.

We searched for ways to think about this. The concept of 'kinship' took us back to the evolutionary and social roots of belonging, cooperation, altruism and compassion. In this context, 'kindness' is an expression of such collective belonging, a 'feeling realisation' that 'your wellbeing is also my wellbeing'. Kindness has, of course, been rather denigrated over recent centuries, relegated to a private, sentimental, soft, domain—certainly not the domain of professionalism. But it offers a crucial perspective on the nature of a culture of cooperation and compassion.

Kinship is also a useful thing to think about because it can also go very wrong. Within kinship groups, and between such groups, conflict, rejection, abuse and discrimination can emerge all too readily. Considering the dynamics of kinship can help us go beyond a simple *demand* for compassion or kindness, to understand the factors that nurture or undermine it. A range of personal, group and contextual factors influences the nature of relationships between people, within the 'family' or reaching out inclusively to 'the other'. These factors can be thought about and addressed in attempting to create and sustain the organisational culture that will deliver effective and compassionate care.

MGM. What is the main difference between intelligent kindness and a normal kindness?

JB. Simple kindness is not enough. We must resist the temptation to move someone with broken bones to a more comfortable place. Soldiers liberating concentration camps after the Holocaust kindly shared their rations with starving prisoners—whose ability to digest was so damaged that many died. The concept of intelligent kindness suggests that all healthcare is relational but stresses the need to exercise both 'technical/professional' and 'emotional/social' intelligence in the caring relationship. Intelligent kindness also involves an understanding of the psychological and emotional factors in the individual, the group and the wider system that require attention to ensure effective, compassionate care.

The patient and the clinical team have to manage the anxiety, pain and disgust that are so often part of experiencing and treating illness and ill-being. They have to be able do this as individuals and as teams and groups. We believe that expecting the individual to manage herself so as to be effective and compassionate is not enough. Though practicing mindfulness or meditation might help that individual, it is through addressing the conditions and dynamics of the wider system that a culture of intelligent kindness can grow. Such a culture sustains its members in working together compassionately, efficiently and effectively. We like your idea of ecological healthcare. I think we both recognise that it is in a system, a culture, that good practice emerges, nourished by the right awareness, values, behaviour and conditions. This is as true of an orchestra or a football team as it is of a healthcare team. All are relational systems, which can be helped to strengthen mutual attentiveness, attunement, trust and effective collaboration. Intelligent kindness is not a commodity or a tool. It is a way of thinking about, developing and participating effectively in a culture that has its roots in our evolutionary history of collaboration and solidarity—our positive kinship.

MGM. Why is kindness so difficult to achieve in the setting of care, paradoxically, since fragile patients are those that need it most?

JB. However skilled and professional the clinicians, they and the patient have to manage the profound anxiety involved in meeting illness and ill-being. They have to resist the temptation to turn away, to deny, to panic. This is as much, if not more, unconscious as conscious, in both patient and clinician. Ignoring or managing this anxiety badly can blind us, distort and cut the human connections between clinicians—with each other and with patients. Anxiety can generate competition, hostility and exclusion. It can cloud the mental space necessary to stay attentive, to be moved, to manage emotions, relationships and clinical skills properly. Anxiety is a factor for individuals, teams and wider systems.

One effect of pervasive anxiety is that organisations can become perverse, as Susan Long notes in her work. In such organisations people, especially leaders, use others as *means to ends*, as instruments to satisfy their own needs or reduce *their* anxiety. As in individual perversion, in such manipulative and demanding cultures, there is a turning of a blind eye, a both wilful and unconscious denial of the cost to the other, of the problems they encounter in meeting the demands, of what is involved in doing their work well. Inevitably, care suffers in healthcare organisations that behave like this.

MGM. What are the causes of this pervasive anxiety in healthcare?

JB. Well, I've mentioned the nature of illness and ill-being. But there is a range of other factors. Many of them are to some degree unavoidable in the modern healthcare organisation, but all, if not managed intelligently, can have dangerous side-effects that undermine effective, compassionate care.

The sheer scale of need and the complex range of skills and resources in healthcare mean that some degree of industrialisation, of systematisation, is inevitable. Working to meet outcome or performance targets, to be efficient, is also unavoidable to some extent. There can also be competition between organisations. At their worst, how these factors are managed can provoke enormous anxiety and distort the human system of healthcare. Leaders may be anxious that their services meet difficult targets, manage limited resources, deliver efficiency, survive. Staff can be drawn in to this anxiety, distracted from the patient and each other, looking over their shoulders to provide data, numbers, measurable outcomes, to try to manage their leaders' anxiety, to deliver for them, to meet *their* needs.

There is always the danger that staff become parts of a machine, delivering fragmented procedures by rote, prevented from thinking and using their imaginations, missing the complexity of the patient. There is no doubt, for example, that check lists can be very helpful in ensuring important basics are done, but their true value is to release space for the attentiveness, creative thinking, feeling and collaboration of the clinical team. Often the procedure or check list is used *instead of* such intelligent practice.

The patients themselves can become products of production-line process, experiencing a fragmented and impersonal journey, measured in numbers and as recipients of assorted commodities. When their needs make meeting targets difficult, they may even become inconveniences! Caught between management and patients, healthcare professionals can become anxious, enraged or grimly despairing—or all these things.

Intelligent kindness requires us to consider minimizing all these factors, and, where they are still necessary, managing them with sensitivity to their potential damage to the thinking, feeling and relationships involved in healthcare. Leaders, especially, but all staff, need help to recognise and manage anxiety and to think about whether it is being healthily contained and how it is influencing culture and practice for the organisation and its members.

MGM. Do you think that kindness is a practice that can be learnt? Do you think that it could reform the healthcare system?

JB. Just as our experience of early relationships can nourish or damage our ability to develop, relate to others, to concentrate, to think, so kindness of the sort we are talking about it can be nourished, and it can emerge from the quality of our experience of the people and culture in which we work. If that ecosystem is properly managed, with the right understanding of what the collaborative task is, then that can promote intelligent kindness. This can be very simple. If you work with others who can bear in mind the pain of illness and death, who can discuss and respond to each other's vulnerability to stress, tiredness and anxiety, then you are likely to develop practice that is based in intelligent kindness.

But, in a time of technical knowledge and skills, it is vital we recognise and teach that their true effectiveness depends on these skills being delivered within a healthy and creative working relationship—with colleague and patient. Attention driven by the kindness that emerges from a sense of kinship (from being 'of a kind' and 'in it together') promotes attunement, trust, a therapeutic alliance and better clinical outcomes. We need to unite the technical and the relational in our teaching, training and language of professional healthcare.

Continuous education and professional reflection is vital. Exposing clinicians (and managers) to authentic narratives—about patients and about staff experience—can promote kindness, empathy and relational skill. It is most powerful when such stories are delivered face to face, though stories on the page can help.

A range of reflective practice approaches, for individuals, teams and organisations, can help. It is concerning that such practice is now squeezed out, almost as a luxury. We also need to recognise that supervisors and mentors of clinical staff need, themselves, support to understand and value the psychological, emotional and the relational aspects of professional work.

MGM. What do you do when you have to teach evidence-based doctors? When can EBM be defined more as an ideology than a science?

JB. There can be an almost Aspergers-like failure or resistance to integrating the psychological, the relational, with the technical, the procedural. I think we need to confront this head-on. Evidence is important. But as scientists, people who cling rigidly to a narrow, 'hard-evidence', technical perspective need to recognise that evidence, like all scientific knowledge, is proved wrong or replaced, changes or develops, over time. Good scientists are always attentive to anomaly, contradictory evidence, special circumstances—and that requires psychological openness. Secondly, I would also refer to the evidence that supports the benefit, in terms of effectiveness outcomes of care and efficiency, of attending to the quality of the relationship between clinician/services and patients. I would point out the enormous range of research about how human beings, groups and wider social systems survive, thrive, cooperate and succeed (or not).

There must be a firm assertion of the integrated technical and relational nature of healthcare practice at all levels. This goes further than semi-optional 'communication skills' training to a clear expectation that all practitioners need to recognise the equally important responsibility to manage themselves and their relationships, alongside any technical learning. In the end, though, there is a strong argument for leaders, especially, but all staff in reality, concentrating on caring for the caregivers, by addressing the conditions in which they work, recognising their experience and openly valuing work to realise intelligent kindness. Just as in any ecosystem, attentive work on such conditions leads to the emergence of healthy developments.

Interestingly, Dr. Ballatt concludes the interview with the definition of healthcare ecosystem, the same words that I used in the preface and across the chapters of this book. In this discussion of languages of care, we have dared to span from EBM and NM to other aspects as linguistic, humanities, mythology, music, sounds, colours, architecture, emotions, consciousness, neuroscience and spirituality. Yet, there are many more languages of care that I have not mentioned, on which I could have been writing pages as body language, scents, flowers, foods, beyond drugs and procedures.

I focused my attention on the 65 primes of the NSM and discovered that even the term *kind* is among those ancestral words that helped our evolution, contributing by transmitting the concept of 'grouping'. If competition was necessary for mere survival, cooperation though grouping allowed us to become thriving and wealthy.

Compassion is related to kindness, and it works as a healer (Davidsons 2013): in a study on volunteers on compassion meditation, people after a baseline fMRI of the brain to measure the amygdala activity were asked to concentrate on a loved one at a time in her life when she was suffering. With this image in mind, people were asked to concentrate on the wish that her suffering end, silently repeating a phrase as 'May you be free from suffering, may you experience joy and ease'. After doing this for a loved one, you expand your circle of compassion little by little, to yourself, then to someone you recognise but do not really know. Using online instructions, this lasted for 2 weeks, 30 min each day of compassion meditation. The other group of people, after a baseline fMRI of the brain to measure the amygdala activity, were told to visualise the suffering, but they were told to reframe which is a cognitive approach through which one can see that the suffering might not be as extreme as other forms of suffering and that it could end up in a good way. The cognitive reappraisal group received instruction online, also for 30 min of reframing a day for 2 weeks. At the end of the 2-week training, Davidson and his group recorded the brain activity through MRI, while all volunteers were looking at images of suffering: participants in the 'compassion meditation' group showed striking changes in brain function, particularly in the amygdala; they tended to show less activation, that means less fear, in response to images of suffering. In people who underwent training in cognitive appraisal, amygdala activity, when pictures of sorrow were displayed, was just high as before the training. Then the same two groups of people were challenged by doing something generous for unknown people: the people who practised compassion meditation were spending 38% more money than the 'cognitive reframing group'. This has confirmed what seen at the brain fMRI scans that not only the amygdala is deactivated but also the connectivity between the brain prefrontal cortex and the brain areas where motivation and reward are processed, with consequent release of dopamine, the neurotransmitter of resiliency and planning, and serotonin which is the gold antidepressive inner agent in the group who practised compassion meditation. This is why kindness and compassion can be considered as healers.

I hope that by reading this book there will be more interdisciplinary cooperation, less walls between the EBM and the other humanistic approaches. Neuroscience is proving how our brain and body are impacted by the words we use or we do not use, the beauty we see or we do not see, the hope we have or we do not have. Neuroplasticity is a tangible hope to bring wellbeing and more joy in our lives and in places of care, where physical pain and sorrows might be dominant. Beliefs on the link between human nature, behaviour and wellbeing that are used to be considered suppositions or wives' tales are now being proved through scientific evidence. We are called now to connect precision medicine with spirituality, target medicine, with target words and target gestures. It shall not take years; the time is now for showing the multiple intelligences of which we are gifted as human being: the logical one, the emotional one, the body postural one, the musical one, the visual one, the artistical one. Intelligence is not fix neither unique.

The challenge is to find the balance among these intelligences, as the woman looking at her scale, concentrated, not distracted by the noise of the outside environment to find, for each one of us, our unique and individual point of balance.

Practice Time

Coping factors: What do you think about the one mentioned by Carver? Are there more? What do you think about their use?

Which of the coping factors do you use in stressful situations?

Consider consciousness and its seven components, which thoughts and feeling do these evoke? Do you think that there could be more? Less?

Consider free will as a coping factor, which are your thoughts about it?

And what do think about social embedding?

Have you ever thought about a possible difference between religion and spirituality? How do you envision religion? How do you envision spirituality?

Take the five-petaled blue flower of spirituality and imagine it empty. Would you like to try to write your personal five issues on spirituality (You may even change the flower and pick a daisy). Would you like to try it with the people around you (carers, patients, colleagues, friends….)?

Intelligent kindness: What do you think about this concept?

Would you like try to think to an act of intelligent kindness for yourself? And for your group?

And now, only if you really wish, read some oddities: the following neologisms are definitions from the Dictionary of Perceptible Joys (Dictionaryofperceptiblejoys Website n.d.):

SOKÄCH

The pleasure of waking up on a weekend morning, by the device of your own internal clock, refreshed with peace of mind for there is no race against time or traffic, the apprehension of deadlines non-existent or postponed, the possibility of doing nearly absolutely nothing attainable—pajamas on all day, coffee tasting more like honey than a drug, eating whilst sitting down, a bygone concept on any other day of the week—able to make plans for the rest of your day that only revolve around you and your simplest desires.

FAMIGLISTIMO

The opulence that no fame or fortune can afford you when you're surrounded by your dearest ones, by choice or by blood, something simmering, boiling, or frying on the fire, its steam emanating the preamble of the expected cuisine, plates and glassware exchanged every which way, attempting to squeeze in just another placemat, just another chair, just another million laughs—the more faces the more exuberance, the more crumbs the more cheer, the more bustle the more hilarity—pupils widened, mouths salivating, stomachs growling, and hearts most gratified to be included.

GNOMESHGH

The tenderness you feel when someone shares an idea, a photo, a song, a passage etc., *accompanied by a note that conveys that you were the face that came to the forefront of his mind when this thing first occupied his senses—that you've organically nestled your way into this other person's cortices so that he no longer just sees remote objects in time and space, but rather a set of associations that lead back to you—recovering you once again from the self-inflicted fallacy of aloneness.*

POLYDEXURY

The comfort of knowing there is an individual out there, maybe near, maybe far, but someone whose chronicle is as close to your own—though seen through a different set of eyes and perhaps even retold with biased and distorted memories, the unique essence of the narrative is shared with this one person and for as long as (s)he is alive (s)he can fill the void left by a "you had to be there" without having to fabricate a duplicated memory, knowing exactly the foundation upon which you now act for (s)he too had a stake in that backbone.

PIACERANCE

The experience of hearing a song for the very first time that stops you in your tracks, your ears perked to the immaculate composite of lyrics, melody, harmony, and chord changes as if each constituent part was given life with you and your narrative in mind, and now eternally stored in your medial pre-frontal cortex so that years from now when you walk into a coffee shop and hear it again, you will immediately see the associated person, place or memory of your past self in your mind's eye, autobiographical details more vivid than ever.

Could we think that these perceptible joys are related to spirituality?
And what about inventing new words, as the children do, to express how we feel? Could it be our unique language of care?

References

Ballatt J, Campling P (2011) Unsettling times. In Intelligent kindness: reforming the culture of healthcare. RCPsych Publications, p 125–138

Carver CS (2010) Personality and coping. Annu Rev Psychol 61:679–670

Carver CS, Scheier MF, Weintraub JK (1989) Assessing coping strategies: a theoretically based approach. J Pers Soc Psychol 56(2):267–283

Davidsons RJ (2013) The emotional life or our brain. Hodder & Stoughton, London

Dictionaryofperceptiblejoys Website. http://dictionaryofperceptiblejoys.tumblr.com/

Durham University Website. https://www.dur.ac.uk/dialogue/signposts/staff/?itemno=30081

Frank AW (1995) The wounded storyteller: body, illness, and ethics. University of Chicago Press, Chicago

Greenhalgh T, Hurwitz B (1999) Narrative based medicine in an evidence based world. BMJ 318(7179):323–325

Juvenal, 2nd-century AD

Kalnbach LR, Lantz BM (1997) The effects of optimism and willingness to trust on work-related attitudes and behaviors: an application to the commercial vehicle industry. MPC Publications

Marini MG, Chesi P, Bruscagnin M, Ceccatelli M, Ruzzon E (2017) Digits and narratives of the experience of Italian families facing premature births. J Matern Fetal Neonatal Med 22:1–7

Online Etymology Dictionary (n.d.) Gentile: https://www.etimo.it/?term=gentile

Oxforddictionaries Website. https://en.oxforddictionaries.com/definition/hope

Ramachandran VS (2012) The tell-tale brain: unlocking the mystery of human nature. Windmill Books

Reale R, Marini MG, Gatti V (2017) Narrare il dolore per guarire. Il Sole 24 Ore Sanità

Sacks O (2013) Hallucinations. Optom Vis Sci 90(4):e124–e125

Thaleb N (2007) The black swan: the impact of the highly improbable. Random House, New York

Glossary[1]

Art therapy A therapeutic approach based on the idea that the creating process supports reparation and recovery could be defined as a form of non-verbal communication of thoughts and feelings: it can help individuals in creating meaning and achieving insight, finding relief from overpowering emotions or trauma, resolving conflicts and problems and reaching an increased sense of wellbeing. The approach is grounded on the belief that people have the capacity to express themselves creatively and that the most important thing is the therapeutic process rather than its product—so the therapist's focus is not on the aesthetic merits of art making but on the therapeutic needs of the person to express him- or herself. What is important is the person's involvement in the work, choosing and initiating helpful art activities (in which some authors include also the blog therapy), assisting the person in finding meaning in the creative process and facilitating the sharing of the experience of image-making with the therapist.

Body It is a prime of the Natural Semantic Metalanguage, a concept that is innately understood, but cannot be expressed in simpler terms, and like other semantic primes (or semantic primitives) represents words or phrases that are learned through practice but cannot be defined concretely. It is universal, because it can be translated literally into any known language and retain its semantic representation (Wierzbicka 1996).

Body language The communication without words is anything someone does to which someone else assigns meaning. Not all of the 'signals' a person sends are intentional, and often they are 'not picked up' or misinterpreted.

Non-verbal behaviour is complex, subtle and multichannel. The sender of the message may be aware or unaware of the non-verbal signals he or she sends. Indeed, receivers may not always be aware of the messages they are actually picking up. For instance, most people are not aware of their pupil dilations, nor are observers aware

[1] The purpose of this glossary is to provide the reader further insight into concepts frequently encountered and investigated in this book, defining them in a systematic and referenced manner.

It is presented in alphabetical order and includes the reference to resources used to create this glossary and a list of further readings.

M. G. Marini, *Languages of Care in Narrative Medicine*,
https://doi.org/10.1007/978-3-319-94727-3

that they can on specific occasions respond positively to dilated pupils (when people are sexually aroused).

We are all 'people watchers' and amateur psychologists, partly because we have to be. In every aspect of communication, we need to observe others carefully to try to understand better what they are feeling as well as (really) saying.

Non-verbal communication is a more primitive and often a more powerful means of communication than verbal one. Body language has a clear biological base and is a product of evolutionary development. Animals touch, smell, gesture and point to each other, and so do we. Consequently, the way we sit, hold a cigarette, smile and shake hands could also be interpreted and read into to reveal both the inner state of mind and social status.

Often non-verbal cues can stress, underline or exaggerate the meaning of the verbal message. But non-verbal cues can also negate verbal cues, such as in contradictory signal where words give one message while voice and expression another.

The doctor-patient approach has been studied in medical and anthropological terms, and the consultation is considered the central moment in the relationship; at the beginning of a consultation in a typical doctor-patient office encounter, a patient arrives with ideas, concerns and expectations which they expect to be discussed and understood. Within communication skills in general, body language becomes extremely important when establishing this relationship.

Observational studies investigated verbal and non-verbal behaviour in the context of patient perceptions, and the results suggest that patients may respond to non-verbal behaviours more than to traditional verbal behaviours. Body language can include at one level posture, active listening, facial expression, but at a wider level, it also includes the arrangement of the room, how the doctor and patient are oriented to each other (sitting, lying or standing), how the doctor is dressed and on a ward round, who the consultant addresses, whether the patient is given time to speak, whether the patient is allowed to have an explanation of what is being discussed between members of the team and so on (Woodhead et al. 2015).

Brain In modern Western medicine, the brain is the most important organ, acting as a command centre for the human nervous system. It is the organ that controls all functions of the body, interprets information from the outside world, receives input from the sensory organs, sends output to the muscles and embodies the essence of the mind and soul. It assembles the messages in a way that has meaning for us and can store that information in our memory.

The brain controls our thoughts, memory and speech, movement of the arms and legs and the function of many organs within our body.

Intelligence, creativity, emotion and memory are a few of the many things governed by the brain. It is divided into two hemispheres, left and right, connected by a bundle of nerve fibres called the *corpus callosum*. Still, there are some important differences between these areas. The left brain contains regions involved in speech and language as the Broca's area and Wernicke's area and is also associated with mathematical calculation and fact retrieval; the right brain plays a role in visual and auditory processing, spatial skills and artistic ability—more instinctive or creative things—though these functions involve both hemisphere.

However, it should be noted that for other cultures, as the Chinese medical tradition, the brain is not the centre of thought: mental functions are attributed to the heart, seat of emotions, consciousness, memory and thought, indicated by the ideogram SHEN (神) [Chinese Fractal Website].

This is not a coincidence. What's really fascinating is that the heart contains a little brain in its own right: in addition to its other functions, actually possesses a heart-brain, an intricate network of several types of neurons, neurotransmitters, proteins and support cells, like those found in the proper brain. The heart-brain is composed of about 40,000 neurons that can sense, feel, learn and remember and sends messages to the head-brain about how the body feels and more. It is like the heart has its own way of knowing. When we experience sincere positive emotions, such as caring, compassion or appreciation, the heart processes these emotions, and the heart's rhythm becomes more coherent and harmonious. This information is sent to the brain and the entire body neurologically, biochemically, biophysically and energetically.

Surprisingly, there are over 100 million of neurons even in our stomach and gut. This other little brain does not do a lot of complex thinking, but it is daily grind involved in digesting food, lots of mixing, contracting and absorbing, to help break down our food and begin extracting the nutrients and vitamins we need. The brain-gut axis describes a network of neurons that connect the human enteric nervous system (ENS) with the central nervous system (CNS). The ENS consists of a series of neurons that exist within the gastrointestinal tract and which govern visceral sensation and perception, as well as the secretion of various chemicals into our gut. And all those neurons lining our digestive system allow it to keep in close contact with the head-brain, via the *vagus* nerves, which often influence our emotional state. And when we experience *butterflies in the stomach*, this really is the brain in the stomach talking to the brain in our head. As we get nervous or fearful, blood gets diverted from our gut to our muscles, and this is the stomach's way of protesting [BBC Website].

(To) care and (to) cure and (to) heal What is the difference between care and cure? Both words originally came from the same word, the Latin noun 'cura'. Cure means to make someone healthy again after an illness. A doctor, a lawyer, a minister, a social worker: they all want to use their professional skills to bring about changes in people's lives. They get paid for whatever kind of cure they can bring about.

But care is something other than cure. Care means have a concern towards about something or someone; care is being with, crying out with, suffering with, feeling with; it is compassion. It is claiming the truth that the other person is my brother or sister, human, mortal, vulnerable, like I am. 'When care is our first concern, cure can be received as a gift. Often, we are not able to cure, but we are always able to care. To care is to be human' (Nouwen 2006).

Often even the words 'healing' and 'curing' are used interchangeably, but their definitions could not be more different. Curing is a restoration of health, an absence of symptoms and a remedy of the disease.

Healing, on the other hand, is a restoration of wholeness—not the level of wholeness before the diagnosis but a restoration of wholeness that is new, different and comparatively better than before the onset of disease. Interesting to note, the etymology of the words 'health' and 'holy' is the same, from the Proto-Indo-European word *kailo—whole, uninjured [Online Etymology Dictionary]: healing is not the removal or cessation of symptoms, but rather an integrative process that transcends the physical and includes mental, emotional and spiritual vitality and wellness. In the case of chronic illness or emotional disease, 'cure' is only lasting when healing happens on a deeper level. Heal probably has the same root as related to holy, whole. Therefore, holistic medicine has to deal with the deep honour of the body and soul, intertwined together. Slight different concept is in our Mediterranean country the concept in Italian for salute, health: its root comes from *Salvus*, to be 'alive', 'survived' to something. This has very much to do with the pragmatic Latin culture.

Caregiver Usually, it is an unpaid or paid member of a person's social network who helps with activities of daily living (Koopmanschap 2008). Caregivers provide direct care and are responsible for looking after someone, for example, a person who has a disability or is ill.

The caregiver's work varies with different sets of duties each day, such as assessing medical and basic needs, transporting people and providing companionship during the illness. They may help with daily activities, such as dressing, bathing and toileting, and are often in charge of preparing meals, monitoring nutrition and doing chores.

Classification of illness narratives according to Arthur Kleinman The illness narrative is the interpretation of the narrative dimension of a social actor's illness experience in a specific historical, cultural, social and family context. For Kleinman the narrative's evaluation of a subjective experience of illness has to be an integrating part of medical knowledge, of a therapeutic routine and of a process of recovery. In fact, pain and subjective meanings of disease can emerge from patients' narrations, from the stories they tell, and that give order and meaning to events, symptoms and pain, and the main point of the observation must be 'illness' rather than 'disease'.

The concept trilogy of 'illness', 'disease' and 'sickness' has been used to capture different aspects of ill health.

Disease is defined as a condition that is diagnosed by a physician or other medical expert, and it is considered as alterations or dysfunction in biological and/or psychological process, a deviation from the recognised 'normal' state, an isolated malfunction of a body part; ideally, this would include a specific diagnosis according to standardised and systematic diagnostic codes. This also means that the clinical specific condition has a known biomedical cause and often known treatments and cures. Nevertheless, according to Kleinman, *health* as well as *ill health* cannot be limited to biomedical observation. It requires an understanding of the biological significance as well as social and cultural one (Kleinman 1988).

On the other hand, *illness* is defined as the ill health the person identifies themselves with, often based on self-reported mental or physical symptoms. It refers to the lived experience, to how the sick person and the members of the family or wider social network perceive, live with and respond to symptoms and disability; it is something being lived through the body and can have many types of meanings, in different contexts, to different people.

Lastly, Kleinman introduces a third term, sickness. Sickness describes a disorder in a generic sense as applied to a population or group. It is related to a different phenomenon, namely, the social role a person with illness or sickness takes or is given in society, in different arenas of life, often used to measure social consequences for the person of ill health (Van-Poppel 2002).

Classification of illness narratives according to Mike Bury This type of classification foresees that analysis must consider three types of narrative forms: contingent, moral and core narratives. Under the heading of contingent narratives, narrative analysis is concerned with those aspects of the patient's story that deal with beliefs and knowledge about factors that influence the start of disorder. If this kind of narratives describes events, their proximate causes and their unfolding effects in relation to the performative of everyday life, moral narratives provide accounts of changes between the person, the illness and social identity and help to (re)establish the moral status of the individual or help maintain social distance, introducing an evaluative dimension into the links between the personal and the social. Core narratives reveal connections between the person's experiences and deeper cultural levels of meaning linked to suffering and illness.

Classification of illness narrative according to Kenneth Burke and Moira Kelly A series of genres that can be seen to underpin all forms of narrative—these include epic or heroic, tragic, comic or ironic, disembodied or romantic, didactic. Although individuals may draw on more than one of these genres, it may be the case that the reconstruction of identity and interaction with others is expressed more or less within a particular narrative form.

Classification of illness narratives according to Arthur Frank Classifies stories into three common story types: restitution, chaos and quest. (1) Restitution narrative: this is the story most favoured by physicians and other medical professionals and poses the emphasis on restoring health. These narratives often have three moments: they start with physical misery and social default, continue with the remedy (what needs to be undertaken) and finish with the moment in which remedy is taken; moreover, the narrator describes how physical comfort and social duties are restored. These are often stories told about patients rather than by patients, also because they give little agency to the narrator: patients simply have to 'take the medicine' and get well. (2) Chaos narrative, which is really a nonstory: there is little narrative drive or sequence, just a list of negative things that will never improve and by which the narrator is almost overwhelmed. The story signals a loss or lack of control, and medicine cannot do anything. (3) Quest narrative: this is the teller's story, where the teller is in control of things. Narrators tell how they met the illness 'head on' and sought to use it, to gain something from the experience; the story is a kind of journey, with a recognised departure, an initiation (the mental, physical and social suffering that people have experienced) and a return (the narrator is no longer ill but is still marked by the experience).

Classification of illness narrative according to John Launer Stories can be divided into three types: progressive, regressive and stable one. Progressive narratives move towards the personally valued goals; regressive narratives move away from such valued goals; and stable narratives sustain the same position in relation to the valued goals throughout the narrative sequence. This last kind of narrative could be seen as less engaging than others, because it tends to relate a sequence of events without great drama—a form of storytelling that goes under the heading of the so-called contingent narratives. The use of a progressive, regressive and stable framework allows an analysis that safeguards against over-interpreting the range reserved of meanings conveyed by patients' accounts. It is important to underline that whatever narrative form may be identified in analysis, many accounts move from one to another, for example, from regressive to stable. Consistency in narrative accounts may be achieved or sought by patients, but it may not: much depends on the context in which narratives are constructed and presented and on the intentional acts which they help to constitute. This classification is very useful to focus on the coping strategies acted by patients: if regressive or stable narrative may show no positive engagement and if narratives are progressive, this may represent an evolving positively situation.

Coping Coping strategies refer to the specific behavioural and psychological efforts employed to master, tolerate, reduce or minimise stressful events. Two main coping strategies have been distinguished: problem-solving strategies, that is, the proactive efforts to alleviate stressful circumstances, and emotion-focused coping strategies, which involve efforts to regulate the emotional consequences of stressful (or potentially stressful) events. Some researches indicate that people use both types of strategies to combat most stressful events. The predominance of one type over another is determined, in part, by personal style and by the type of stressful event. An additional distinction, often made in coping literature, is between active and avoidant coping strategies: active strategies are behavioural or psychological responses to change the nature of the stressor itself or how one thinks about it; avoidant strategies lead people into activities or mental state that keep them from directly addressing stressful events. Generally, active strategies are thought to be better ways to deal with stressful events, whereas avoidant strategies appear to be a psychological risk factor or marker for adverse responses to stressful life events. Broad distinctions, such as problem-solving versus emotion-focused, have only limited utility for understanding coping, and so research on coping and its measurement has evolved to address a variety of more specific coping strategies.

Coping according to Carver Coping is defined as the conscious effort to solve personal and interpersonal problems and seeking to master, minimise or tolerate stress or conflict. As reported by Carver, the effectiveness of coping does not only depend on the type of stressor—which can be the onset of a disease, the death of a beloved, or a job loss, but also on personality traits—but rather on other attitudes such as optimism, extraversion, openness to new experiences, agreeableness and consciousness, which are positive markers to engage with coping (Carver and Connor 2010). Conversely neuroticism, with obsessive thought, is related to disengagement with coping, and among the other social factors influencing maladaptive coping, there are hopelessness, helplessness, fatalism, avoidance and denial. At baseline, the use of these maladaptive strategies correlated with a higher incidence of depression.

Defensive medicine The practice of medicine based on requesting tests, procedures or visits or avoiding high-risk patients or procedures, primarily—but not solely—to reduce their exposure to malpractice liability. When clinicians provide extra tests or procedures to reduce malpractice liability, they are practising the so-called positive defensive medicine; when they avoid certain patients or procedures, they are practising the so-called negative defensive medicine. This definition recognises that practices defined as 'defensive' may be motivated by a range of factors and may either enhance or reduce quality of care. It's difficult to classify most practices as totally 'good' or 'bad'; in addition, a substantial proportion of defensive medicine may occur unconsciously, and physicians receive 'signals' from the malpractice system in a variety of ways, such as personal litigation experiences, their colleagues' one, the media, risk management and quality assurance activities and their malpractice insurance premiums.

Digital humanities Digital humanities could be defined as research and education that relies on information technology as a central part of its methodology for creating and processing data. From many points of view, all the Humanities are now involved with the digital sphere: virtually most of researchers use generic digital resources of various kinds, but digital humanities go beyond this to make more systematic use of specialist digital technologies. Digital technologies have the potential to transform research in Humanities field, making it more efficient, enabling new ways of working, stimulating questions and creating new knowledge or answering existing questions more systematically; they provide to integrate collections of research materials, find new ways of processing and representing data and create new connections between different types of data and new support for collaboration, networking and community building. Digital humanities are most successful where there is a two-way collaboration between scholars and technologists. In the education pattern, digital humanities are a resource for linking healthcare and humanistic professionals through digital to organise webinars, knowledge-sharing platforms and Internet libraries.

Digital Narrative Medicine The so-called digital revolution impact has been considered as explosive and very different in respect to technological innovation in the past: many authors think that this digital turn could change the disease pathway and the patient's role in the diagnosis and care process, facilitate the use of Narrative Medicine as a tool to improve the patient-physician relationship and collect information that contributes to the diagnosis, to the management of care and to the compliance. Researchers in Digital Narrative Medicine want to inquire how narratives could positively and efficaciously complete those innovative processes that use new technologies in the digital health field, starting from the prerequisite that the technologies are a means and not a purpose, a tool in the field of a personalisation and care pertinence process. Patients and carers can type their illness narratives freely on social media, as Facebook, or in private blogs and forums, or can leave their witness in dedicated platforms. More often Digital Narrative Medicine is fostered by patient and caregivers' associations.

Digital storytelling: According to the Digital Storytelling Association, digital storytelling is the modern expression of the ancient art of storytelling: throughout history, storytelling has been used to share knowledge, experiences and values. Stories have taken many different forms and have been adapted to each successive medium that has emerged—now, the computer screen. Collecting and preserving histories have become an academic endeavour since 1970; digital storytelling is not just about the transfer of knowledge, it is also a movement designed to amplify the voice of a community. Digital storytelling is an online personal narrative in digital format, supported by the use of multimedia components of narrative, text, images and so on. Physical and social media communities are engaging in digital storytelling to give voice to themselves and others: digital communication has the potential to revolutionise the sharing of knowledge, ideas and culture in the way that written communication did in the past, and people are creating digital stories in order to participate in what has become a massive and meaningful conversation. Community engagement in digital storytelling involves sharing human experiences, and this phenomenon reveals the power of the individual voice to influence positive change: digital storytelling has the potential for connecting a community through shared experiences and developing tolerance by understanding someone else's story.

Disease The biomedical definition of the 'pathological condition', objectified as system alteration and named in a nosological label in biomedical knowledge, on the strength of signs and symptoms interpreted from an external point of view to the suffering body—the physician's diagnostic gaze. Moreover, the practitioner reconfigures the patient's illness problems as narrow technical issues and disease problems: in this process, the healer interprets the health problem within a particular nomenclature and taxonomy, a disease nosology, that creates a new diagnostic entity—the disease. Disease is a problem from the practitioner's perspective, and in narrow biological terms of the biomedical model, it is reconfigured merely as an alteration in biological structure or functioning. So, if we think the pathological condition as a symbolic reality, ignoring the patient's perspective, it means keeping out from clinical action a fundamental dimension of health process: the significant elaboration of experience. Cultural predilection for the disease brings biomedicine to the therapeutic structural ineffectiveness because it eludes the patients' need to give sense to their suffering experience.

Dopamine Dopamine is a neurotransmitter, one of those chemicals that are responsible for transmitting signals between the neurons of the brain. Once released from the first neuron, it floats into the synaptic space and bumps against receptors for it, on the other side, then sends a signal down the receiving neuron.

The effects of dopamine release depend on where it's coming from, where the receiving neurons are going and what type of neurons they are, what receptors are binding the dopamine (there are five known types) and what role both the releasing and receiving neurons are playing. Very few neurons actually make dopamine. Some, in a part of the brain called the *substantia nigra*, and others are located in a part of the brain called the *ventral tegmental area*.

Dopamine is involved in many different important pathways, for example, it plays a big role in starting movement, and the destruction of dopamine neurons in an area of the *substantia nigra* is what produces the symptoms of Parkinson's disease. It also plays an important role as a hormone produced by the hypothalamus, inhibiting prolactin to stop the release of breast milk.

But when most people talk about dopamine, particularly when they talk about motivation, addiction, attention or lust, they are talking about a dopamine pathway known as the mesolimbic pathway, which starts with cells in the *ventral tegmental area* and where dopamine can play a role in psychosis, and many antipsychotics for treatment of schizophrenia target it. Dopamine is also involved in the frontal cortex in executive functions like attention, and increases in its release in the *nucleus accumbens* occur in response to sex, drugs and rock and roll: the signalling in this area is changed during the course of drug addiction. Dopamine neurons become activated when something good happens unexpectedly, such as the sudden availability of food and all abuses of drugs.

Dopamine neurons also play a key role in controlling stress vulnerability: indeed, the noradrenergic neurotransmission promotes resilience against chronic stress by inhibiting the *ventral tegmental area* (Isingrini et al. 2016).

Emotions From the Latin emovère—move out, remove, agitate [Online Etymology Dictionary]—emotions include specific reactions to a particular event. Everyone experiences emotions, but it's complex to say what emotions are, because there are both physical and mental components.

As stated by the American psychologist Paul Ekman, the most fundamental emotions, known as the basic emotions, are those of anger, disgust, fear, happiness, sadness and surprise. The basic emotions have a long history in human evolution, and they have developed in large part to help us make rapid judgements about stimuli and to quickly guide appropriate behaviour. Ekman added to this list in the 1990s other emotions: amusement, contempt, contentment, embarrassment, excitement, guilt, pride, relief, satisfaction, sensory pleasure and shame.

According to the book *Discovering Psychology* of Sandra Hockenbury, science writer specialised in psychology, 'An emotion is a complex psychological state that involves three distinct components: a subjective experience, a physiological response, and a behavioral or expressive response' (Hockenbury 2007). The component of emotions that scientists call subjective feelings refers to the way each individual person experiences feelings, and this component is the most difficult to describe or measure because it cannot be observed; plus, we don't always experience pure forms of each emotion. Mixed emotions over different events or situations in our lives are common, but the person experiencing the emotion can describe it to others, and each person's description and interpretation of a feeling may be slightly different (e.g. two people falling in love will not experience or describe their feeling in exactly the same ways).

Physiological responses are the easiest part of emotion to measure: many of the physical reactions we experience during an emotion, such as sweating palms, racing heartbeat, blood rushing to the face or rapid breathing can all be measured with scientific accuracy and are controlled by the sympathetic nervous system, a branch of the autonomic nervous system. Brain scans have shown that the amygdala, part of the limbic system, plays an important role in motivational states such as hunger and thirst as well as memory and in emotion, fear in particular.

The final component is the actual expression of emotion, the behavioural outwards, which can include fainting, a flushed face, muscle tensing, facial expressions, tone of voice or other body language. The outward expression of an emotion gives other people clues to what someone is experiencing and helps to regulate social interactions: every person unconsciously learns to 'read' the outward expressions of other people and apply past experience to determine what these outward signs indicate about what the other person is feeling. Our ability to accurately understand these expressions is tied to what psychologists call emotional intelligence, and these expressions play a major part in our overall body language. Researchers believe that many expressions are universal, such as a smile indicating happiness or pleasure or a frown indicating sadness or displeasure. Cultural rules also play an important role in how we express and interpret emotions. In Japan, for example, people tend to mask displays of fear or disgust when the authority figure is present [Verywellmind Website]. For many people, strong emotions are one of the fundamental traits associated with being human, are linked to creativity and expression and give us depth and differentiation. Great art, music and literature deal on a fundamental level with arousing emotions and creating an emotional connection between the artist and the public. We can also interpret our experiences to create a more complex array of emotions that often do not have a descriptive term. As we have seen in Chap. 9, one of the most used classifications in the medical humanities and narrative medicine field is that one based on the wheel of emotions by Robert Plutchik (1991).

The poet John Koenig defines neologisms for emotions, based on his research on etymologies and meanings of used prefixes, suffixes and word roots. The terms are often based on 'feelings of existentialism' and are meant to 'fill a hole in the language'; in fact he created *The Dictionary of Obscure Sorrows* with the purpose of including emotions that had never been linguistically described [Dictionaryofobscuresorrows Website].

An example? *Occhiolism* (the awareness of the smallness of your perspective, by which you couldn't possibly draw any meaningful conclusions at all, about the world or the past or the complexities of culture, because although your life is an epic and unrepeatable anecdote, it still only has a sample size of one) or liberosis (the desire to care less about things—to loosen your grip on your life, to stop glancing behind you every few step).

Empathy Generally defined as the ability to sense other people's emotions, to share someone else's feelings coupled with the ability to imagine what someone else might be thinking.

From an etymological point of view, its linguistic roots in ancient Greek but the concept of empathy is of recent intellectual heritage, and the term was introduced in the English language in the nineteenth century by the psychologist Edward Titchener as the translation of the German term *Einfühlung* (feeling into) [Stanford Encyclopedia of Philosophy Website]. Contemporary emotion researchers often differentiate between two types of empathy. The 'affective empathy' which is the understanding of the Other's feelings and refers to the sensations we get in response to Others' emotions; this can include mirroring what that person is feeling, or just feeling stressed when we detect another's fear or anxiety. 'Cognitive empathy', sometimes called 'perspective taking', refers to our ability to identify and understand other peoples' emotions and point of view (Marini 2016). Empathy seems to have deep roots in our brains and bodies and in our evolutionary history. Elementary forms of empathy have been observed in our primate relatives, in dogs and even in rats. Empathy has been associated with two different pathways in the brain, and scientists have speculated that some aspects of empathy can be traced to mirror neurons, cells in the brain that fire when we observe someone else performs an action in much the same way that they would fire if we performed that action ourselves. Research has also uncovered evidence of a genetic basis to empathy, though studies suggest that people can enhance (or restrict) their natural empathic abilities.

Endorphins Etymologically from 'endogenous' + 'morphine', intended to mean a morphine-like substance originating from within the body (Goldstein and Lowery 1975), because they are natural pain relievers: enter endorphins are our own private narcotic.

Their principal function is to inhibit the transmission of pain signals, and they may also produce a feeling of euphoria very similar to that produced by other opioids in general, and if our body isn't producing enough endorphins, we might experience depression, anxiety, moodiness, aches and pains.

Endorphins are neurotransmitters, playing a key role in the function of the central nervous system and either prompting or suppressing the further signalling of nearby neurons. They are produced as a response to certain stimuli, especially stress, fear or pain, but they're also released during other activities, like eating, exercise or sex, and they also surge during pregnancy. Originating in various parts of your body—the pituitary gland, the spinal cord and throughout other parts of the brain and nervous system—endorphins interact mainly with receptors in cells found in regions of the brain responsible for blocking pain and controlling emotion.

Our body naturally produces endorphins, for example, during sex, which is an activity that balances our hormone levels. Being intimate with our partner greatly enhances our mood and alleviates tension in the body; this leads to a subsequent release of endorphins that promote joy and satisfaction. Also eating chocolates stimulate the release of endorphins, which directly affect the brain to generate emotions of pleasure. In fact opioids released in response to ingestion of sweet and other pleasantly palatable foods can increase central opioidergic activity, in turn stimulating the immediate release of beta-endorphin in the hypothalamus and producing an analgesic effect (Parker et al. 2006). Also the creating music or art, dance and meditation helps us: scientists believe that yoga can reduce stress, thanks to endorphin release, because the controlled breathing during yoga contributes to the release of the said hormones.

And another way to liberate these hormones is by smiling.

Indeed, the facial contractions, associated with the emotional experience connected with them, would appear as a standard brain signal: interesting are the findings of changes in endorphin modifications implied in the neurophysiological smiling and laughing mechanism (Torta et al. 1998).

So, whenever we are feeling down, one way to lighten up the mood is by attempting to smile, even if it is a fake one, because any smile, even a faux one, still stretches the facial muscles and contributes to increased endorphin release.

Since laughing increases endorphin levels, we might assume that crying does the opposite effect. However, this is not the case, because crying also promotes endorphin increase: after crying, a person becomes comfortable and relieved after releasing the tension. This further enhances endorphin levels in the body.

Evidence-based medicine Evidence-based medicine (EBM), the philosophical origins of which extend back to the mid-nineteenth century, remains a reference topic for clinicians, researchers, health practitioners, planners and the public. EBM has been defined as the conscientious, explicit and judicious use of current best evidence in making decisions about the care of individual patients. The practice of EBM means integrating individual clinical expertise, that is, the proficiency and judgement that individual clinicians acquire through clinical experience and clinical practice, with the best available external clinical evidence, that is, clinically relevant research, often from the basic sciences of medicine but especially from patient-centred clinical research into the accuracy and precision of diagnostic tests, the power of prognostic markers and the efficacy and safety of therapeutic, rehabilitative and preventive regimens from systematic research: increased expertise is reflected especially in more effective and efficient diagnosis and in the more thoughtful identification and compassionate use of individual patients' predicaments, rights and preferences in making clinical decisions. External clinical evidences replace previously accepted diagnostic tests and treatments with new ones that are more powerful, more efficacious and safer. In this perspective, 'good doctors' use both individual clinical expertise and the best available external evidence: without clinical expertise, practice risks becoming tyrannised by evidence, and without current best evidence, practice risks becoming rapidly out of date, to the detriment of patients.

Grounded theory Is composed by inductive data collection and analytic methods; it's a set of iterative techniques designed to identify categories and concepts within text that are then linked into formal theoretical models. Grounded theory can be also defined as a set of methods that consist of systematic but flexible guidelines for collecting and analysing qualitative data to construct grounded theories in the data themselves. This methodology uses systematic and exhaustive comparison of text segments to build thematic structure and theory from a body text; theoretical models are created and continuously revised as data are progressively collected and analysed. In-depth interviews and focus groups are the most common data collection techniques associated with grounded theory; sample sizes for grounded theory are more limited than for inductive thematic analysis, because the analytic process is more intensive and time-consuming.

Health The World Health Organization defines 'health' a state of complete physical, mental and social wellbeing and not merely the absence of disease or infirmity. There are other generally accepted definitions of 'health': it could be defined as a dynamic state of wellbeing characterised by a physical and mental potential, which satisfies the demands of life commensurate with age, culture and personal responsibility, or a condition of wellbeing free of disease or infirmity, and a basic and universal human right. Some societies, for example, Australian Aboriginal people, assert that health does not just mean the physical wellbeing of the individual but refers to the social, emotional, spiritual and cultural wellbeing of the whole community, a whole of life view that includes the cyclical concept of life-death-life. So, there are many critics arguing that the WHO definition of health is utopian, inflexible and unrealistic and that including the word 'complete' in the definition makes it highly unlikely that anyone would be healthy for a reasonable period of time. Health economics can be defined as a branch of economics that addresses issues relating to efficiency, effectiveness, value and behaviour and consumption of healthcare: health economists analyse the functioning of healthcare systems and health-affecting behaviours. It is standard to consider 'health economics' as the discipline of economics applied to the topic of health: their philosophical and methodological bases are, as a result, founded upon their similar bases in economics. Health services research has become a multidisciplinary enterprise first because of the complexity of health, healthcare and the organisation of services: multidisciplinary research entails not just practitioners of different disciplines but also the opportunity to develop innovative ways of researching particular questions in a cross-disciplinary manner. Health economics—as a component of health services research as well as economics—has the opportunity to draw on these innovative cross disciplinary ways of working. Particular questions can be addressed by using qualitative methods such as interviews, focus groups, observation—with the aim of obtaining an overview of this area of study and to understand the ways in which people think and act in their everyday life in relationship to action of care. Outcomes are investigated in healthcare economics, and they can be clinical, epidemiological, economics, organisational and humanistic. Among humanistic outcomes, patient's preference and quality of life measurement are considered: patient's preferences are related to the informed consent ethical issue as far as the personalisation of care is concerned and to a wider population approach if new intervention therapies have to be implemented. A new stream deriving from outcome research is the health technology assessment to evaluate the economic, clinical, organisational and patient's point of view as a consequence of a new intervention in medical practice.

Healthcare provider A professional involved in the context of care, whose role in the setting of narrative medicine is pivotal towards the improvement and progress in patient care. In the specific case of physicians, their ordinary professional actions are naturally filled by narrative and can be made more effective once recognised as such. Students become physicians by functioning as a medium for medicine's continuity of knowledge, learning about in the process of living through their passages. In professional life, physicians rely on one another for honesty, criticism and the courageous blend of uncertainty and authority in the phrase 'We see this'. Medicine is considered a profession in part because of the strength of these bonds among physicians, who accrue responsibility for one another's competence and conscience. However, specialised physicians seem isolated from other specialists and from their colleagues in nursing, social work and other health professions.

The most effective methods to reinforce professionalism, perhaps, are to endow them with the competence required to fulfil their narrative duties, to envision the stories of science, to teach students responsibly, to give and accept collegial oversight and to enforce bonds among healthcare professionals.

Humanities Set of academic disciplines that study what is defined as 'human culture' and the ways through which people process and document human experiences: they involve inquiry into consciousness, values, ideas and ideals as they seek to describe how these experiences shape the understanding of the world. Philosophy, literature, religion, art, music, history and language are modes of expression that have become some of the traditional subjects falling under the 'Humanities umbrella', areas that are sometimes regarded as social sciences and sometimes as Humanities include anthropology, area studies, communication studies, classical studies, semiotics, and linguistics. Humanities use methods that are primarily critical, or speculative, and have a significant historical element—as distinguished from the mainly empirical approaches of the natural sciences. Human disciplines like history and cultural anthropology study subject matters that the experimental method does not apply to—and instead mainly use the comparative method and comparative research.

Illness The innate human experience of symptoms and suffering. Illness refers to the way a sick person and the members of the family or close social network perceive, live with and respond to symptoms and disability. Moreover, illness is the lived experience of monitoring bodily processes, and this illness experience includes categorising and explaining, in ways that are comprehensible and accessible to all lay persons in the social group, the forms of distress caused by those pathophysiological processes. When we speak about illness, one must include the patient's judgements about how best to cope with distress and practical problems in daily living it creates, and one must consider that it is shaped by cultural factors governing perception, labelling, explanation and valuation embedded in a complex family, social and cultural nexus.

Language The skill of speaking developed approximately between 40,000 and 50,000 years ago, during the period of the migrations of the *Homo sapiens*: we cannot go back to the time, but the sources tell us that a proto language—the centre of linguistics of Mark Pagel in England with the project 'the Tower of Babel'—has identified the roots of a common language developed in that period. The written language comes much later than that oral one; the transition from the hunter-collector society to the shepherd-agriculture society has probably induced the development of the writing: it could be dated around the 5,000 BC, and it was invented for management control, that is, for counting the goods in a warehouse, or in a barn, or in a stable, not only to tell stories. In fact, narratives were narrated since the 30,000 BC.

The words become therefore a system to make order, or that somewhat embanks the river of liberty of thoughts. The evangelist Giovanni writes us that *In the beginning was the Word*—logos, in Greek—*and the Word was with God, and the Word was God* [John's Gospel—The Holy Bible: King James Version, 2004]. The 'logos' is the word that becomes the mean to reach the divinity and that it turns itself into a divinity. Without the word there is not even a beginning, and the history of our humanity has been articulated by the word.

The word is one of our tools of communication, deliberately risen to divinity, but perhaps this occurred mainly for the development of a linguistic code that could highlight the difference between humanity and animals. In Greek, the word 'kaleo' means 'to give a name'. The adjective 'kalos' means beautiful: they have the same root.

In short, the language is extraordinarily ambiguous and correlated to the point of view of who speaks and of who listens.

Medical humanities A field of inquiry in which Humanities and social sciences perspectives are brought together to explore human aspects of medicine. These perspectives play a key role in analysing our expectations of medicine (term which includes biomedicine and other medicines) and the relationship between medicine and our broader ideas of health, wellbeing and flourishing. As some authors highlight, despite a lack of clarity on what exactly the medical humanities involve and how they should be integrated into medical education, medical humanities share several characteristics. First, they use methods, concepts and content from one or more of the humanistic disciplines to investigate illness, pain, suffering, disability, healing, therapeutic and care relationships and other aspects of medicine and healthcare practice. Second, they employ these methods, concepts and practices in teaching health profession students how to better understand and critically reflect on their professions with the intention of becoming more self-aware practitioners. Third, their activities are interdisciplinary in theory and practice and necessarily nurture collaboration among scholars, healers and patients. These conditions imply that medical humanities have a moral function: an important goal for them is to reconceptualise healthcare, through influencing students and practitioners to query their own attitudes and behaviours while offering an integrated perspective on the fundamental aspects of illness, suffering and healing. Mixed methods approach involves collecting and analysing different forms of data in a single study: the first researchers in this field recognised that all methods have limitations and felt that biases inherent in any single method could neutralise or cancel the biases of other methods. There are three main strategies of inquiry. The first, the sequential procedures, in which researchers seek to elaborate or expand the findings of one method with another method. This may involve beginning with a qualitative method for exploratory purposes and following up with a quantitative method with a large sample, or it may begin with a quantitative method in which theories or concepts are tested, to be followed by a qualitative method involving detailed exploration. The second, the concurrent procedures, in which the researcher converges quantitative and qualitative data in order to provide a comprehensive analysis of the research problem. The third, the transformative procedures, in which researchers use a theoretical lens as an overarching perspective within a design that contains both qualitative and quantitative data; this lens provides a framework for topics of interest, methods for collecting data and outcomes or changes anticipated by the study. One can talk about 'narrative' (or story) when somebody shares with another person through narration that considers a teller, a listener, a time course, a possible plot.

Broadly speaking, narrative does not require language: it can be expressed by means of dancing, art and music as well as speech and writing. The form of the narrative also conveys information and meaning. Narratives are about particular events, rather than about events in general, although several narratives can share the same narrative type in that they can be the same kind of story. Representing real-life dimensions, narrative allows to elaborate interpretations that concern the discourse of a specific reality. The narrative form is influenced by precedent models of storytelling; narrative groups several genres, made by a variety of styles that go from complex (spoken or written) language to images; it is present in myth, legends, stories, tragedy, comedy, books, movies and so on. Even if the central importance of narrative in medicine has been understood centuries ago, it has been only in the last 20 years that narrative has become an essential area of research in health sector. In medicine, narrative survives in several forms that can model future interactions in different contexts. However, these forms become constantly fragmented: the recognising of narrative is central in clinical methodology because it puts together and communicates what symptoms mean to patients, inquires their perspectives, why they are searching for help and why now and recognises their role in facing difficult situations.

Metaphor Metaphor, the figure of speech that makes an implicit or hidden comparison between two things that are unrelated but which share some common characteristics.

Elena Semino, an Italian-born British linguist focused on figurative language, in *Metaphor in Discourse* claims that metaphor involves the phenomenon whereby we talk and, potentially, think about something in terms of something else.

Over the last three decades, much attention has been paid to the presence of large numbers of metaphorical expressions in language, which we often use and understand without being conscious of their metaphoricity.

In a series of influential works, the linguist George Lakoff and his colleagues pointed out that metaphorical expressions are pervasive in language and that they tend to form systematic sets such as the following:

Your claims are *indefensible*.

He *shot down* all of my arguments.

He's without *direction* in his life.

I'm at a *crossroads* in my life.

In *Metaphors We Live By* (1980), Lakoff and Johnson famously showed that these expressions are not simply ways of talking about one thing in terms of another, but these set phrases are known as 'conceptual metaphors' and defined as systematic portions of our background knowledge that relate to particular experiences or phenomena (Semino 2008).

Even medical language is soaked in metaphor, and this way of thinking and talking is central in medical culture and clinical practice. Many writers have looked beyond the day-to-day language to discover the basic model or the metaphor we use when thinking about medicine:

Disease is the *enemy*.

He's a good *fighter*.

The *war* on cancer.
Disease is *malfunction.*
He's in for a *tune-up.*
Something's wrong, doc… you *fix it.*
It's obvious the rapid advance of the engineering and war metaphors.

The literary critic and novelist Susan Sontag published a book entitled *Illness and Metaphor* in which she argued that the disease called 'cancer' evokes in the population a pervasive cultural myth or metaphor. Cancer is an obscene, unspeakable and shameful condition. On the other hand, medical practitioners approach cancer with a different metaphor based on military images. Cancer is aggressive and invasive; it seeks to infiltrate and colonise by battering down the body's defences (Sontag 1978).

There are also other, more humane, metaphors for medicine, for example, physician-as-teacher. We need many such images to capture the truth, and some are more useful in healing than others; indeed everyday medicine is replete with evidence of the power of language and narrative to heal or to harm (Coulehan 2003). Metaphors are a useful device to grasp an unknown concept by using a known concept, thus naming and explaining a phenomenon, i.e. illness, which otherwise would remain unintelligible, obscure. They make it easier to have a broader understanding of the disease in its aspects not only biological but also psychological and emotional, helping to grasp meanings that are otherwise not expressed and not said.

Mind Though the word *Mind* is very often used in scientific literature, the definitions given often are more descriptions of its functioning aspects and do not set out what it actually means. The mind holds the power of imagination, recognition and appreciation, and it is responsible for processing feelings and emotions; it involves describing something that is subjectively experienced in the first person and explaining it in an objective form.

In most of the scientific literature, particularly conventional psychology, it is considered an epiphenomenon on the body, and the brain is considered the seat of mind. The neurobiological approach tries to explain the mind as a byproduct of physicochemical processes involving the billions of neurons in the human brain, and its various components are the thought process, emotions, intelligence and awareness (Aravinda and Bhat 2013).

The American Heritage Dictionary of the English Language defines mind as follows: 'The collective conscious and unconscious processes in a sentient organism that direct and influence mental and physical behavior'. This definition attributes mind to sentient organisms and identifies it with processes that control behaviour.

Since the concept of mind is understood in many different ways by many different cultural and religious traditions, some see it as a property exclusive to humans, whereas others ascribe properties of mind to nonliving entities (e.g. panpsychism and animism), to animals and to deities. Others still think that there is nothing within the body that can be identified as being our mind because our body and mind are different entities.

The earliest recorded speculations linked mind, sometimes described as identical with soul or spirit, to theories concerning both life after death and cosmological or natural order, for example, in the doctrines of Zoroaster, the Buddha, Plato, Aristotle and other ancient Greek, Indian and, later, Islamic and medieval European philosophers.

In Buddhist scriptures, mind is formless, or non-physical by nature, our body is compared to a guest house and our mind to a guest dwelling within it. When we die, our mind leaves the body and goes to the next life, just like a guest leaving a guest house and going somewhere else. Oriental psychologies and philosophies considered mind and body as the gross and grosser aspect of the underlying unitary reality which is described in Vedantic texts as S*oul* or *Atman* or B*rahman*. Swami Vivekananda, a key figure in the introduction of the Indian philosophies of Vedanta and Yoga to the Western world, explained the mind-body relationship from his own transcendental experience: 'The body is just the external crust of the mind. They are not two different things; they are just as the oyster and its shell, they are but two aspects of one thing; the internal substance of the oyster takes up matter from outside, and manufactures the shell. In the same way, the internal fine forces which are called mind take up gross matter from outside, and from that manufacture this external shell, the body. We shall find how intimately the mind is connected with the body: when the mind is disturbed, the body also becomes disturbed' (Papers read at a seminar at Ramakrishna Mission Institute of Culture Gol Park, India, 2004).

Music Beyond the physical impact of producing endorphins, it is one sort of language which has an intrapersonal effect, as evoking past memories, cheering up mood, softening harsh times of life and interpersonal effect as developing empathy, interconnecting our minds and souls and evoking similar emotions, of course, depending on our contextual environment and on our taste.

Music is known to produce wellbeing in our bodies and minds and maybe souls, if they exist. It is well established all over scientific journals that music produces endorphins in the brain. They are the internal opioids which give us a feeling of excitement. They act somehow on the same receptors as those of analgesic drugs and have the same effect of gymnastic, meditation and sex. Music causes a relaxation of the tensions and can help in performing with sports, as shown by the fact that turning up your tunes can also up the effort you exert during exercise.

Music has been used as a therapeutic tool for centuries and has been shown to affect many areas of the brain, including the regions involved in emotion, cognition, sensation and movement. This fact, combined with the engaging nature of music and the diversity of music forms, makes music uniquely effective in the treatment of a wide array of physical and mental problems, including depression, anxiety and hypertension.

Mythology Mythology (from the Greek *mythos* for story of the people and *logos* for word or speech, so the spoken story of a people) is the study and interpretation of the myths, which tell the stories of ancestors, of the origin of humans and the world, the gods, supernatural beings (satyrs, nymphs, mermaids) and heroes with superhuman, usually god-given, powers. Myths also explain natural events such as the sunrise and sunset, the full moon or thunder and lightning storms.

Since the early days of the history, there has been a relation between faith and mankind, and the emergency of the myths is the reflection of the faith of the humans, as they interpret their world and purpose by means of myths (Berk 2016). Every culture has some type of mythology. The classical mythology of the ancient Greeks and Romans is the most familiar to people and it has subsequently had extensive influence on the arts and literature of Western civilisation. Poets and artists from ancient times to the present have derived inspiration from Greek mythology and have discovered contemporary significance and relevance in classical mythological themes.

But every society has its own form of myth, cultural identity generally associates with mythology and, interestingly, often these myths are retellings of archetypal stories changed to fit different cultures and experiences.

The same types of stories often can be found in myths from different parts of the world, and they can be described as sacred tales that help men understand the world and his place in it and seem to give guidance to every generation. Taking one example, the hero's quest, such as *The Odyssey*, is a kind of model for youngsters to imitate as they go through the process of growing up and accepting adult responsibilities.

To the ancients the meaning of the story was most important, not the literal truth of the details of a certain version of a tale. It was understood in the ancient world that the purpose of a myth was to provide the hearer with a truth which the audience then interpreted for themselves. The ancient myths still resonate with a modern audience precisely because the ancient writers crafted them towards individual interpretation, leaving each person who heard the story to recognise the meaning in the tale for themselves.

Myths open the window of the timeless and the essential, and this remains true whatever period of history we come from.

Narrative analysis Narrative analysis is based on the study of discourse and the textual representation of discourse. Narratives, in this context, refer to stories that represent a sequence of events: they can be generated during the data collection process, such as through in-depth interviews or focus groups, or they can be incidentally captured during participant observation, or they can be embedded in written forms (e.g. including Internet). Narrative analysis is represented within a large range of academic tradition sciences, anthropology, health sciences, cultural studies—and it can be used for a wide range of purposes: formative research for a subsequent study, comparative analysis, diagnosing medical conditions.

Parallel chart: An informal patient chart, in which physicians can collect their impressions as opposed to clinical data invented by Rita Charon in 1993 and first introduced as a teaching tool, in some settings also considered as a practice tool of narrative reflective strategy for medical students. Its primary goal was to enable students to recognise more fully what their patients endure and to examine explicitly their own journeys through medicine, and not (as Charon distinguishes) as a form of support group therapy, venting sessions or group therapy intended to support students' emotional wellbeing. This textual work is a practical and essential part of medical training, designed to increase the student's capacity for effective clinical work. Reflective writing in medicine should be thought of as a mainstream part of the training of clinicians; parallel chart must be part of clinical training: it is not a general exploration of one's life and times; it is, instead, narrative writing in the service of the care of a particular patient. In the course of writing about patients, students write a great deal about themselves. The patient's biography is always intertwined with the student's autobiography. Students recognise this presence of the self very forcefully while writing their own parallel charts and reading and listening to one another's.

Pathography: The genre of narrative descriptions of illness, most often used to designate patients' first-person accounts; the construction of a pathography, in this sense, is an interpretive and narrative act that gives coherence, unity, and form to an event or experience. Sociocultural metaphors that invade and consecrate medical narratives enable patients to achieve 'transcendence' over their illness.

Patient: The 'patient' can be defined as a person receiving healthcare, for acute or chronic disease or a traumatic event. In particular, the use of this term as in patient-centred care is intended to underline the active involvement of patients and their carers according to a new model of care and treatment decision-making, built around and in consideration of the patient's story, experience, preferences, needs and values.

Narrative research Qualitative research methods are often used to answer questions regarding human behaviours, opinions and experiences: difficult information to obtain through more quantitatively oriented methods of data collection. Despite the interdisciplinary recognition of its value, qualitative research—theoretically and practically—is not a unified field: a plethora of viewpoints exist on the subject of qualitative analysis. Some authors emphasise the research purpose and focus, others highlight an epistemological stance, others focus more on the process and context of data collection. We can propose an outcome-oriented definition, that is, qualitative research involves any research that uses data that do not indicate ordinal values. Such a definition avoids generalisations and the dichotomy between qualitative and quantitative research: furthermore, it allows for the inclusion of different kinds of data collection and analysis techniques, as well as the diversity of theoretical and epistemological frameworks that are associated with qualitative research. In this model of inquiry, the epistemological landscape is as complex as the various disciplines that employ qualitative methods. The two main perspectives, here, are the interpretive and the post-positivistic ones. Authors from the first school (like Geertz) argue that the scientific method is reductionist; instead, stemming from a hermeneutic tradition, this approach is more interested in interpreting deeper meaning discourse that is represented in a collection of personal narratives or observed behaviours and activities. An interpretive perspective is based on the idea that qualitative research efforts should be concerned with revealing multiple realities as opposed to searching for one objective reality. On the contrary, a post-positivistic approach is based on the fundamental ideas that interpretations should be derived directly from data observed and that data collection and analysis methods should be systematic and transparent. Post-positivism is closely associated with the scientific method, and it distances itself from the strict epistemological position that a truly objective reality can be assessed and represented. Indeed, from a theoretical and philosophical perspective, the notion of being able to observe and document one true objective reality is a dubious concept, particularly for social and behavioural phenomena. Post-positivists accept the premise that a completely objective reality is impossible to apprehend but assume that research accounts can approximate, or at least attempt to approximate, an objective truth. The main approaches to collecting and using qualitative data are phenomenology, ethnography, inductive thematic analysis, grounded theory, case study, discourse/conversation analysis, narrative analysis and mixed methods—this last defined as integrating quantitative and qualitative research methods in one study. Therefore, qualitative research is a valid tool for listening, observing and understanding multiple realities brought by patients and carers throughout the illness process.

Narrative medicine What is narrative medicine? There are many different definitions of narrative medicine given by experts.

According to what was written by Brian Hurwitz and Trisha Greenhalgh, it's *everything happens between the healthcare profession and the patient.*

According to Rita Charon, it enters in the depth of daily clinical practice, and it is based on the skill of the professionals to observe, listen, interpret and being moved by the patient's narrations.

According to John Launer, narrative medicine means understand if there are a positive adaptation after the beginning of the disease, or if the stories remain 'stopped', with the patient's trauma facing the new undesired condition.

The Superior Institute of Healthcare with the CNMR (National Centre for Rare Diseases) defines that with the term narrative medicine, we mean a methodology of clinical-helpful intervention based on the specific communicative skill.

According to Maria Giulia Marini and Fondazione ISTUD, narrative medicine is placed side by side with evidence-based medicine (EBM), and we don't have to make confusion with the medical humanities. At the basis of narrative medicine, there is an approach to the care more focused on the human being: the analysis of the text written by patients, by healthcare professionals and by relatives allowed to understand the culture, the values, the needs, the passions, the personal and the professional projects, and it's on this that we concentrate to create or maintain an ecological healthcare.

Narrative medicine rewrites the medical and scientific terminology to make it more coherent with the living and the way of thinking of the patient.

Narrative medicine isn't an 'artistic and fancy representation of the stories of illness' but a science that helps all the healthcare system professionals and host with attention the experiences of people that lives with a pathology and of the caregivers, through the research and the clinical practice.

Narrative Medicine is democratic. It is able to unite ill people and healthcare operators, to associate Evidence-Based Medicine and Narrative-Based Medicine, as well as clinical sciences and human sciences. Narrative Medicine belongs to anyone is involved, both as patient and as carer, in the therapeutic process; it belongs to patients, to their families, to doctors, to nurses, to other healthcare and administrative professionals, to General Directions, but most of all to citizens. (from an interview to Maria Giulia Marini on La Repubblica, June 12 2012)

Natural semantic metalanguage Natural semantic metalanguage (NSM) is based on a shared core of simple words called *semantic primes* that could be translated in many different languages evoking exactly the same concept. It was the main result of an intensive studies lasting beyond 30 years by Anna Wierzbicka, Professor of linguistics at the Australian National University in Canberra University, Australia. Sixty-five semantic primes emerged from her long-lasting study, a group of words that could be used as linguistic and cultural analysis tool to explain the meaning of more complex sentences or cultural-specific concepts as values and cultural attitudes. Actually, the NSM represents a universal language that allows us to formulate analysis: firstly, reducing the risk of any sort of misunderstanding and secondly, without the problem of traducing from the 'Anglo-centric' sense of meaning.

I, me, you, someone, something-thing, people, body	**Substantives**
Kind, part	**Relational substantives**
This, the same, other, else	**Determiners**
One, two, much, many, little, few, some, all	**Quantifiers**
Good, bad	**Evaluators**
Big, small	**Descriptors**
Think, know, want, don't want, feel, see, hear	**Mental predicates**
Say, words, true	**Speech**
Do, happen, move, touch	**Actions, events, movement, contact**
Be (somewhere/someone/something), there is, is mine	**Location, existence, specification, possession**
Live, die	**Life and death**
When, time, now, before, after, a long/short time, for some time, moment	**Time**
Where, place, here, above, below, far, near, side, inside	**Space**
Not, maybe, can, because, if	**Logical concepts**
Very, more	**Augmentor, intensifier**
Like	**Similarity**

Neuroaesthetics In the last few decades, cognitive neuroscience has extended its field of investigation to the domain of art, focusing in particular on visual arts. The term neuroaesthetics was coined by Semir Zeki referring to the study of the neural bases of beauty perception in art; it uses neuroscience to explain and understand the aesthetic experiences at the neurological level and investigate the 'perception, production and response to art, as well as interactions with objects and scenes that evoke an intense feeling, often of pleasure' (Chatterjee 2011).

Many artists have been inspired by scientific investigations and some have undertaken their own. Leonardo is a shining example, and others have included Piero della Francesca, Brunelleschi, Delacroix, Seurat, Duchamp and Mondrian.

So the study of the brain as it responds to art implies the existence of neural mechanisms entailed in art appreciation that are common to all individuals.

The aesthetic experience of visual artworks begins with the visual analysis of the stimulus, which then undergoes further processing. This progression may lead to an aesthetic experience likely based on biological mechanisms, and our fruition of art is certainly cognitively mediated because the peculiar quality of our aesthetic experience is influenced by our culture, by the environment in which we were educated, by the aesthetic canons informing our time and by our level of expertise and familiarity with the artworks we contemplate.

A lot of researchers have investigated the underlying neural foundations of aesthetic experience, and two main methods have been used: analysing the effects that brain lesions and neurodegenerative diseases have on the appreciation of art and using non-invasive neuroimaging technique, which allows to measure the activity of brain regions in controlled situations and to draw general conclusions about the neural processes underlying this kind of experience.

The results suggest that our experience of art emerges from the interaction among the nodes of a broadly distributed network of cortical and subcortical brain regions: prefrontal, parietal and temporal cortical regions are involved in evaluative judgement, attentional processing and memory retrieval; about the relationship between aesthetic experience and emotion, the areas involved are the insula and the amygdala (Gallese and Di Dio 2012), and the general consensus is that the medial orbitofrontal cortex, particularly its subdivision A1, is maximally engaged during the perception of beautiful stimuli, regardless of whether they are visual, musical or mathematical (Ticini 2017).

None of these areas are specialised in responding to art alone, and the distributed and unspecific quality of the neural underpinnings of the aesthetic experience might be the reason why it is resilient to neurological disorders. In spite of the different effects that these disorders seem to have on the experience of art, patients continue to engage with art in personally meaningful ways, even though perceptual, memorable or affective qualities might escape them.

Neuroscience Neuroscience is a multidisciplinary branch that studies the nervous system and deals with the anatomy, biochemistry, molecular biology and physiology of neurons and neural circuits. It also draws upon other fields, with the most obvious being pharmacology, psychology and medicine.

From a historical point of view, manuscripts dating to 1700 BC indicate that the Egyptians had some knowledge about symptoms of brain damage (Mohamed 2008) and that they thought the seat of intelligence was in the heart. Because of this belief, during the mummification process, they used to remove the brain but leave the heart in the body.

The view that the heart was the source of consciousness was not challenged until the time of the Greek and Roman physicians. Then a lot of active in the Medieval and Renaissance world described a number of medical problems related to the brain; in the first half of the nineteenth century, studies of the brain became more sophisticated after the invention of the microscope and the development of a staining procedure by Camillo Golgi, who reveal the intricate structures of individual neurons. His technique led to the formation of the neuron doctrine, the hypothesis that the functional unit of the brain is the neuron (Guillery 2005). During the twentieth century and today, the scientific study of the nervous system made huge advances, mainly because of the progress achieved in other and related fields, such as computational neuroscience, electrophysiology and molecular biology. This has allowed neuroscientists to study the nervous system in all its aspects: how it is structured, how it works, how it develops, how it malfunctions and how it can be changed or repaired.

Modern neuroscience education and research activities can be very roughly categorised into a lot of branches based on the subject, such as affective neuroscience, which looks at how neurons behave in relation to emotions, cognitive neuroscience—the study of higher cognitive functions that exist in humans and their underlying neural basis, or computational neuroscience—attempting to understand how brains compute, using computers to simulate and model brain functions and applying techniques from mathematics, physics and other computational fields.

Oxytocin Oxytocin is a hormone produced by the hypothalamus and then secreted into the blood by the posterior lobe of the pituitary gland, a pea-sized structure at the base of the brain.

It acts as a neurotransmitter and regulates social interaction and sexual reproduction, playing a key role in behaviours from pair bonding to milk release, empathy, generosity and orgasm.

Oxytocin is often called 'the love hormone'. When we hug or kiss a loved one, oxytocin levels increase; the hormone is greatly stimulated during sex, birth and breastfeeding. It is the hormone that underlies trust and is also an antidote to depressive feelings.

Brain oxytocin appears to reduce stress responses, including anxiety, and it has been described as 'an important component of a complex neurochemical system that allows the body to adapt to highly emotive situations'. Oxytocin levels are high under stressful conditions and, acting in part through effects on the autonomic nervous system, might allow 'immobility without fear'. In other words, oxytocin may in general protect the nervous system from shutting down in the face of stressful circumstances, especially those that require holding still rather than fighting or fleeing. That includes even events that may seem positive from a societal standpoint, such as birth, a tremendously stressful experience in which oxytocin may play an important role in helping females manage both emotional and physiological responses and convert potentially stress into opportunities for expressing joy and love.

Recent researchers found that intranasal oxytocin improve self-perception in social situations and increase personality traits such as warmth, trust, altruism and openness. Scientists have proposed that it might help improve interpersonal and individual wellbeing and that it could have applications for people with some neuropsychiatric disorders, proposing it as a possible treatment for social phobia, autism and postpartum depression.

For all its positivity, however, oxytocin has a dark side, and its role in human behaviour is not easy to pin down. While it appears to enhance bonding and the forming of communities among those who share similar characteristics, the hormone fosters distinctions between in-group and out-group members, giving rise to envy, prejudice and possibly aggression. Double-blind experiments showed that oxytocin creates intergroup bias motivating in-group favouritism and, to a lesser extent, out-group derogation. These findings call into question the view of oxytocin as an indiscriminate 'love drug' or 'cuddle chemical', suggesting that it may have a role in the emergence of intergroup conflict (De Dreu 2011).

Patient's journey In all literatures the journey is a symbol of adventure and quest, a search for truth, peace and immortality. The patient's journey describes all the sequential steps in providing a patient's care, and as in every journey, there are a starting point, encounters, crucial moments, discoveries and obstacles, until an end point.

The healing process begins when patients tell of symptoms or even fears of illness, first to themselves, then to loved ones and finally to health professionals, and in the patient's mind, the journey may often start well before an episode of care and continue on after the discharge. This kind of journeys is rarely linear and always unique.

The underlying scenario is the healthcare system, where traditional approach to the assistance problems solving is that of professionals often focused more on the activities they control and barely observers and supervisors of all the pathway phase.

On the contrary, patients have the overview of the care pathway: they live it as protagonists, crossing several care settings, meeting different professional figures and everyday managing disease. From their perspective it is possible to comprehend the care pathway.

To develop the patient's journey, it is necessary to know deeply the experience of the patients before and during the illness: the life before the illness, the appearance of the symptoms, the progression of the disease, repercussions on the family and on the job, etc. The emotional side should not be neglected: the patient's emotionality makes a sort of journey within the journey, which must be carefully evaluated because a patient confused, unresponsive or with depressive tendencies is difficult to adhere to the therapy. The true keys to the success are therefore the profound knowledge of the patient and his needs, the ability to empathise with the patient and the uptake of his emotional needs as well as physical.

The methodology used to reconstruct patient's journey derives from process mapping, a new and important form of clinical audit which includes collection of information relative to 'what really happens' and aims to reconstruct how care activities occur and in which sequence, reconfiguring the journey from the patient's perspective (Trebble et al. 2010). Mapping helps to find possible actions of change, focusing on critical aspects and allowing to work on solutions. Anyway, it is important to not reduce this precious tool to the mere chronicle of the single activities (disease-centred approach), that is, the typical risk when only professionals realise patient's journey; simultaneously, there is also the risk to see only the perspective of patients and caregivers. According to Fondazione Istud, the most appropriate methodology to analyse the patient's journey is the combination of several methodologies: to reconstruct the pathway, in order to outline the journey collecting data relative to professionals, activities, structures and so on; this together with the collection of narratives through narrative medicine, in order to catch the core of the care experience, emotional, relational and social aspects of the journey. In this way we pass from the mere 'pathway reconstruction' to the research of the sense of the journey [Narrative Medicine Website].

Psychosomatic illness Psychosomatic illness, in strictly medical terms, is any physical dysfunction where the primary or major cause is psychological rather than physical; therefore, it refers to a dysfunction primarily caused by some form of emotional or mental stress.

The link between stress and illness is well known, because the body reflects our mental, emotional and spiritual health, but we often ignore or underestimate it in our day-to-day lives.

When something is bothering us and we can't deal with it appropriately, our brain transforms it into a negative emotion that has organic consequences: it increases the nerve impulse activity in order to release neurotransmitters like adrenaline; this neurotransmitter, along with cortisol whose levels also increase in the bloodstream, can cause emotional blockages, increased heart rate, tremor, headaches or stomach aches. Therefore any disruption to our mental, emotional or spiritual health (fear, anger, guilt, sorrow, jealousy, hurt, anxiety) creates stress in our energy centres, and the more extreme or prolonged the stress is, the more likely we are to experience a change in our physiology; sometimes these changes go unnoticed until there is a severe dysfunction that causes us pain or discomfort.

Furthermore, the effects of the stressors on the body are additive, which means that stress accumulates with each additional small level of stress.

How long we can operate under this reaction all depends on our tolerance—or our 'stress threshold'. Each person has a different tolerance level for stress: some people handle stress well, while others don't, and when we reach our threshold for stress, some form of breakdown occurs, either physically, emotionally or both.

Quantitative research Quantitative research can be defined as explaining phenomena by collecting numerical data that are analysed using mathematical based methods (in particular, statistics). A quantitative approach is the one in which the investigator primarily uses post-positivists claim for developing knowledge (e.g. cause and effect thinking, reduction to specific variables and hypotheses and questions, use of measurement and observation and the test of theories) and uses strategies of inquiry such as experiments and surveys and collects data on predetermined instruments that produce statistical data. In this scenario, the researcher tests a theory by specifying narrow hypotheses and the collection of data to support or refute the hypotheses, and it uses an experimental design in which attitudes are assessed both before and after an experimental treatment. Data are collected on an instrument that measures attitudes, and the information collected is analysed using statistical procedures and hypothesis testing. Evidence-based medicine, for example, heavily relies on quantitative research with its metrics and statistics. Nowadays, quantitative research is even applied to narrative medicine in the analysis of occurrence patterns within the stories narrating about living with the disease.

Reflective writing Reflection is a process of personal insight and exploration of an issue of concern; it is generally triggered by having lived an experience, and it helps the individual to create and clarify meaning of the event in terms of self, and that results in a changed conceptual perspective. In recent years, reflective writing exercises have been used in the education of medical trainees presenting in many forms, as critical incident reports and clinical journal writing. The student is asked to describe clinical scenarios in which he or she is on the doctor side of the doctor-patient relationship. Exercises in writing a clinical story from the patient's point of view or rewriting a patient's narrative from a first-person perspective encourage students to reduce the emotional distance between self and patient. These narrative writing exercises require students to reflect upon clinical experiences from the perspective of themselves as clinicians and from the perspective of the others. In particular, exercises such as personal illness narratives have been shown to enable medical students to articulate and examine feelings about bodily realities of illness, health and selfhood. Students are able to interpret and translate their experiences and gain a better understanding of themselves as practitioners and of their patients. The personal illness narrative allows the physician to enter more fully into the reality of the patient's world by recognising and integrating the similarities in his or her own personal experiences and those of the patient. Also, from the patient's point of view, reflective writing can be defined a therapy, with the benefit of having less stress during the visits, a better functioning immune system, a decrease of blood pressure, a deeper breath and fewer depressive symptoms. Writing allows to face unexpressed emotions, the cognitive elaboration of disease and traumatic experiences: it allows to reveal reason and feelings of a suffering person.

Semantic alignment: Semantic alignment is a constant and iterative planning co-construction with the patient and can be defined as the tool that allows to reduce the ambiguities in patient-physician relationships. Alignment implies thinking on an analogue level, comprehending and sharing identities—a purpose achievable during and after a process made by listening, accepting the non-linearity of thinking and feeling of the 'Other'. The act of giving a sense is allowed by active listening, writing, reflection and interpretation of the patient's story.

Serotonin Serotonin is an important chemical and neurotransmitter in the human body. It is primarily located in the enterochromaffin cells in the gastrointestinal tract, where it is used to regulate intestinal movements, in the blood platelets and in serotonergic neurons of the brain, where it transmits messages between nerve cells modulating many aspects of brain functions. These include the regulation of appetite, constriction of smooth muscles and regulation of the body's sleep-wake cycles. Serotonin also has some cognitive functions, including memory and learning. Serotonin helps in boost and intensification of social behaviour, while it appears to inhibit sexual activity, because increased serotonin levels, brought on by medication, are thought to decrease arousal (Young 2013).

Serotonin is believed to influence both directly and indirectly a variety of psychological aspects, and it is sometimes called the *happy chemical*, because it contributes to wellbeing and happiness, and in the brain, it impacts on mood and anxiety. Low levels of the chemical have been associated with depression, while when our serotonin levels are normal, we feel happier, calmer, more focused a less anxious.

Sickness The social meaning of the pathological condition, the patient's social role formalised with the diagnostic act. If sickness is defined as the understanding of a disorder in its generic sense across a population in relation to macrosocial (economic, political, institutional) forces, this term can also be understood as process of production of medical knowledge and pathologies: social processes determine what is considered a 'medical problem', just like validation processes determine what counts as 'medical knowledge'. Accordingly, one can move from an individual-centred vision to a social perspective able to contextualise its object of inquiry. It is interesting to note that the sickness perspective tries to correct a sort of 'individualism', such as the Harvard Medical School one, but at the price of eliminating every consideration for personal dimensions of suffering experience. Software Semantic Analysis Researchers engage in projects involving interpretation of unstructured or semi-structured data for several reasons, such as exploration, description, comparison, pattern analysis, theory building, testing and evaluation. Qualitative methods are chosen in situations where a detailed understanding of a process or experience is wanted, where more information is needed to determine the characteristics of the investigated issue or where the only information available is in a non-numeric form—such investigations typically necessitate gathering intensive and/or extensive information from a purposively derived sample.

Transactional analysis Berne's transactional analysis can be defined as the method for studying interactions between individuals. The basic interest of this approach is the investigating of what Berne called the 'ego states', that is, coherent systems of thought and feeling manifested by corresponding patterns of behaviour. Everyone exhibits three types of ego states. A first to develop is the little boy/girl inside us who feels, thinks, acts, talks and responds just the way when we were children. A second ego state modelled on parental figures—the parent, which performs the functions of a conscience and the moral law. A third one, last in developing, the ego state in which individual appraises his/her environment objectively and calculates its possibilities and probabilities on the basis of past experience—the adult. Therefore, when two people enter in a relationship, there are six possible ego states involved, three in each person. Since these ego states are as different from each other as actual people are, it is important to know which ego state is active in each person when something takes place between them. When analysing transactions, one must look beyond what is being said, at how the words are being delivered as the non-verbal signs accompanying those words: transactional analysis will pay attention to all of these cues when analysing a transaction and identifying which ego states are involved. Written text narrating on health and disease can be analysed through transactional analysis to evaluate which ego state is the prevalent mode of a story if inner transactions are present due to the inner dialogue. When a patient is told about a disease, he or she generally is pushed back to the child ego state, often twisting with a critical parent when not accomplishing the construction of a trustful relationship with the carers. The adult is a desired ego state, the one which enables the person to react positively and to actively coping with the disease.

Wellbeing Wellbeing is a growing area of research, but the question of how it should be defined remains unanswered: there is a greater necessity to be clear about what is being measured and how data should be interpreted, in order to undertake a valid assessment. Any new definition must go beyond an account or description of wellbeing itself and be able to make a clear statement of the meaning of the term. The knowledge of the historical background of the study of wellbeing can be necessary for this purpose, and one can focus on two main approaches—the hedonic tradition, which accentuated constructs such as happiness, positive affect, low negative affect and satisfaction with life, and the eudaimonic tradition, which underlined positive psychological functioning and human development. Despite these two different approaches, most researchers now believe that wellbeing is a multidimensional construct—and, consequently, the diversity dimensions have created a confusing and contradictory research base. To move closer to a new definition of wellbeing, we may focus on three key areas: the idea of a set point for wellbeing, the inevitability of equilibrium/homeostasis and the fluctuating state between challenges and resources. Consequently, the research has proposed a new definition of wellbeing as the balance point between an individual's resource (psychological, social and physical) pool and the challenges (psychological, social and physical) faced.

Appendix

Case 1: The Ability to Communicate with Autistic People: Help from the Natural Semantic Metalanguage

As a brief background, in recent years, there has been a steep increase in new cases of autism, 1 in 110 children today; accordingly, efforts have multiplied to understand and accommodate the condition in childhood. Children with autism today will account for approximately 500,000 adults with autism in this decade alone. Donald Gray Triplett, now 77 years old, lives in Forest, Mississippi. He was the first person ever diagnosed with autism, and his long, happy, surprising life may hold some answers. Donald's parents had secured him a consultation with the nation's top child psychiatrist at the time, a John Hopkins' professor named Dr. Leo Kanner. The term *autistic* was already in use in psychiatry, not as the name of the autistic syndrome but as an observational term describing the way some patients with schizophrenia withdrew from contact with people around them. Like the word *feverish*, which described a symptom, not an illness. But Kanner used it to pinpoint and label a complex set of behaviours that together constituted a single, never-before-recognised diagnosis: autism. Curiously, the Austrian Hans Asperger was working at the same time in Vienna with children who shared some similar characteristics and independently applied the identical word, autistic to the behaviours he was seeing; his paper on the subject would come out a year after Kanner's but remained largely unknown until it was translated into English in the early 1990s.

ASD is a neurological and developmental disorder that begins early in childhood and lasts throughout a person's life. It affects how a person acts and interacts with others, communicates and learns. It includes what used to be known as Asperger syndrome and pervasive developmental disorders. It is called a 'spectrum' disorder because people with ASD can have a range of symptoms. People with ASD might have problems talking with you, or they might not look you in the eye when you talk to them. They may also have restricted interests and repetitive behaviours. They may spend a lot of time putting things in order, or they may say the same sentence again and again. They may often seem to be in their 'own world'. The causes of ASD are not known. Research suggests that both genes and environment play important roles and there is currently no one standard treatment for ASD. Treatments include behaviour and communication therapies, skills training and medicines to control symptoms [NIH, National Institute of Child Health and Human Development].

A Guidance to the Art of Conversation for Children and Young Adults with Autism

Paul Jordan, master of translation from the Australian National University, 'is on the autism spectrum'. He lives in Canberra and is author of the book entitled *How to Start, Carry on and End Conversations*, written for adolescents and young adults with ASD (Jordan 2017). The main aim of this book is to teach people with autism how to make sense of and dealing with the most common social situations, as school, university, relations with friends and strangers. The manual specifically deals with the interpretation of speech since *people with ASD tend to consider speech literally* and are thus unable to distinguish the truth from irony or fiction in what is being said. One of the approaches Jordan uses is that of explaining concepts using universal concepts as NSM and structuring his text in *scripts* along with the *thinking* and *saying* parts of the speech. Here, we report some examples of *scripts* in the book.

Making Friends

"You may desperately want to make friends, yet you don't exactly know what to do. You may be avoiding talking to or interacting with other children, because they will probably not tell you when you're saying or doing something inappropriate—something that they think you shouldn't say or do."

Script 1—MEETING UP WITH SOMEONE WHOM YOU HAVEN'T SEEN FOR A WHILE…

<u>Context—It can be like this:</u>

I know someone well.

I haven't been with this someone for some time.

I see this someone now.

<u>Suggestions—When it is like this, it will be good if I say something like this to this someone:</u>

I see you now, I feel something good because of this, I haven't seen you for some time

I want to know some things about you

I want to know what you did during this time

I want to know what happened to you during this time

"It's easy, don't you think, to talk to an adult, because they're more understanding. It's much more difficult, however, to talk to other kids of your own age when you feel you have nothing in common with them."

This chapter is a mirror clearly reflecting the difficulties of autistic people in dealing with social situations, especially with other children.

Conversation

In order to develop friendships, the book suggests to young Aspies to apply their skills and to deal with short conversations. The author indeed explains rules that normal people consider obvious, while Aspies have to learn and apply in their real life.

"In the next chapter, we'll look at how to relate to other children, using this mini-language" in order to explain what happens and what we have to do.

Script 1—BEGINNING A CONVERSATION...

Context—It can be like this:

I see someone somewhere

I know this someone well

I can say some things to this someone at that time

When it is like this, it will be good if I say some things to this someone

It will be good if I say something like this:

I want to know how you are

Examples, you can think something like: *There's Laura who works with me at the supermarket. She was in a different part of the country for 6 months and I have not seen her. I wonder how she is*

You can say something like: *Laura, how are you? I haven't seen you all year! What are you up to? How was Perth? We should catch up. What are you doing on Friday? We could meet somewhere.*

Script 2—KEEPING A CONVERSATION GOING...

Context—It can be like this:

I am talking to this someone for some time

When it is like this, I have to do some things with my body during that time:

I have to look at this someone's face at many times

I have to look at their eyes at many times

It is good if I am on one side of this someone

It is good if I am not very far from this someone; It is good if I am not very close to this

someone

It is good if my arm cannot touch this someone

Suggestions—At the same times, I have to think like this:

When this someone is saying some things to me, I can't say anything to this someone at

the same time

I can say something a very short time after this

I twill be good if I say something about the same thing

"Finally, a conversation has to come to an end- it can't drag on and on, but you may find it difficult to know how to get out of a conversation"

Special Interests

Adults and children with autism often have special interests, something they are particularly fond of and in which they generally achieve high levels of knowledge such as animals, transport means, languages of the world, music or numbers.

The book suggests to young adults with autism to use their interests as a strategy of coping (*coping skills*).

"Because my interests is mini-language, it seems appropriate for me to use it here to outline some ways in which people with autism can use special interests as coping skills."

"…we tend to go on and on about our special interests to the exclusion of anyone else's interests"

Script 1—DEALING WITH THE UNEXPECTED…

Context—I know that it is like this:

I think about many things not like many other people think about these things

Because of this, I feel something bad when things happen not like they happened before

At times like this I think like this: These things are not now as they were before; I don't know why

it is like this

Suggestions—It will be good if I think like this:

I want to know why these things are not now as they were before. I can know it if I do

Something [for example, read about these things, talk to someone about these things]

I want to do it because of it

Thinking Differently Can Be a Problem

Because people with ASD have a very different way of thinking, it is important for them to learn which these differences are so that they can overcome possible difficulties in the social situations they live.

"Sometimes you can feel that you are much more intelligent than the rest of your classmates. You have what is called advanced intellectual ability. While the other pupils in the class are learning other things, you probably find yourself distracted by things like bright lights, loud noises and language issues (especially taking expressions literally)."

Script 1—COPING WITH THE EFFECTS OF THINKING DIFFERENTLY FROM HOW OTHERS THINK…

Context—I know that it is like this:

I am someone not like other people

My brain does things not like other people's brains

Because of this, I think about many things not like other people

Sometimes good things can happen because of this

Sometimes bad things can happen because of this

It is good if I know this well

Suggestions—It will be good if I think like this

I can think about many things very well. Not all people can think like this

"Staying in the present: This is the way, using technique called mindfulness, to stop yourself before bad memory comes back and upsets you, causing you to get angry for no apparent reason. When something bad happens to you like this, just to be still, close your eyes and concentrate on gentle breathing."

Final Considerations

It's surprising learning that the mental processes which are so natural for 'us' since we were infants are not as spontaneous for people with ASD, as Paul Jordan explains.

The book, which was conceived as a conversation handbook using NSM, addressed people with autism. Yet, it could be considerable a manual for everyone, not only for Aspies but more than these, a 'Galateo of the Art of Communication' that reports rules from acceptance, regards, listening, self-respect and respect for others. Looking at people in their eyes is one of the first body language for communications, and perhaps our society, not only Aspies, is losing this welcoming gesture. Not interrupting the other, when someone is talking, waiting until the end of his/her speech, this also is something that we should bring back, not only at the doctor's site during consultations but in our daily lives.

The main actor of this book is the rationalisation process in learning, understanding a phenomenon, searching in a backward logical process the connections between the phenomena they experience and going back to their cause (the door slammed; why did it slam?), giving explanations that hand out peace against anxiety born from unknown and unpredictable things.

Furthermore, through the reading of the scripts, we can experience for the first time the way a person with autistic spectrum thinks (and apply it also in social and emotional fields).

Facing the unpredictability of thoughts, Paul Jordan concluded the book making us remember the importance of plan breathing, of mindfulness, diving us into the oriental philosophies, an unexpected field for the world of autism. Mindfulness is, by the way, present as one element of spirituality and coping and does belong to the languages of care.

Case 2: The Difference Between Medical Language and Metaphoric Language for Chronic Obstructive Pulmonary Disease

COPD, Chronic Obstructive Pulmonary Disease, is defined by the Global Strategy for the Diagnosis, Management and Prevention of COPD, Global Initiative for Chronic Obstructive Lung Disease (GOLD) 2017 as a 'common and preventable and treatable disease that is characterized by persistent respiratory symptoms and airflow limitation that is due to airway and/or alveolar abnormalities'. COPD is currently the fourth leading cause of death all over the world (Bettoncelli et al. 2014), with an estimated prevalence in Italy of 2.83% (Cazzola et al. 2011); its incidence is rising, and experts estimate that it will become the third cause of death by 2020. This forecast is not only due to the ageing of the population but also due to a low awareness on the disease and its risk factors (Roche et al. 2011).

The aim of this research was to raise awareness of this pathology through listening to the real narratives of patients, caregivers and pulmonologist to 'enlighten' the hidden aspects of living with COPD. The second objective was to give clinicians new means to take care and cure COPD patients, trying to limit the increase of the disease due to continued risk factor exposure.

We used a mix of quantitative and narrative method to embrace the guidelines of WHO on how narrative research should be conducted. Three different points of view: patients living with COPD, their caregivers and physicians were analysed.

The study has been carried out from October 2016 to July 2017. The collection of quantitative and qualitative data was carried out by two distinct tools: a specific questionnaire enriched with a narrative plot (designed based around words of NSM but also including words specific of our context and the issue of smoking as shown in Tables A.1 and A.2) addressed to patients and caregivers and a five-item questionnaire addressed to the physicians inquiring on their approach to COPD key topics (See Table A.3).

From October 2016 and July 2017, 235 patients, 55 caregivers and 60 physicians participated to the study, for a total of 350 experiences collected.

Patients

The narratives collected reflected from a representative group coming from the Italian regions, and gender distribution is almost homogeneous: 46% of respondents were women and 54% were men. The most represented age range was from 60 to 70 years old (42%), but there were also younger people: 22% of patients were less than 60 years old. The severity of the disease has been self-evaluated by patients: 12% declared a very severe COPD, 33% severe, 41% moderate and 14% mild.

Caregivers

Regarding the gender of caregivers, the majority of respondents were women (76%), and this can be linked to the traditional role of the woman in the family, considered as the person who has to take care of the eldest and of children.

Table A.1 The semi-structured plot created for patients

I am […]
The past
I noticed that something was different […] When they told me that I had COPD […] At that moment I felt […] I decided to […] And take care of me […] Smoking for me was […]
The present
To have this illness for me is […] Today, the treatment for me is[…]Smoking is […] My activities at home are[…]Going outside for me is […] Walking for me is[…]Travelling for me is […] Working for me is […] Meeting other people for me is […] The difficulties I face […] My achievements […] The relationship with health professionals […] The relationships with my family and close friends are[…] If I have to describe my disease with an image it would be […] My breath is like a […]
The future
If I have to imagine tomorrow It would be […]
Thanks for your time, energy, and thoughts. A last question: How did you feel in writing your experience? […]

Table A.2 The semi-structured plot created for caregivers

I am [...]
The past
I noticed that something in my relative was different [...] When they told me that he/she had COPD [...] At that moment I felt [...] I decided to do for him/her [...] My role has been [...] Smoking was [...]
The present
Taking care of him/her for me is [...] My life today is [...] Our relationship today is [...] Smoking is [...] At home my relative is [...] Outside he/she is [...] Activities for which my relative needs my support [...] The difficulties that I face during caregiving activities [...] From this experience I learnt [...] The other family members [...] If I have to describe my relative's disease with an image it would be [...]
The future
If I have to imagine tomorrow for me It would be [...]If I have to imagine tomorrow for my relative It would be [...]
Thanks for your time, energy, and thoughts. A last question: How did you feel in writing your experience? [...]

Table A.3 The questionnaire for physicians

1. In your opinion what are the best strategies for communicating COPD?
2. How do you face the issue of smoking with your patients?
3. How do you address the issue of therapeutic adherence?
4. Do you think the patient management tools with COPD are sufficient to ensure good patient management? If not, what tools could help it?
5. The name 'COPD' is...

Diagnosis and Care for Patients

The first symptoms perceived by the person affected by COPD are usually lack of breath, fatigue, cough and difficulty in making efforts. These symptoms are referred during everyday activities; in other cases, the first reporting is done during a hospitalisation for other health problems or after a respiratory crisis.

At the moment of the diagnosis communication, 30% of patients declared to have had a neutral reaction, as reported in some narratives' sentences: *I felt normal, I felt calm, I didn't care about it.* The high percentage of 'neutral reaction' can be motivated by a low awareness of COPD; indeed 55% of the patients at the beginning didn't know anything about this pathology and its implications.

Another obstacle to the perception of COPD severity is given by the harsh technical acronym that means chronic obstructive pulmonary disease. Patients reported that they could not fully understand what the disease was about and they usually understand that it is a *recurrent, easy-to-treat* bronchitis.

Diagnosis and Care for Caregivers

Forty-four per cent of caregivers expressed that at the moment of the diagnosis, they felt concerned about the health of their relatives, 28% felt lost and 22% sad, while the 6% decided to react; independently from their emotions, all the caregivers decided to assist the patient by taking care of him/her and helping him/her in everyday activities.

Considering the caregiving activities, 60% of the caregivers express a high dedication to the relative, 24% shows a mix attitude between dedication and burden of caring activities, while 16% describes the burden of caring activities as particularly high: *It is very heavy both physically and psychologically.*

Activities of Daily Living for Patients

Considering patient's daily activities, only in 30% of narratives home activities are described as 'normal', and 40% consider it 'limited' because patients have to implement strategies to do activities without getting tired or to save breath. Here are some sentences of patients: *I do almost all the housework but with a lot of effort and in different 'episodes', I can't lift heavy stuff, I cook fish sitting on a chair, I do almost all activities but very slowly, I don't do the spring-cleaning.* Thirteen per cent of patients do only 'soft' activity like watching TV, using PC and reading, while in 17% of narratives, the patients declare that they don't do any domestic work; obviously patients with moderate severity are less limited, but no relation was found between severity and activities.

Relationships with other people are 'positive' in 74% of narratives, since patients can maintain bonds and are supported by their relatives and friends. In some cases, patients declare that it is possible to meet friends inviting them at home to overcome the limitation imposed by going out.

The outdoor activities are one of the main problems of a person with COPD; 32% of patients say that they are difficult and hard to perform and consider them as a problem to solve. The three main influencing factors found in narratives are weather conditions, obstacles like climbing stairs and going uphill and oxygen management (35% of patients use oxygen daily). An interesting data is represented by the 29% of people who describe as 'positive' going out. This 'positive' has a meaning of 'liberation' or something that is not expected *going out is a liberation*: *I like to go out, do shopping, drive my car, going out make me feel happy as long as I can do it.*

Activities of Daily Living for Caregivers

The disease condition of the partner or of a parent can have an impact on the activities of the relative, who has to change her or his routine. In a list of five items ('going out for short period, going out for long period, travel in Italy, travel in foreign countries, have leisure time'), the most influenced items are the ones about travelling. Fifty per cent of caregivers consider very difficult to have a trip in foreign countries and 50% even in Italy; but also going out for a long period is defined very difficult by the 33% of participants.

The difficulties to face the situation are caused not only by the caregiving activities, as underlined in some expressions, *finding outside and suddenly arriving at an attack, not having the cortisone to intervene, do not know how to intervene immediately, waiting for the arrival of a doctor*, but also by the psychological support, patient requires *to make him understand that he still has residual capacities to exploit, to console him and give him courage and patience.*

Smoke for Patients and Caregivers

The 60% of the patients declares to have a past as smoker and 60% of them has quitted after COPD diagnosis, the 20% is still smoking, and the remaining 20% has never smoked. The most frequent words used by patients to describe the smoke were *poison, enemy, problem, nightmare, harmful* but also words like *important* and *memory*. Caregivers consider smoking the cause of their relative's disease, so their feeling towards smoke was hate: the most frequent words in the narratives are *bad, bad habit, to abolish, cancer*.

Language of Narratives

Analysing the language of the narratives following the Kleinman classification, the majority of patients' and caregivers' narratives resulted *illness centred*, with a few patients' narratives, and none of the caregivers' narratives *sickness centred*. Using Launer's classifications it was possible to see that caregiver's narratives were more progressive than patients' narratives.

Metaphors for Patients

The images chosen to describe the COPD can be clustered in four categories: breathlessness, sadness, fragility and desperation. They are threatening sentences, so metaphors tell that despite the initial neutrality at the diagnosis communication, the illness is felt by the patient with fear (*a tsunami, an ordeal*), anxiety (*I'm closed in a bag, an iron cage that tightens your chest and prevents you from breathing*) and sadness (*a completely bare tree*). Many of the metaphors indicate how COPD strongly limits their activities.

In particular, the metaphor 'My breath is like….' gave this word cloud (Fig. A.1).

Metaphors for Caregivers

Caregivers choose images that evoke fragility, sadness and anguish. About half of the caregivers choose images particularly evocative. Some of these images suggest the *lack*: *a fish out of water, swallow without wings, a plant without water*; others indicate the *impossibility*: *a sparrow who wants to fly, flaps his wings but fails, a person in the sea who asks for help because he is drowning, a lion that advances and retracts*. Some caregivers imagine something that makes it difficult to breathe: *something that compresses the chest, that generates breathlessness* or *London wrapped in smog*; others chose natural elements, with negative (*tornado, storm*) or positive connotation (*sea, breeze*).

The physicians' Approach

The Diagnosis

The physicians communicated the diagnosis using different kinds of approaches, the majority of which can be considered as illness centred.

The communication of the diagnosis in the case of COPD can be more difficult due to the name of the disease; indeed 89% of physicians think that the name of the pathology—COPD, or in Italian BPCO, *broncopneumopatia cronico ostruttiva*—is

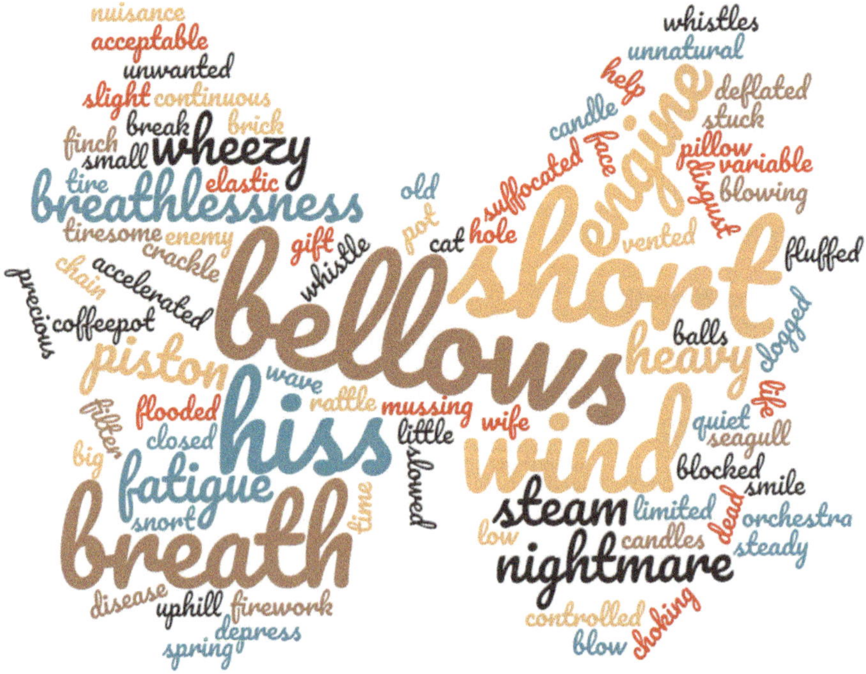

Fig. A.1 The metaphors 'My breath is like…' given by patients

difficult for the patients to understand, it is ineffective and the definition must be explained to patient. Only 11% of the respondents find it appropriate.

Analysing the physician approach to this issue, 39% of the respondents have a 'counselling' attitude towards the patients: they try to understand the reason why the person still smokes and which are her/his psychological needs. Fourteen per cent of physicians attempted the way of reaching an agreement with patient, for example, choosing goals in terms of number of cigarettes per day, and 47% choose an intimidating approach listing all the negative consequences of smoking in an attempt to scare the patient: *I tell them that for a COPD patient, smoking is like healing a wound with acid.*

This research is the first one that includes all the three points of view on national scale.

The emotional reaction to the diagnosis is 'neutral' for 30% of patients; the main cause of this reaction is possibly the fact that patients don't know this disease. While diagnoses of other lung disease such as 'lung cancer' or 'emphysema' immediately alert patients and family members, the 'disease' alert is not perceived as threatening.

In this case, raising of awareness could help people understand immediately the seriousness of COPD and the consequences of neglecting the disease. The impact of COPD on daily activities is quite high, only 30% of patients consider 'normal' activities at home, and a lower percentage (17%) consider 'normal' outdoor activities. Patients are obliged to limit the activities outside: the house becomes the safe place, but this can cause isolation and loneliness and becoming the prison represented by the metaphors.

The caregivers were all involved in the assistance of the patient and shared the COPD burden of the disease, with change in their lives and working activities. Hence, this evidences the need for caregivers as well to be included in the pathway of care and to be supported by an eco-friendly healthcare system (Bryant et al. 2016).

The analysis of the language gives some hints for possible strategies that can be adopted by physicians. The language used by doctors is technical; they talk about tests' results, therapy and disease in a factual way, while patients would need another type of language to better understand the real meaning of COPD and the importance of the therapy. Metaphorical language could be an example since it is useful to express in easy words complex concept (Thibodeau and Boroditsky 2011). In this research, metaphors chosen by patients and caregivers are full of fear and panic and give the idea of suffering caused by the COPD: *I'm captive in a glass bubble, I'm closed in a bag, (COPD is) an iron cage that tightens your chest and prevents you from breathing, the fog, a prison, a grip that tightens my throat.* Images like those ones could be used more also by physicians at the beginning, when symptoms are not very severe and the daily activities are not limited to make patients understand how COPD could eventually evolve.

Clinicians consider the term COPD (in Italian BPCO) difficult to understand by patients. For these reasons, it is very problematic for physicians, mainly pulmonologists, to communicate COPD diagnosis and give to the patients a correct and full idea of this chronic pathology and what the pathway of care would be. Physicians are challenged to find new ways to communicate COPD, perhaps by finding a new name, to raise the awareness on this pathology.

References

Aravinda HR, Bhat PS (2013) Mind and consciousness in yoga - Vedanta: a comparative analysis with western psychological concepts. Indian J Psychiatry 55:182–186

Berk FM (2016) The role of mythology as a cultural identity and a cultural heritage: the case of phrygian myhtology. Procedia, 225, 67–73

Bettoncelli G et al (2014) The clinical and integrated management of COPD. An official document of AIMAR (Interdisciplinary Association for Research in Lung Disease), AIPO (Italian Association of Hospital Pulmonologists), SIMER (Italian Society of Respiratory Medicine), SIMG (Italian Society of General Medicine). Multidisciplinary Respiratory Medicine 9:25

Bryant J, Mansfield E, Boyes AW, Waller A, Sanson-Fisher R, Regan T (2016) Involvement of informal caregivers in supporting patients with COPD: a review of intervention studies. Int J Chron Obstruct Pulmon Dis 11:1587–1596

Carver CS, Connor J (2010) Personality and coping. Annu Rev Psychol 61:679–704

Cazzola M, Puxeddu E, Bettoncelli G, Novelli L, Segreti A, Cricelli C, Calzetta LN (2011) The prevalence of asthma and COPD in Italy: a practice-based study. Respir Med 105(3):386–391

Chatterjee A (2011) Neuroaesthetics: a coming of age story. J Cogn Neurosci 23(1):53–62

Coulehan J (2003) Metaphor and medicine: narrative in clinical practice. Yale J Biol Med 76(2):87–95

De Dreu CKW (2011) Oxytocin promotes human ethnocentrism. PNAS 108(4):1262–1266

Gallese V, Di Dio C (2012) Neuroesthetics: the body in esthetic experience. In: Ramachandran VS (ed) The encyclopedia of human behavior, vol 2. Elsevier Academic Press, Amsterdam, pp 687–693

Global Strategy for the Diagnosis, Management and Prevention of COPD, Global Initiative for Chronic Obstructive Lung Disease (GOLD) (2017). https://goldcopd.org/wp-content/uploads/2016/12/wms-GOLD-2017-Pocket-Guide.pdf

Goldstein A, Lowery PJ (1975) Effect of the opiate antagonist naloxone on body temperature in rats. Life Sci 17(6):927–931

Guillery RW (2005) Observations of synaptic structures: origins of the neuron doctrine and its current status. Philos Trans R Soc Lond Ser B Biol Sci 360(1458):1281–1307

Hockenbury DH (2007) Discovering psychology. Worth Publishers

Isingrini E et al (2016) Resilience to chronic stress is mediated by noradrenergic regulation of dopamine neurons. Nat Neurosci 19(4):560–563

Jordan P (2017) How to start, carry on and end conversations: scripts for social situations for people on the autism spectrum. Paperback

Kleinman A (1988) The illness narratives: suffering, healing, and the human condition. Basic Books

Koopmanschap et al (2008) An overview of methods and applications to value informal care in economic evaluations of healthcare. PharmacoEconomics 26(4):269–280

Marini MG (2016) Narrative medicine: bridging the gap between evidence-based care and medical humanities. Springer

Mohamed W (2008) The Edwin Smith Surgical Papyrus: Neuroscience in Ancient Egypt, International Brain Research Organization, IBRO, History of Neuroscience. http://www.ibro.info/Pub/Pub_Main_Display.asp?LC_Docs_ID=3199
Nouwen HJM (2006) Our greatest gift: a meditation on dying and caring. Hodder & Stoughtton, London
Parker G et al (2006) Mood state effects of chocolate. J Affect Disord 92(2–3):149–159
Plutchik R (1991) The emotions. University Press of America
Roche N, Perez T, Neukirch F, Carré P, Terrioux P, Pouchain D, Ostinelli J, Suret C, Meleze S, Huchon G (2011) High prevalence of COPD symptoms in the general population contrasting with low awareness of the disease. Rev Mal Respir 28(7):e58–e65
Semino E (2008) Metaphor in discourse. Cambridge University Press, Cambridge
Sontag S (1978) Illness as metaphor. Farrar, Straus and Giroux Publisher
Thibodeau PH, Boroditsky L (2011) Metaphors we think with: the role of metaphor in reasoning. PLoS One 6(2):e16782
Ticini LF (2017) The role of the orbitofrontal and dorsolateral prefrontal cortices in aesthetic preference for art. Behav Sci 7(2):31
Torta R et al (1998) Transmethylation and affective disorders. Arch Gerontol Geriatr 26:499–506
Trebble TM et al (2010) Process mapping the patient journey: an introduction. BMJ 341:c4078
Van-Poppel J (2002) Measuring sick leave: a comparison of self-reported data on sick leave and data from company records. Occup Med 52(8):485–490
Wierzbicka A (1996) Semantics: Primes and Universals: Primes and Universals. Oxford University Press, Oxford, UK
Woodhead S et al (2015) The Doctor Patient Relationship; what if Communication Skills are not used? A Maltese Story. Psychiatr Danub (Suppl 1):S34–S40
Young SN (2013) Acute tryptophan depletion in humans: a review of theoretical, practical and ethical aspects. J Psychiatry Neurosci 38(5):294–305